Peter Carnley was ordained as a priest in the Diocese of Bathurst in 1964. He became Archbishop of Perth in 1981 and Primate of the Anglican Church of Australia in 2000. In 1998 he received an Order of Australia award for his contributions to theology, ecumenism and social justice. His other writings include *The Structure of Resurrection Belief*, an essay in *Faithfulness in Fellowship: Reflections on Homosexuality and the Church*, and *The Yellow Wallpaper and Other Sermons. Reflections in Glass* is his third book.

Also by Archbishop Peter Carnley and published by HarperCollins:

The Yellow Wallpaper and Other Sermons

REFLECTIONS IN GLASS

ARCHBISHOP PETER CARNLEY

Trends and tensions in the contemporary Anglican Church

HarperCollinsPublishers

HarperCollins*Publishers*

First published in Australia in 2004
by HarperCollins*Publishers* Pty Limited
ABN 36 009 913 517
A member of the HarperCollins*Publishers* (Australia) Pty Limited Group
www.harpercollins.com.au

HarperCollinsPublishers
25 Ryde Road, Pymble, Sydney, NSW 2073, Australia
31 View Road, Glenfield, Auckland 10, New Zealand
77-85 Fulham Palace Road, London W6 8JB, United Kingdom
2 Bloor Street East, 20th floor, Toronto, Ontario M4W 1A8, Canada
10 East 53rd Street, New York NY 10022, USA

National Library of Australia Cataloguing-in-Publication data:

Carnley, Peter.
    Reflections in glass: trends and tensions in the
    contemporary Anglican Church.
    ISBN 1 8637 1755 2.
    1. Anglican Church of Australia. 2. Spirituality –
    Anglican Church of Australia. 3. Anglicans – Australia.
    I. Title.
283.94

Cover image: Getty Images
Cover concept: Luke Causby
Cover design: Judi Rowe
Internal design: Louise McGeachie
Author photograph: Geoff Fisher, Fisher Studio
Typeset in Centaur MT 12.5/15 by HarperCollins Design Studio
Printed in Australia by Griffin Press Pty Ltd on 79gsm Bulky White

6 5 4 3 2   04 05 06 07 08

For
my brothers and sisters in the faith of Jesus Christ
of the
Anglican Church of Australia

CONTENTS

PROLOGUE

On 3 February 2000 I was elected Primate of the Anglican Church of Australia. The election was held in Sydney, the most convenient and, when the cost of air fares for people coming from all over the country is calculated, the cheapest gathering place for national church meetings in this vast continent. For essentially the same cost-saving reasons, the formal primatial installation ceremony was also set with Sydney as the venue. The date for this liturgical event was to be 30 April, which coincided with a meeting of the Standing Committee of General Synod, followed by the annual meeting of all Australian bishops. A very representative group of lay and clerical church leaders from across the country would thus be in town to form the nucleus of the congregation for an occasion with a national colouring.

Between these two dates I was approached by the editor of *The Bulletin*, Australia's premier news and political comment magazine, to write a piece for the pre-Easter edition. I was more than happy to seize the opportunity do this. In the Church we suffer from a seemingly incurable disposition to talk our own theological jargon amongst ourselves. The monthly 'Letter from the Bishop' in the ecclesiastical press often tends to settle into a kind of low-temperature piety addressed to the converted. The chance to break out of this straitjacket and try to communicate religious truth to a wider audience through the columns of an essentially secular publication was too good to miss.

The ensuing short article was originally entitled 'Christ the Victim', though this was changed in the editorial process to 'The Rising of the Son'. The particular edition of *The Bulletin* that carried it went on sale at newsstands at the end of Lent, during the week prior to Easter. Within a day or two it was clear that the article had at least triggered sufficient interest for a number of national radio programs to seek on-air interviews to pursue some of its key points. Given that it was Holy Week, this provided a further opportunity to explain something of the significance of the coming Easter celebration to Christians. Radio program presenters to a man (for as I recall there were no women) focused on the central point of the article: that a fundamental aspect of the meaning of Easter is the chance to experience the profound forgiveness of God and the offer of new life as a consequence of the death and resurrection of Christ.

In the course of this discussion about the forgiveness of God, I pointed out that there is one respect in which the Easter experience is different for us in the present age from the experience of those who first heard the proclamation of the Gospel two thousand years ago. Unlike us, the original hearers of the message that Jesus had been raised from the dead were people who had actually been involved in his execution, either as part of the crowd of people who demanded his death, or as those who passively stood by and let it happen. For them on Easter Day it was their very own victim who was now declared to have returned from the dead. And part of the astonishingly good news that the first Christians proclaimed to them was not just that Jesus had returned from the dead and had in this way been vindicated by God, but also that he had come back, not vindictively to confront those who had persecuted him, or hellbent on revenge, but rather as one who was prepared to forgive even those who had persecuted and killed him. Jesus, now with the upper hand, did not return to condemn and punish those who had victimised him; rather, he came with an attitude of generous forgiveness.

The *Bulletin* article was thus about the depth of the divine forgiveness that is revealed in the story of the death and resurrection of Jesus, and it then went on to cite some echoes of the healing power of this kind of forgiveness that we experience today in the ordinary business of living our lives. In other words, when we bring ourselves by grace to forgive those who treat us badly, or when we experience the grace of forgiveness from our own victims, we encounter something of the same spiritual reality.

This immediate experience of the saving liberation of God within broken interpersonal relationships is what radio presenters found interesting enough to pursue in conversation. None of them misunderstood the article or missed its chief point. It was not a point for which I could claim any great originality, and at that stage there was little, if anything, that was thought to be controversial in it.

But then, in the following week, the media machine of the Diocese of Sydney got to work. A number of key Sydney Anglicans had their attention drawn to the *Bulletin* article or were provided with faxed copies of it, and were invited to write critical responses. These began to be posted on the Sydney Diocesan webpage. In this process another and quite different spin was put on the article. Moreover, the Sydney responses were expressed with unmistakable overtones of hostility. 'The Rising of the Son' quickly became the subject of public controversy that was picked up by just about every media outlet in Australia. If the Anglican Church wanted to get itself in the news it certainly succeeded. Whether what was communicated was an enhancement of the Christian Gospel, given that the media delighted in exploiting the apparent rifts and divisions of opinion within the Church, is another matter.

In the ensuing debate, and especially in the flood of correspondence that I received in following weeks, it became clear that some Sydney Anglicans had difficulty in thinking about the saving significance of the Cross and Resurrection in terms of the depth of divine forgiveness they revealed. To understand this difficulty it is important to know that there is a mind-set amongst some Christians, exemplified by Sydney Anglicans, that tends to think of the Cross of Christ and its meaning almost exclusively in terms of justice. Indeed, this particular theory of the saving effect of the Cross tends to be promoted as the essence of the Gospel.

This theory of the Atonement is usually called the penal substitutionary theory. It is an attempt to explain the saving efficacy of the Cross based on the contention that justice dictates the need for someone to bear the burden of punishment for human sinfulness and disobedience to God. This is alleged to be required so as to meet God's own demand for justice to be done: somebody had to bear the punishment for the sins of the world, and Jesus filled the bill. Thus the justice of God, rather than the forgiveness or self-giving love of God, becomes the governing concept.

The penal subsitutionary theory has been criticised in the course of the history of Christian theology right from the moment it was first articulated by St Anselm in the Middle Ages. It has nevertheless enjoyed great popular appeal, and some theologians of the past, such as the sixteenth-century reformer John Calvin, even sought to defend and improve on it. However, it is today generally regarded as inadequate. During the last two hundred years particularly, its logical shortcomings have been very regularly pointed out on two grounds in particular. The first is the offensive view it projects of an uncompromisingly cruel and punishing God; the second is the inadequacy of the rough-and-ready kind of justice it depends upon, given that it is the innocent Christ who suffers the required punishment to satisfy God instead of the guilty.

The penal substitutionary theory is also very much the time-bound product of a feudally ordered society, in which satisfaction regularly had to be made to amend for the slighted honour of an overlord, and is actually very insecurely rooted in the biblical tradition. We shall explore this more in Chapter 4. For the moment it is sufficient to note that, despite the criticism levelled at this theory over the last two hundred years, it survives amongst some local pockets of Christians. It is certainly clear that some Sydney Anglicans still think of the Gospel message predominantly in terms of this particular understanding of the Atonement. And it is therefore understandable that some feel threatened whenever its shortcomings are pointed out, even by implication.

Some readers also seemed to have difficulty in working with the article's method of drawing an analogy between the depth of the divine forgiveness revealed in the Raised Christ's return with the offer of salvation and forgiveness even to those with blood on their hands, and the forgiveness extended to us by those whom we have victimised in some way.

This focus on the contemporary religious experience of divine forgiveness appears to have raised a substantial problem. Even an interest in identifying and talking about religious experience, or 'spirituality', as we tend to call religious experience these days, can be uncongenial to some. Rather, they favour a more rationalistic understanding of faith in terms of an intellectual assent to abstract doctrines, rather than a more experiential engagement with the divine. This tendency to adopt a rationalistic mentality necessarily locates the object of faith in the past, essentially as something to be thought about or assented to rather than as something to be experienced in the present. In this way of thinking, faith becomes the belief *that* certain things happened long ago, rather than a commitment of trust within an interpersonal relationship with God in the present. Hence the necessity to assent to the penal substitution theory of the Atonement as something that happened two thousand years ago. But this kind of rationalistic and historical focus leads to a tendency to avoid talk of the human experience of the divine in the present.

This same rationalistic impulse leads to a number of other idiosyncratic commitments, particularly characteristic of Sydney Anglicans. For example, Christ's promise that the Spirit of God will lead his disciples into all truth (John 16:13) tends to be interpreted as a reference only to the first generation of Christians up to 'the death of the last Apostle. At that point the revelation of God is understood to be complete, which means that the Spirit's leading into all truth is also understood to have ended at the same time. Once the first Christian witnesses were led into all the truths that were written down and that are now found within the pages of scripture, the Spirit's leading into all truth ceased. Today we may assent in a rationalistic way to the truths to which they were led and which they recorded in scripture, and the Spirit may illumine our minds as we read and apply the scriptural truths in our own lives. But the leading of the disciples into all truth is something that happened to them and not to us. The experience is not ours to have; rather, we in faith assent in a rationalistic way to the truths into which they were led.

Likewise, Christian claims to encounter the presence of Christ in the breaking and sharing of the bread of the Eucharist tend to be set aside by Sydney Anglicans in favour of an approach to the Eucharist also as a rationalistic mental act, a remembering with gratitude of the saving death of Christ upon the Cross in the past. Instead of *doing* something in liturgy of an experiential kind in commemoration of the death of Christ, it is a matter of mentally remembering in the course of doing something. An entry into liturgical experience thus becomes incidental to the having of right thoughts.

Such an essentially non-experiential style of religious commitment derives from a somewhat abstract and rationalistic, or purely propositional, approach to faith. It furthermore appears to operate as an inhibitor that prevents people from thinking outside a particular rationalistic frame of reference. A spirituality focused on an encounter with the saving and forgiving activity of God or of the Holy Spirit or with the presence of Christ at the Eucharist seems almost to be studiously avoided in favour of a more rationalistic fixation on the need to assent to abstract and speculative propositional truths. More will be said of this in Chapter I. For the time being it is sufficient to note that the concentration of attention on the need to assent to a particular theory of the Atonement is what seems to have made it difficult for some to entertain the thought of entering into the actual living experience of Atonement with God, by concrete acquaintance with the divine forgiveness within the texture of contemporary human living.

The second charge against the *Bulletin* article was that it did not proclaim the uniqueness of Jesus Christ as 'the only way to salvation'. Indeed, it was held that the article categorically questioned Christ's uniqueness. Though the article had been very carefully written, it was, unfortunately, in many cases not very carefully read. Indeed, a whole train load of baggage was projected onto it, apparently fed by the nervous fear that adherents to other faiths might somehow 'get to God' by following another religious path. One sometimes has the sense that some Christians are secure in their own faith only so long as they can be sure that most other human beings will perish in the fires of hell!

One of the points my article was making was that, in the early chapters of Acts, when Luke recounts the first Christian preaching of the Easter good news and records that the first believers proclaimed that 'only through Jesus can you be saved' (see Acts 4:12), he was not just distinguishing Jesus Christ from other world religions and religious leaders. Indeed, the modern question of 'other religions' was for Luke miles away. Buddhism was far off geographically; the advent of Islam was centuries into the future. There were, of course, plenty of competing religious movements in the Roman world, but when Luke recorded the preaching of the early Christians to their first-century Jewish audience, he was not *just* contrasting Jesus with other religious teachers and leaders but was also underlining the fact that it was the Jesus whom they had crucified, *their very own victim*, who had returned with the offer of salvation. It was only though this particular person with whom they had already had dealings that they could be saved. In other words, Luke was making the central point that the one who had been raised and through whom the salvation of God would come to them was the very one they had persecuted: 'this Jesus whom *you crucified*' has been made Lord and Christ (see Acts 2:36).[1] Thus, the original experience of those who first heard the Easter good news embodied the truth that it is only in the experience of forgiveness received in a very concrete way from one's own victim that the limitless depth of the forgiveness we call divine can be known and received. That is why Jesus was uniquely significant as the bearer of salvation for those who had mistreated him. In the return of the Easter Jesus that experience of forgiveness was thus known in the most immediate, poignant and definitive of ways.

The question of the relation of Christianity to 'other faiths', and the specific way to God that Christians find uniquely through Jesus Christ, particularly the way to God understood as 'Father', is of course a very important subject of theological reflection.[2] But the question of who is within and who is outside of the salvation of the God whom Christians know and address as 'Father' raises yet another set of issues. Jesus himself taught by parable that the prerogative of separating the sheep from the goats belongs to God alone. We humans need to use a little caution before presuming to exercise the judgment that belongs to God. Self-righteously condemning attitudes are alien to the Christian mentality.

Certainly, particularly since September 11, we have become very conscious of the need to enter into a respectful dialogue with the adherents of other great world religions, especially Islam. It is also clear, of course, that the world's monotheistic faiths share a great deal in common. Despite obvious differences, there *is* ground on which adherents of the three great Abrahamic religious traditions — Judaism, Christianity and Islam — stand together. Nevertheless, it is a fundamental principle of dialogue with other faiths that we must also appreciate one another's differences. Each of the great world religions has its own distinctive set of beliefs and we do no service to any of them by opting for a lowest common denominator of shared beliefs and values that does not honour their respective emphases. If all religions are regarded as being more or less the same, then none of them can really be taken seriously.

However, the distinctive and unique claims that Christians make for Jesus Christ in contrast with the teachings of the leaders of other world religions were in fact not the central point of the article I published in *The Bulletin* back in April 2000. Rather, the article simply drew attention to the sinful tendency of some Christians to victimise others. By way of particular example, the adherents of other religions were said sometimes to be victimised by Christians. By adopting self-righteously condemning attitudes towards them we put them down. The article thus pointed out that we are all prone to look down on those who think differently from ourselves; it is easy to subject them to a subtle kind of low-grade victimisation. We have to be aware of the human propensity to diminish others in this way and make them into our victims. And it may then come to us as a surprise when we are the recipients of forgiveness and welcome instead from them. This example was used in the *Bulletin* article as a way of illustrating one area of human experience where we can receive forgiveness of the kind we call divine even from those whom we tend to write off or put down. The question of the ultimate destiny beyond the grave of adherents of other religions was quite simply not treated in the article.

† † †

If the debate triggered by the publication of the *Bulletin* article was already lively, it intensified wildly after a summarised version of it appeared on the Sydney Diocesan website, apparently posted so that overseas readers who had no access to the original article would be able to understand what the website debate was all about. The summary was published without my permission to reproduce my article in a shortened form, and without any attempt to check that the gist of the article was being preserved.

This inept and cavalier piece of journalism was made worse by the fact that one key passage of the original *Bulletin* article was reproduced incorrectly, entirely misrepresenting its meaning! As outlined above, I had written that when St Luke says that the first Christians proclaimed that salvation could come 'only through Jesus' they were not *just* distinguishing Jesus from other religious leaders and religious movements, but were underlining the fact that it was the very Jesus whom they had themselves crucified who had returned with the offer of forgiveness and salvation. But his sentence was reproduced with the word 'just' entirely left out. The effect of this was to say quite simply that Luke does not distinguish Jesus from the leaders of other world religions. This journalistic gaffe more than anything else was what fanned a lively media discussion of the uniqueness of Jesus in relation to other world religions which entirely missed the point about the Easter Jesus' being the limitlessly forgiving resurrected victim. From then on it was not the original *Bulletin* article, but the Sydney website version of it, that became the focus of debate.

As soon as I noticed that the press reports of the ensuing controversy were reproducing statements in the incorrect form that had appeared on the Sydney Diocesan website, I drew the problem to the attention of Anglican Media Sydney officer Margaret Rodgers. Obviously appreciating the gravity of the mistake, she undertook to correct the offending statement. I suggested that in order to avoid further confusion, a footnote would need to be included to explain the earlier faulty version of the text, and indicated that an apology would be appropriate. As a consequence, a corrected version of the offending statement reinserting the crucial word 'just' immediately appeared, with an asterisked footnote admitting that a mistake had been made and regretting 'any inconvenience'. Later Miss Rodgers wrote to the national bishops, pleading that it was a simple mistake involving the omission of only a single word, but apparently not appreciating that the omission of this single word entirely reversed the meaning of the sentence and thus of my original text.

Though this was a very minimal statement of apology, I was prepared to accept that the publication of the original incorrect text had been a genuine mistake. In other words, I doubt if this textual tampering was the result of some sinister and deliberate attempt to misconstrue or misrepresent the article. Though some thought at the time that this might have been the case, I myself think it is more likely that the key word 'just' was omitted as the actual text of the *Bulletin* article was unwittingly brought into line with the particular interpretation that was being put upon it in Sydney. Nevertheless, the damage had been done. From that point all hell broke loose.

† † †

The ensuing public controversy, largely about the uniqueness of Christ and whether Christians claim to have a monopoly on salvation, produced over three hundred separate press items in the form of commentary, opinion pieces, letters to the editor, cartoons, and even leading articles in major newspapers right around Australia. A huge wave of written correspondence and e-mails flowed into my office. While the large majority received from across the nation were generously supportive, some hostile correspondence clearly indicated that people were responding to and commenting not on the *Bulletin* article itself, but on the interpretation of it projected in the propaganda columns of Anglican Media Sydney. This was particularly so with regard to about fifty very aggressive letters, mostly from Sydney addresses. Indeed, it was clear that some of these writers who were quick to cry 'heresy' had not so much as read the original article. Given that the particular edition of *The Bulletin* was by this time a sellout on the newsstands, it was perhaps unavoidable. It nevertheless struck me as sadly odd that good Christian people were so readily prepared to put pen to paper to vent their hostility without having read what they were complaining about.

Generally speaking, the secular Australian press was very tough on the Sydney critics of the *Bulletin* article. The Sydney Archbishop of the time, Harry Goodhew, who had been drawn into the fray by his hapless media people, was savaged for expressing exclusivist views about Jesus Christ's being 'the only way to salvation'. This was said to be quite out of place and inappropriate in a broadly tolerant and increasingly multicultural society. One cartoon showed heaven divided between 'Sydney Anglicans' and 'The Rest of Humanity', with a barbed wire fence in between.

Meanwhile, I was a little bemused to find that I was being supported and commended for the generous inclusiveness of the view that there were 'other paths to heaven'! While this is certainly a topic worthy of serious discussion, the curious thing was that, apart from pointing up the inappropriateness of self-righteously condemning attitudes towards people of other religions, this was not really what I had addressed in the *Bulletin* article. In fact the *Bulletin* article was about a particular path to the experience of the divine forgiveness in this world!

In the course of the ensuing controversy, a petition was organised, probably initially to head off the holding of the Primatial installation ceremony in St Andrew's Cathedral in Sydney on 30 April and urge a boycott of the event. The Reverend Deryck Howell, of St Matthias' Church, Centennial Park, Sydney, was instrumental in promoting this. In a letter commending this petition for others to sign, Howell engaged in *ad hominem* abuse of an unfortunately intemperate and insulting kind instead of engaging in a rational discussion of the theological issues. In academic circles we are schooled in the view that ideas and not people are to be attacked, but this principle does not seem to have penetrated far into the thinking of the inner sanctum of St Matthias', Centennial Park.

Nothing much came of this petition, but it is an example of a tendency amongst some people to resort to abusive protest as a low-grade alternative to contributing more positively to rational conversation and debate. Its only continuing value resides in the invitation it contains for others of us to try to understand the underlying insecurities of faith that lead to this kind of projected hostility.

It did have the consequence that some Sydney clergy declared publicly that they would not attend the installation ceremony in St Andrew's Cathedral on 30 April. All this was said to be in the cause of 'speaking the truth in love'. In supporting a boycott, the Reverend Dr John Woodhouse, the then rector of the northern Sydney parish of St Ives, declared on national television that the inauguration ceremony was 'never going to be a big event anyway'. Sydney people were said not to be much interested in primates. Press reports also listed a number of assistant bishops of the Diocese of Sydney among those who intended to boycott the ceremony, even though two of these had told me long before the *Bulletin* episode that they unfortunately had other commitments on the day that had been set for the installation and would not be able to attend. Another bishop who was identified as a supporter of the boycott had written months earlier to explain that he would be absent because he was going to be overseas. Among those who did boycott the event was the Right Reverend Reg Piper of Wollongong, apparently under pressure from a group of 'Sydney Anglicans'. Piper actually tried to explain his reasons in a written statement.

Despite these tactics the primatial inauguration did go ahead as scheduled, and the noisy public controversy of course ensured that the event that was 'never going to be big' was blessed with a huge to overflowing congregation.

While all of this is now history, what is of continuing importance is the clarification and exploration of the actual theological issues that were raised in the course of the controversy. Of particular interest to me are the views of those in Sydney who imagined that they were the champions of Christian orthodoxy. These people have regularly been categorised in the Australian media as 'Sydney fundamentalists' and a number of press articles and TV programmes subsequent to the *Bulletin* episode have dealt with the 'Sydney phenomenon' in a less than sympathetic way.

Many people in the pews of our churches and in the Australian community generally are still left in the dark about what the underlying issues of this debate with 'Sydney Anglicanism' really were. Exactly why they triggered such a passionate response is yet to be understood, let alone explained.

Certainly, the deeply held convictions underlying the public frenzy following the publication of 'The Rising of the Son' have not gone away. Indeed, at the General Synod of the Anglican Church of Australia that was held in Brisbane in July 2001, one perceptive Sydney clergyman spoke of the differences of opinion within Australian Anglicanism as being so profound as in effect to create a stratified Church, almost two different Churches in one. Within the Anglican Church of Australia two quite different mind-sets rub up against one another, he said, like two great tectonic plates that occasionally move and grate upon one another. This book will attempt to clarify some of the issues that surfaced amongst Australian Anglicans in April 2000. It then seeks to make a contribution to the continuing discussion of them. This quest is pursued in the belief that the resolution of the conflict of ideas can only be achieved by the grace of God in generosity of spirit through reasoned conversation and debate.

† † †

Curiously, the incoming Archbishop of Canterbury, Rowan Williams, has encountered some similar and not unrelated hostility since his election to office late in 2002. In England a group called Reform, which claims to represent about one hundred and fifty parishes, has taken issue over Rowan Williams' alleged views on the pastoral handling of homosexual people. The current Archbishop of Sydney, Dr Peter Jensen, has acknowledged similar concerns about Dr Williams' views on homosexuality, observing that 'The present Archbishop is teaching something which I regard as untrue ... To have the Archbishop of Canterbury, of all people, being ambivalent about or commending it [homosexuality] in a small form creates a great tension.'[3]

I myself do not know Rowan Williams' precise views on this subject. However, his opponents are clearly of the view that the Bible speaks unequivocally on this matter, whereas many of us take note of the fact that the term 'homosexual' was coined only in the middle of the nineteenth century, and prior to that people assumed that they were dealing more simply with the deviant behaviour of heterosexual people. It thus seems to many of us that the relevant ancient texts do not directly address the essentially modern question posed by the need to minister to homosexual people in long-term committed relationships. For this reason many of us see this as a rather more complex and difficult moral question than the critics of Rowan Williams, who appear to assume that the Bible speaks unequivocally about what we refer to today as homosexual behaviour amongst exclusively homosexual people.

However, this English dispute about the interpretation of biblical texts relating to homosexual behaviour is clearly only the current manifestation of a more deeply rooted division of opinion about the nature of revelation. It may be that the English theological debate about this issue can throw some light on underlying differences of opinion that we experience in Australia. It is clear enough that the Reform group believes that, while the Anglican Church has always been a broad and comprehensive Church, many Anglicans have in recent times embraced doctrine and ethics 'that go beyond a breadth that a Reformation Church can or should celebrate'. Rowan Williams' namesake Garry J. Williams has produced a brief outline, *The Theology of Rowan Williams,* in which it becomes clear that there is a basic concern about the Archbishop of Canterbury's understanding of revelation. Indeed, Garry Williams charges the new Archbishop of Canterbury with having no doctrine of revelation at all.

The trigger for this assessment of the Archbishop of Canterbury's theology is his use of the image of the Christ-child as an index to the character of God. The fact that the Christ-child is unable to speak clearly to us points us to the abiding reality of the silence of God. As Archbishop Williams puts it: 'Ask a baby about the ordination of women, about divorce legislation, violence on television, who will win the election: it is not a fruitful experience.'[4] The baby Jesus thus challenges us with his silence. And this alerts us to the silence of God generally, which challenges the human tendency to overconfident knowledge claims and assertive uses of knowledge in the exercise of power. For Archbishop Williams the silence of God challenges our human propensity to put our faith in systems of alleged truth which are then taken to be God's truth and used against others. Instead, the inarticulate silence of the incomprehensible mystery of God cautions us about making arrogantly overconfident claims. 'This is at its heart', says Garry Williams, 'a theology which negates all theologies, a *via negativa*, a radical apophatic theology, that is one which moves us away from speech and into the darkness.'[5]

While Garry Williams thinks this means that Rowan Williams has abandoned the concept of revelation, it may be more true to say that what Rowan Williams is affirming is something very important about the self-revelation of God. This is that when God is revealed God is revealed precisely as a transcendent mystery, which is beyond all attempts to capture him in the net of our human conceptions. The transcendence of the infinite God dictates that God will not be reduced to petty formulas or contained in any single finite form of words. After all, if God is infinite, no finite form of words will be adequate to the task of expressing the truth about him. Indeed, not a little ambiguity may attach to God's surpassing mystery. On this side of the full revelation of God at the eschaton, as St Paul said, we see in hints and glimpses, like dim reflections in glass, but not with the clarity of face-to-face encounter (I Corinthians 13:12).

Whether Garry Williams has rightly understood Rowan Williams or not, his observation about the apophatic nature of the Archbishop of Canterbury's theology is a pointer to one of the most profound differences of opinion within contemporary Anglicanism. Within Australian Anglicanism it is fairly clear, for example, that 'Sydney Anglicans' think of revelation in terms of a body of information of a propositional kind that is found within the pages of scripture. This presupposes that there can be a single reading of the scriptural texts of a very clear and distinct kind and that the revelation of God can be understood to be communicated in matter-of-fact, black-and-white terms. Others of us, in contrast, appreciate the Word of God not so much as a body of information, but as a form of questioning of the inner motives of our hearts, or as an invitation to relate with God, who ultimately remains essentially an unfathomable mystery to us, and as a Word of promise to be with us always as we wrestle to discern his truth for the living of our lives.

The ramifications of this for our understanding of God are important to all religions at a time when fundamentalism appears to be on the rise. And an appreciation of the mystery of the transcendence of God as against all overconfident fundamentalisms is a theme of subsequent chapters of this book.

† † †

There are a number of other matters that continue to trouble and divide Australian Anglicans. In particular, these are issues that set so-called 'Sydney Anglicanism' at odds with mainstream Anglicanism as it is found not only in Australia but elsewhere in the world. Of these, some of the most troublesome are those that focus on the nature of the ministry of the Church.

The question of whether women may be ordained to ministerial priesthood and to the episcopate is a case in point. The ordination of women has been a live issue since the Lambeth Conference of 1968 in most Churches of the Anglican Communion. It has been a particularly contentious issue here in Australia, where the Diocese of Sydney and a few country dioceses still forthrightly resist such developments, though for different reasons. It is over ten years since the first women were ordained to the priesthood in Australia, but there are still differences of opinion and unresolved tensions within the national Church over this issue.

More recently, the idea that lay people might be authorised to preside at celebrations of the Eucharist in place of an ordained priest has been promoted with enormous enthusiasm from within the Diocese of Sydney and to a lesser extent in the Diocese of Armidale in rural New South Wales. The importance of the continuing consideration of this matter for the whole Church has been heightened by a majority Opinion of the Church's Appellate Tribunal of 1997 which upheld the openness of the Church's Constitution to this development should the Church choose to pursue it. Once again we currently find ourselves confronted with the challenge of having to resolve the conflict of ideas in relation to this matter.

Chapters 6, 7 and 8 of this book are therefore devoted to the continuing discussion of issues relating to ordained ministry, including the legal and technical complexities that confront the Church.

† † †

It may also be of use to select and discuss some interrelated moral issues that have recently divided the Christian community, if for no other reason than to illustrate the way in which Anglicans today might approach the task of moral reasoning in relation to difficult topics. If the Anglican Church is to move beyond an extreme kind of liberalism that simply leaves the individual to make up his or her own mind in relation to what these days are termed 'lifestyle issues', we must corporately make a serious attempt to provide and commend some agreed moral advice to people, at the very least for their serious consideration.

An excessive individualism that focuses on the human subject as a self-contained atom of direction and moral decision-making has been a feature of moral debate in the Western world since the Enlightenment. A contrasting communitarian approach to discerning what is right and what is wrong, what is good and what is evil, and what is important for the living of life well, contends that the Church must think through the difficult issues that face us today. The Church may wisely avoid giving the impression that it has ready-made answers to every conceivable question and has nothing much to learn. But equally, it cannot allow people to live with the illusion that it has nothing much to teach.

It is also true that the Church today cannot do its moral reasoning in a self-contained cocoon, at arm's length from the rest of the world. Bishops are constantly expected to make a contribution to the public debate of moral issues. Often these are complex questions involving considerable ambiguity, for moral reasoning rarely has the precision of mathematics. Inevitably, there will be differences of opinion both within and outside of the Church. But that does not mean that the Church can afford to remain silent. It is imperative that the Church should think through moral issues so as to enter the public debate as a positively contributing voice.

I have therefore chosen to discuss, by way of example, the area of human reproductive technology and embryo research, this being one of the most difficult and potentially divisive issues we face, at least in the immediately foreseeable future.

But there are wider difficulties facing most Western liberal democratic societies, in which individual autonomy and freedom bulk so large. The need for a more communitarian ethic is canvassed, along with a discussion of the way in which the doctrine of the Trinity of diverse persons in one unity of being may be helpful in working towards a balance between the interests of the individual and those of the community. The need for much more community discussion and debate to develop a shared set of moral commitments and as much shared belief as may be possible then invites a discussion of what kind of contribution Judaism, Christianity and Islam might be able to make towards achieving a more harmonious and peaceful world society.

† † †

That religion could be the subject of such media interest as was whipped up across Australia early in the year 2000 convinces me that there is a huge thirst for some mature, commonsense thinking about religious and moral issues. It was not unusual in that period for Perth telephones to ring in the early evening. On the other end of the line would be people at a dinner party at an Eastern States venue, where heated discussion had developed. Given the two-hour time difference, it was for them well into the night. A bottle or two of red wine may well have already been consumed. The kind of question that would be regularly asked was: 'Does what you said in *The Bulletin* mean that ...?' This convinced me at the time that the discussion of religious issues is probably much more a part of the texture of Australian life than many imagine.

Given Australia's reputation for being a very secularised and matter-of-fact society, it may also come as a surprise to learn that Australia leads the entire world in sales of Bishop John Shelby Spong's books, ahead of New Zealand, Canada, the United States and Britain. Some people clearly find what Jack Spong has to say refreshingly helpful;

others may not agree with all that he says, but given that Australia is his best market, it has to be acknowledged that he is clearly filling a vacuum in this country. I think we have to work at input into that vacuum ourselves.

But why is there a vacuum? In my view the Anglican Church is not alone in this country in labouring to overcome an inability to engage at any real depth in civilised theological and moral conversation. Committed religious people often seem to prefer retreating into the false security of a set position, a fundamentalism of one kind or another, that claims access to a prepackaged set of answers to a wide range of questions. Unfortunately, there are many Christians who find it difficult to work other than in absolute, black-and-white terms. Alternative ways of thinking are very challenging. For such people it is second nature to cry 'heresy' in relation to the views of those who think differently from themselves, while not making much of an attempt to engage in genuine theological conversation and debate with others. Making themselves vulnerable to the public testing and justification of their own views is probably too disturbing to contemplate. Often the views of a perceived opponent are simply declared to be a departure from 'Christian orthodoxy' without any demonstration of how this is the case. With little more debate than defensive assertions arising from private fears, such exchanges sadly do not get far beyond name-calling.

'Speaking the truth in love' (Ephesians 4:15), however, calls us all to careful listening in a spirit of attentiveness to the views of others. It demands a willingness to come to terms with subtleties of thought hitherto overlooked, a preparedness to shift position from time to time. It is salutary to remember the condemnation that Augustine of Hippo leveled at the Donatists, the superior self-confident Christians of his day in North Africa: These, he said, were like frogs 'who grunt from their little pond: "Christians? None but us."'

It is, of course, true that the Anglican tradition, like the theological tradition of any Church, is enormously rich and diverse. We should not expect to live and work with a bland uniformity of viewpoint. Indeed, scripture itself includes a range of different approaches to various issues, and individual texts obviously admit of a variety of different interpretations. It is understandable if elements of the scriptural record that strike some as significant and determinative for further doctrinal development may strike others as being of equal importance. However, given the unavoidable diversity of viewpoints, not all accounts of what Christianity involves will be internally coherent, or valid in equal measure. Where we encounter theological expressions that are not only different from one another but incompatible and thus in competition with one another, some careful assessment of the question of truth becomes particularly necessary.

It has been said that the Christian Church is essentially a community of unlikeminded people. Christianity does not involve the gathering of people around some kind of beautiful idea that is uniformly shared. We come together as Christians not because we recognise one another as entertaining the same mind-set, or because we perceive the desirability of pursuing a commonly held agenda together, or even because of the wish to promote a particular set of interests together, like stamp collectors might. Rather, Christians are drawn together for no reason other than that they are called together by the Word of God. The Christian community comes together not around a shared set of ideas, but essentially around the person of Jesus Christ. The basic elements of its shared faith in Jesus Christ are expressed in the affirmations of the Creeds, which focus upon the relation of the incarnate Jesus the Father and the continuing presence of the Spirit. Apart from the basic dogmatic affirmations of the Creeds, and the ruling principles of its Prayer Book, the Anglican Church is not a confessional community that is held together by some kind of enforced conformity to an authorised set of theological opinions or doctrinal glosses on Christianity's basic dogmas. Beyond its shared dogmatic or credal centre it is a community of diverse people, often of disparate views, who find themselves living and worshipping together only because they acknowledge themselves to have been called together by God. Finding themselves united in the faith of Christ, they then have to struggle for unity of heart and mind, 'having the same love' (Philippians 2:2). And the quest for doctrinal and moral truth is often arduous.

However, even though the resolution of questions of truth is a matter of importance, which we must pursue wherever it may lead, at the end of the day we Christians must acknowledge that a rich diversity of doctrinal viewpoints will nevertheless remain. This will be made up of all those complementary and non-competing insights into truth that contribute to the full complexity of the Christian tradition. If the Church is not a gathering of the likeminded, perhaps we should not be surprised to find continuing differences of opinion in relation to doctrinal and moral issues. Indeed, this book will argue that a more inclusive approach to life that is open to a wide-ranging diversity of viewpoints in Christian theology is the necessary outcome of the surpassing mystery of God. In the Church we are constantly wrestling to discern the truth of God and the direction of his will for the living of our lives. The end of that quest will only manifest itself on the last day when the truth of God will be fully revealed and we shall know even as we are known. Meanwhile, we are on a journey of discovery and learning and of ever-deepening communion together as we enter into the truth of Christ.

In this quest we inevitably have to deal with humanly defective expressions of faith, including misinformation and misrepresentation of one another's ideas as a result of the sinful human need always to be right, the inevitable products of human fallenness. It would be a vain hope therefore to imagine that we might avoid all tension in dealing with the conflict of ideas within the Church. But we do have an obligation to try to understand one another's opinions. It is certainly very important that the Anglican Church of Australia should itself face up to the issues that divide it with openness and candour as it seeks to achieve a more profound communion. Without a free and open debate of different theological viewpoints it will not be possible to transcend current tensions in order to enter into that unity of heart and mind for which our Lord prayed for his disciples (John 17). My hope is that this book may contribute positively to such a debate.

CHAPTER I

GOD: MANIFESTATION OR MYSTERY?

I suspect many people in the community have a stereotypical understanding of an Anglican, of what an Anglican believes or does not believe. To a significant degree the predominant contemporary stereotype of Anglicanism has been created by the media. Anglicans have had to contend with the received TV stereotype of the wimpish and dithering parish vicar of the 'All Gas and Gaiters' Derek Nimmo variety, who has been surpassed in more recent times by the image of the Vicar of Dibley and her highly dysfunctional parish council. This is not to mention the celebrated episode of 'Yes, Prime Minister!' in which, when proposing a candidate for Crown appointment as a bishop, Sir Humphrey Appleby questions whether belief in God is really a necessary part of the job description!

While many in the Anglican community will judge such stereotyping to be false and unfair, others may be prepared to agree that there is some value in images of this kind. We may at least accept that they help us not to take ourselves too seriously. Indeed, we may even acknowledge that such benign and whimsical projections of Anglicanism and Anglicans could contain at least a grain of truth. There is quite a firmly held view in the wider community, for example, that Anglicans are not big on dogma; that they do not believe a great deal, and they are not required to believe anything in particular. By contrast with conservative born-again or card-carrying fundamentalists on one hand, and Roman Catholics on the other hand — who in another stereotype are imagined to have to assent on pain of excommunication to a catalogue of required dogmatic teachings and moral directives — Anglicans are thought not to have to believe anything with a firm conviction.

According to this stereotype, Anglicanism is understood to allow a certain latitude to its adherents, a certain freedom for believers to hold their own private opinions and make moral judgments according to the dictates of their own conscience. Sometimes the apparent freedom of members of the Anglican Church to do or believe more or less anything they might wish is even spoken of as a virtue, the so-called virtue of 'Anglican comprehensiveness': the broad and expansive tolerance of a wide variety of possible moral and doctrinal positions. So we Anglicans are often stereotyped as woolly liberals, who stand for nothing in particular, and muddle along with no really clear moral directives. It is all a matter, as Archbishop Robert Runcie used to say, of 'the bland leading the bland'.

When I speak of 'liberalism' in relation to this stereotype I mean, of course, small 'l' liberalism, marked by the Enlightenment ideal of individual autonomy, the tolerance of alternative moral and religious viewpoints, and freedom of choice to decide between them. This is the Enlightenment ideal of the freedom to believe or do as one might wish so long as the equal right of others to do likewise is respected. Somebody has said that if God had been a liberal he would not have given us the Ten Commandments; instead he would have given us the Ten Suggestions!

The principle of individual freedom of religious choice mirrors other expressions of liberalism, also inherited from the Enlightenment. For example, in the world of commerce and politics the same emphasis on the freedom and autonomy of the individual finds expression in a commitment to free enterprise, small and unintrusive government, and a minimum of regulation. I think it is understandable that the Anglican Church in its original home-grown

English expression, the Church of England, has sometimes therefore had to bear the jibe of being the Conservative Party at prayer.

The most positive spin to be put on all this would be to appeal to the supreme authority of individual conscience. We can fully appreciate that the moral precepts and doctrinal norms of the Church's day-to-day teaching cannot be imposed on individuals contrary to the dictates of their own inner conscience. The supremacy of conscience has had some notable supporters. Even John Henry Newman, a lifelong critic of liberalism, which he thought of as a dangerous tendency to accommodate Christian truth to worldly knowledge, nevertheless upheld the sovereignty of conscience. He consistently condemned liberalism as the enemy of the Church's received dogmatic teaching, yet saw no inconsistency in upholding the importance of the inner voice of conscience as the 'aboriginal vicar of Christ' — the sin against the Holy Spirit being to call right wrong and wrong right, or knowingly to act contrary to one's conscience.

Inevitably, however, an appeal to individual conscience tends to open the way for the development of a huge diversity of theological and moral viewpoints within the Church. This brings with it the obvious difficulty that the free exercise of private judgment, informed simply by the dictates of individual conscience, may lead to doctrinal vagueness and even to an almost unprincipled tendency to compromise between conflicting opinions.

If we were to look for a biblical warrant for this liberal position, it would most likely be found in St Paul's advice, when he tells us frankly that his missionary strategy was to keep the Jewish law when he lived and preached amongst Jews so as not to alienate them from his message, but that, when he preached to those who were outside the world of Jewish law, he himself stood more loosely to it so as to identify as much as possible with his Gentile listeners. He was a Jew to the Jews and a Gentile to the Gentiles. He was, indeed, in the interests of influencing and converting people, 'all things to all people' (I Corinthians 9:22). This, according to the received stereotype of Anglicanism, could be our motto, though less as a missionary strategy and more as a regular way of being: Anglicans are 'all things to all people', thus taking a stand for nothing in particular by being utterly accommodating and tolerant of diversity.

The fear of liberalism in the Church, understood as a bland presentation of the Gospel without a clear cutting edge, appears to bulk large amongst contemporary conservative-minded Anglicans as a fundamental enemy which they must confront. For example, the fear of liberalism in the Church tends to be cited by 'Sydney Anglicans' more often than secular materialism as the polar opposite against which they define themselves. Archbishop Peter Jensen of Sydney, in his 2001 Diocesan Synod Charge, thus spoke negatively of theological liberalism as a force to be resisted at all costs. The danger he perceived to be inherent in it is that it blunts the Church's ability to present the Gospel in a straightforward and clear way. Archbishop Jensen was explicitly hostile to the liberal views of John Shelby Spong for this reason.

We can agree that the Church does not need to be so committed to individual human freedom that it surrenders the responsibility of providing advice and leadership as though it has nothing much of importance to teach. But there is another side to the coin. While there is certainly some element of truth in the stereotyping of Anglicanism as exceedingly inclusive and broad, and while Anglicanism is therefore known for its liberal-minded tolerance and for giving believers the freedom to make up their own minds and the psychological space to make judgments according to the dictates of their own conscience, I think there is a more exact truth of things which we may profitably explore.

Indeed, if we admit that it is probably inevitable, as we live our daily lives, that we experience a natural tendency to pigeonhole people by stereotype in some kind of way, then it is also true that we resort to this kind of stereotyping strategy as a way of understanding ourselves. I am on record as saying that I do not see myself as a theological liberal, and certainly not a biblical fundamentalist. Instead, I prefer to think of myself as 'progressive orthodox'. One of the things I want to do in this chapter is to unpack what I mean when I describe myself in this way. This can be done by touching down at various points in the historical pedigree of this particular way of being an Anglican Christian.

† † †

As suggested, there is an element of truth in the view that Anglicans are not big on dogma. I think it is certainly true, for example, that Anglicanism exhibits a measure of prudence, a certain cautious reticence, when it comes to the defining of doctrines. It gets by with an economy of expression, if you like. It is possible to detect this mood right at the beginning of the English Reformation in the writing of Erasmus. In a letter to Cardinal Campegio early in 1520 he said:

> *Every definition is a misfortune ... True religion is peace, and we cannot have peace unless we leave the conscience unshackled on obscure points ... If we want the truth, every man ought to be free to say what he thinks without fear. If the advocates of one side are to be rewarded with mitres and the advocates of the other with rope or stakes truth will not be heard.*[1]

But caution in relation to the definition of nice theological points does not mean that Anglicans are free to believe anything they might choose — or next to nothing at all. For a start, Anglicans are firmly committed to the fundamental tenets of the catholic and apostolic faith of the undivided Christian Church, particularly as these are summarised in the basic dogmatic affirmations of the Apostles' and Nicene Creeds. Assent to the Apostles' Creed is an essential element in our baptismal liturgies; the Nicene Creed is recited by Anglicans at the Eucharist Sunday by Sunday. However, the Churches of the Anglican Communion are reluctant about adding to those ancient Creeds further dogmatic definitions and deeming them to be 'generally necessary for salvation'. Thus we have difficulty with what John Henry Newman once referred to as the 'luxury dogmas' of the Immaculate Conception of the Blessed Virgin Mary (1854) and the infallibility of the papal teaching office in matters of faith and morals (1870). Anglicans usually also have difficulty with the more recently defined dogma of the Bodily Assumption of the Blessed Virgin Mary of 1950. For Anglicans such matters as these somewhat speculative Marian dogmas at best fall within the category of 'pious opinions' that individuals might choose to entertain, rather than being imposed as required dogmatic commitments of the whole Church.

This reticence about adding to the Church's dogmatic nucleus (as this was credally defined in the ancient Councils of the undivided Church) is something we Anglicans share with the Orthodox Churches of the East. Orthodoxy continues to be irritated by the Western addition of the *filioque* clause ('and the Son') to the Nicene Creed's affirmation about the Holy Spirit 'proceeding from the Father', for example. The chief problem here for the Orthodox Churches is one of unauthorised tampering with the text of the Councils of Nicaea (325 AD) and Constantinople (381 AD). The worldwide conference of Anglican bishops, the Lambeth Conference (held once every ten years), has also recognised this as something that should be addressed by Anglicans. Indeed, at the 1988 Lambeth Conference a resolution was passed that encourages the Churches of the Anglican Communion to reverse this development of the Western Church in future liturgical reform.[2]

Anglican reluctance about adding to the required dogmas of Christianity spills over into a characteristic Anglican reticence and caution towards doctrinal definition more generally. What is not often appreciated, however, is that this is fed by some very firmly held and shared fundamental theological convictions. It is not a matter of lack of belief so much as an implicit corporate commitment to a very fundamental and particular belief. Let me explain what I mean.

The first thing that I think is essential to the understanding of the ethos of Anglicanism, and which I particularly value as an important ingredient in Anglicanism understood from the perspective of 'progressive orthodoxy', is the basic theological truth that God, by definition, is an infinite mystery, an ineffable, transcendent reality. This means that by definition God is beyond all our finite images of him, and beyond all our attempts to express or describe him in finite human words. For this reason, when we humans speak of God we are obliged to speak haltingly and with the help of symbols and metaphors: in the biblical tradition God is a rock, a mighty wind, a flame of fire, a shepherd, a father, a judge, a king, and so on, even a milkmaid, for as the suffering Job says in words addressed to God, 'Did you not pour me out like milk and curdle me like cheese' (Job 10:10). Given the radical invisibility and transcendence of God, humans have no alternative but to picture God by analogy with the finite rocks, winds, fires, shepherds, fathers, judges, kings and milkmaids of our acquaintance in the course of living our lives within this finite world. We project these earthly images onto a heavenly screen, as it were, in the exercise of our theological imagination, but these symbols and metaphors of the biblical revelation cannot be unpacked in any more literal or prosaic form of language. In this sense they are irreducible, for at the end of the day God is, by definition, beyond our words and images rather than limited and contained by them. The representations we use point towards God as a transcendent mystery, who is acknowledged to be always beyond our conceptions of him. And to think that we can reduce the infinite God to the proportions of our finite categories of mind would be as mistaken as to think that we could fit the Indian Ocean into a teacup. Even worse, to mistake the representational image for the reality would be to worship a humanly crafted idol, for mental images can become as idolatrous as metal ones.

It is important to recognise that this does not mean that Anglicans do not believe anything in particular, or that God has no reality beyond our language about him. On the contrary, one of the first things to which Anglicans are very firmly committed is this very particular foundational and ultra-orthodox Christian belief in the reality of the transcendent mystery of God. Iris Murdoch, taking issue with Don Cupitt's anti-realist tendency to abandon belief in God as an objective reality, embodies this fundamental insight of Christian orthodoxy when she speaks of her 'interest in and respect for the high and orthodox emphasis upon divine transcendence'.[3] In the classical traditions of Eastern Orthodoxy, this is expressed in what is called apophatic theology, by stressing what God is *not* — not finite (infinite), not material (immaterial), not in time (atemporal), not subject to change (immutable), and so on. Indeed, Maximus the Confessor saw that only negative statements about God could really be said to be true, for any affirmation of a positive kind had to be qualified. If it is positively affirmed that God is a rock, a wind, a fire, a shepherd, a father, judge or king, these affirmations are true but only in a certain yet-to-be-explicitly-defined sense. Orthodox Anglicanism, as I hope to illustrate in this chapter, shares with the Churches of the

East this essential apophatic tradition, which flows from a sense of engagement with the transcendent mystery of God.

This commitment to God's mystery brings with it, as the other side of the coin, an awareness of the limits of human understanding. In other words, we are humbly conscious of our intellectual and perceptual poverty. By definition God always transcends our human attempts to encapsulate him and have him on our own terms, and even when we speak of him in biblical terms we are aware of the inchoate and halting nature of our theological discourse. God's 'thoughts are not your thoughts'; and God's ways are not our ways', as Isaiah says (Isaiah 55:8). St Paul also puts the point clearly in Romans 11:33: 'O the depth of the riches and wisdom and knowledge of God! How unsearchable are his judgments and how inscrutable his ways! For who has known the mind of the Lord, or who has been his counselor?' 'God as God is in himself', or 'God as God is in God's self', as we say these days, is essentially a hidden God, in ultimate terms unknowable and in an important sense incomprehensible to finite human intelligence. We must speak of God, of course, but when we do so we have no alternative but to resort to images and metaphors as the best tools we have. At the end of the day we must confess that 'God as God is in God's self' is an unsearchable mystery. This is the reason why the object of our religious conviction can only ever be perceived dimly, like reflections in glass.

Just as we are a mystery to ourselves, and as the spiritual journey of each one of us is the lifelong journey of self-knowledge and self-discovery, and just as we are mysteries to one another and with the best will in the world are only ever able to reveal part of ourselves even in our most intimate relationships with one another, so 'God as God is in God's self' always remains a mystery to us. When God is revealed we *apprehend* the presence of a reality that surpasses our understanding, but we do not *comprehend* God's inner nature and being. As we shall see, this also means that we wrestle with moral complexities as we respond to the moral pressure of God's perceived will in relation to the issues that confront us in daily living.

It is important to be clear that even when he is revealed in and through the person of Jesus Christ, God is revealed in his essential nature as mystery. The earthly Jesus always pointed beyond himself to the one to whom he referred as his transcendent heavenly Father. The consequence of God's essential mystery and transcendence as they are worked out according to the principles of apophatic theology is that when we affirm a biblical understanding of God as Father, we have in the next sentence to say an important qualifying 'but not'; God is not literally a father as we know the fathers of this finite world. God does not bring home a pay packet; God does not sit in front of the telly; God does not have a beard (despite many representations of him in Christian art); indeed, God does not have a body! Such anthropomorphic images have to be subtracted from our conception of God as Father. And as we say how God is not like the fathers of this world, the image that we have projected onto the heavenly screen is gradually and systematically rubbed out, as it were, and all we are left with is a kind of after-image. It is then that we encounter something of what Archbishop Rowan Williams speaks of as the silence of God.

Because something of God has been revealed, but not everything, we Christians have been able to develop a disposition for the use of some images to the exclusion of others. Thus we register a heavy preference for this image of God as a loving father. This says what we want to say about God in a way that other competing images that could be used of God do not. In the Christian tradition it is used as a dominant image to communicate our apprehension of God's nature in and through what he has revealed of himself in the life and witness of Jesus Christ. The use of this particular image of God is thus sufficient to give us a practical sense of wellbeing, of being cared for as by a loving father, but a clear and distinct speculative knowledge of 'God as God is in God's self' nevertheless evades our grasp. We are conscious of the danger of reducing the infinite God to the limited proportions of our finite understanding. The transcendence of God thus makes all our systematising relative and reminds us of the need to be humbly aware of our human limitations.

In the next chapter I will seek to draw out the fundamental implications of an appreciation of the abiding mystery of God, both for worship and for doctrinal theology. But first let us make the connection between belief in the mystery of God and Christian orthodoxy as this has been understood quite explicitly over the last three hundred years or so in the tradition of Anglican theological reflection.

† † †

There was one key point in the history of ideas when the importance of an appreciation of the mystery of God as the index to Christian orthodoxy surfaced with some very helpful clarity. This was in the *Dialogues Concerning Natural Religion* of the eighteenth-century philosopher of the Scottish Enlightenment David Hume. In these dialogues, which date from around 1751, belief in the transcendent mystery of God is expressed by a fictitious but theologically representative character named Demea, whom Hume presents in conversation with another character named Cleanthes.

The theological position articulated by Demea, with which I myself have a great deal of empathy, represents the position of those who in Hume's day emphasised faith and revelation, the otherwise unknowable mystery and 'otherness' of God, and thus the essential dissimilarity between human and divine nature. Cleanthes represents an alternative theological stance that enjoyed enormous popularity in Hume's own day — that of the physico-scientific theologians, who, by observing the natural order, concluded that there must be a designer of the universe. The natural theology represented by Cleanthes focused upon the use of reason and the apprehension of an alleged design in the material universe in order to ground claims to an inferential knowledge of the being and nature of the divine. This inevitably entailed the essential similarity between the divine mind and human intelligence, the designer of the universe being understood to have been involved in design work like that of a human architect. In the context of the post-Newtonian world, the position Hume articulates through the voice of Cleanthes was the position espoused by thinkers such as John Ray, Robert Boyle and William Paley. It is a viewpoint that was also very vigorously defended by the Anglican philosopher-bishop George Berkeley.[4]

A third participant in Hume's dialogue, Philo, is a sceptic whom Hume uses as a kind of devil's advocate to bring a critical mind to bear on the reflections of Demea and especially of Cleanthes. Thus, in the *Dialogues*, Hume first has Cleanthes argue from design in the universe to the similarities between divine and human intelligence:

> *Look round the world: Contemplate the whole and every part of it: You will find it to be nothing but one great machine, subdivided into an infinite number of lesser machines ... The curious adapting of means to ends, throughout all nature, resembles exactly, though it much exceeds, the productions of human contrivance; of human design, thought, wisdom, and intelligence. Since ... the effects resemble each other, we are led to infer by all the rules of analogy, that the causes also resemble; and that the Author of Nature is somewhat similar to the mind of man; though possessed of much larger faculties, proportioned to the grandeur of the work, which he has executed. By this argument a posteriori, and by this argument alone, do we prove at once the existence of a Deity, and his similarity to human mind and intelligence.*[5]

In other words, because 'like effects arise from like causes' Cleanthes argues that an inference may be drawn from the created order to divine contrivance.

The basic flaw in this position is indicated by Hume in the *Dialogues* through the voice of Philo, who draws out with incisive critical probes the disastrous anthropomorphic implications of the design argument: God has 'a mind like the human? said Philo. I know of no other, replied Cleanthes. And the liker the better, insisted Philo. To be sure, said Cleanthes.'[6]

By contrast, Demea defends 'the adorable mysteriousness of the divine nature' God; he understands to be radically unlike humans, incomprehensibly inscrutable and sublime, and unknowable as he is in himself. This entails a certain agreement about the limitations of human reason between Demea and Philo, in a way that contrasts dramatically with the position espoused by Cleanthes. For example, Philo is made to say:

> *Let us become thoroughly sensible of the weakness, blindness, and narrow limits of human reason: Let us duly consider its uncertainty and endless*

contrarieties, even in subjects of common life and practice ... who can retain much confidence in this frail faculty of reason as to pay any regard to its determinations in points so sublime, so abstruse, so remote from common life and experience?[7]

In response to these words of Philo, Hume writes, 'Demea seemed to imply an unreserved satisfaction in the doctrines delivered.'[8] Hume makes it clear that the position espoused by Cleanthes slips perilously close to the idolatry of fashioning God in a human form, for 'by representing the Deity as so intelligible, and comprehensible, and so similar to the human mind, says Demea, we are guilty of the grossest and most narrow partiality, and make ourselves the model of the whole universe'.[9] For Demea the divine is essentially other than we are.

In reaction to the rationalism of Cleanthes' position, and to a degree anticipating the nineteenth-century German theologian Friedrich Schleiermacher, Demea's God is apprehended not so much by rational inference from data gathered within the natural order as more directly and intimately, through the inner life of the religious subject:

> *It is my opinion, I own, replied Demea, that each man feels, in a manner, the truth of religion within his own breast; and from a consciousness of his imbecility and misery, rather than from any reasoning, is led to seek protection from that Being, on whom he and all nature is dependent.*[10]

Philo, apparently agreeing with Demea's self-standing faith — or fideism — asks, '...is it necessary to prove what every one feels within himself?'

However, Demea does not entirely reject a natural theology based on the evidence of the physical universe and the use of reason, but simply proposes the postponement of the teaching of it in favour of an initial concentration on piety. Faith and piety, devotion and worship, or in other words, religious experience, or what we would speak of today as spirituality, come first; only then does reason have a role as faith seeks further understanding.[11]

Cleanthes' rationalistic bent in turn finds what is referred to as the 'rigid inflexible orthodoxy' of Demea all too mystical and difficult to manage from a critical point of view; such theologians are said to be 'mystics, who maintain the absolute incomprehensibility of the deity'.[12]

Hume goes on to reveal that he is aware of the orthodox pedigree of the Demea position when he has Philo say that it represents the position of 'all the sound, orthodox divines almost who have ever treated of this subject ...'[13] Nevertheless, Hume appears not really to have understood this orthodox tradition of the incomprehensibility and ultimate unknowability of God. He is certainly uncomfortable with it and seems to have had difficulty in handling it. His presentation of the Demea position is therefore somewhat undeveloped and thin. While being confident in his criticism of the argument from reason and design expressed by Cleanthes, the tradition of theological orthodoxy expressed by Demea was much more troublesome to him.

Given that it was acknowledged to be the position of 'all the sound orthodox divines' who had ever treated of the subject, however, we should be able to fill out the chief characteristics of Anglican Demea theology by referring to a selection of actual theologians from the historical tradition. Indeed, at this point we can really begin to engage with the pedigree of Demea theology within the history of Anglicanism. Meanwhile, we can note that the connection between orthodoxy and the transcendent mystery of God has been explicitly and clearly established.

† † †

The seminal thinker of the Demea tradition of the actual Anglican past was William King, who was the Archbishop of Dublin early in the eighteenth century. In an enormously important treatise that was first delivered as a sermon before the Irish House of Lords in 1709, King laid out the basic elements of what was to become known some fifty years later at Hume's hands as the Demea position. Indeed, King's treatise, entitled 'Divine Foreknowledge Consistent with the Freedom of the Will',[14] is the classic historical expression of the theological ideas that Hume presents in very brief outline in the *Dialogues* though the mouth of Demea.

King's work of 1709 triggered such interest that it went through seven editions during the following century. It was known to Hume, even though he did not draw on it to fill out his presentation of the Demea position in the *Dialogues*. This was probably because Hume was more concerned with critically assessing the design argument as it was presented through the mouth of Cleanthes.

The basic thesis of King's famous Sermon was that no contradiction could be drawn between divine predestination and human freewill, precisely because humans are not given to have an intimate knowledge of the inner workings of the mind of God and are therefore not in the position to make such a judgment. After all, predestination could be understood more as a kind of divine foreknowledge than as a form of determinism. But, given that the inner nature of the divine mind remains an unknowable mystery from a human point of view, and that human beings do not really know what predestination in God is like in any exact sense, there is no way of knowing whether it is incompatible with human freewill or not. All this is shrouded in mystery, for God is beyond all feeble human attempts at the precise conceptualisation of his nature. To intrude into the inner mind of God is an overconfident and rationalistic presumption.

William King's thesis about divine predestination and its apparent incompatibility with human freewill became important for subsequent Demea theologians, given that it was the vehicle for articulating a distinctive appreciation of the incomprehensibility and unknowability of God. This in turn has implications for an understanding of the nature of the Church's doctrine and the function of religious language.

King pointed out that, just as a person born blind can only imagine what colours might be like, so humans generally can only speculate about what it might be like for God to be God. Indeed, he argued that the workings of our own minds are by and large hidden from us and we even have to speak of our own mental processes in what are often quite basic physical metaphors and analogies. We speak of 'reflecting on an idea' or of 'embracing an idea' or 'weighing an argument'. Such language, says King, actually tells us very little about the nature of these processes as they are in themselves, and it is only when we stop to think about it that we become aware of how figurative this language actually is. Likewise, for the purpose of living our religious lives we are obliged to work with fragmentary hints and glimpses, and tentative analogical representations or images of the divine. These, King argues, are sufficient for their pragmatic religious purpose without being clear and distinct. But we must be aware of their limitations, for they are not in any unequivocal way sufficiently informative to ground further speculative thought.

✝ ✝ ✝

During the course of the nineteenth century, in the wake of the study of Hume's *Dialogues*, the design argument and its reliance on human reason came under sustained scrutiny. At the same time, Anglican Demea theology flowered, particularly in the first decades of the nineteenth century at Oxford. At Oriel College, William King's work was studied with enormous seriousness at this time. Indeed, it is at this point in the historical development of distinctively Anglican theology that we are able to pick up the Demea tradition as a fundamental influence, in the work of John Henry Newman, who very quickly perceived the tension between an orthodox awareness of the importance of 'mystery' and the rationalistic temper of his contemporaries. These, he believed, placed far too much confidence in the capacities of human reason and so claimed to have a deceptively clear and distinct, but nevertheless mistaken, propositional knowledge of God.

If we are to place Newman by theological type, he is certainly to be aligned with Demea as opposed to the kind of theology articulated by Cleanthes. It is abundantly clear from his writings, for example, that Newman inherited the post-Humean suspicion of the argument from design. In fact, a belief in the nature and existence of God based on the evidence of the alleged design of the universe seemed to Newman singularly unconvincing. He saw clearly that observation of the universe with all its evil and distress could as easily lead to a belief in a God of whim, if not of a fiendish and vengefully punishing disposition. Certainly, a reasoned assessment of evidence derived from the observation of nature did not necessarily lead to the God of moral goodness of the biblical revelation in Christ.

In order to arrive at an awareness of the nature of God, Newman therefore consistently favoured an apophatic theology grounded in a more fideistic acknowledgment of the unknowable mystery of God. The existence and nature of God, he concluded, are beyond the unavoidable anthropomorphisms that result from drawing rational inferences from the alleged design of the universe.

Newman scholars have generally failed to discern the increasing dominance of the Demea position in the emerging theology of the Anglican Newman, but it is possible to connect him securely with the Demea tradition by observing some of the formative influences upon him. From the time he arrived at Oriel in 1822 he came under the sway of two card-carrying Demea theologians, Richard Whately and Edward Copleston. Copleston, who became a Fellow of Oriel in 1795 and Provost in 1814, was in office when Newman arrived on the scene, though he was personally a little removed from Newman. But Richard Whately, who was also a Fellow of Oriel until his marriage, became Newman's close friend and mentor.[15]

It has often been observed that Newman's original religious conditioning by a Calvinist evangelical family was very self-consciously abandoned during the period when he came under the direct influence of Whately and Copleston, though the dynamics of his transition are not so well understood. However, both Copleston and Whately were self-conscious and uncompromising Demea theologians who, at the precise time when Newman was so closely associated with them, were aggressively promoting the work of William King. Indeed, Whately actually republished King's treatise of 1709 in the belief that it contained the essential index to the right method of interpreting scripture, particularly in relation to the understanding of the nature of God and his dealings with humankind. As it happens, King's treatise was published by Whately in 1821, just prior to Newman's election as a Fellow of Oriel.[16]

Newman developed a close working relationship on matters of logic with his mentor, and it is not insignificant that Whately in his *Elements of Logic* (1826), on which Newman actually collaborated, embraced and expanded upon some of the insights of King's Sermon, particularly relating to the analogical nature of religious discourse. Indeed, he actually quoted and discussed King's work at some length.[17] On its first appearance Whately sent a copy of his *Logic* to Newman, who wrote in response on 14 November 1826 saying not only that Whately had taught him 'to think correctly', and to rely on himself, but that Whately 'broke' him of his Calvinistic views.[18] It is important to appreciate that it was a distinctive set of theological insights as much as a capacity to think logically and independently that released Newman from the religious tradition of his family upbringing.

At exactly the same time, King's work was having enormous influence on Copleston, who found the 1709 Sermon a helpful resource in developing his own approach to reconciling the apparent conflict between divine predestination and human freewill. This was a subject that continued to be troublesome to Anglican theologians exposed to Calvinism. Copleston's own *Enquiry into the Doctrines of Necessity and Predestination in Four Discourses* also coincided with the year of Newman's arrival at Oriel in 1821.

Whately's republication of King's Sermon, and Copleston's work, which was so heavily dependent upon it, along with the enthusiastic promotion of views deriving from King by both Whately and Copleston gave Anglicans at Oxford at the time an alternative to the inherited Calvinistic option of the period.[19] It is therefore understandable that Newman shared the same mind-set. Indeed, Newman's expressed dislike of the design argument and his conviction of the impossibility of coming to an understanding of the divine nature on the basis of it clearly echo the thought of Whately, who had argued, against William Paley, that God's moral qualities, his perfection and love, cannot be inferred from the mere inspection of the universe using inductive processes of reasoning. Indeed, it was Whately in his commentary on King's Sermon, long before Newman, who observed that if such a bare inspection were attempted it would more likely than not lead to the conclusion 'that the Deity was a being of a mixed or a capricious nature'.[20] For these theologians it was better to be soberly aware of our human limitations and silent before the incomprehensible mystery of God, who remained remote, sublime and ultimately unknowable as 'God is in God's self'.

This emphasis on the hiddenness of God, who remains a mystery even when revealed, entails that human images and analogical concepts of the divine are representations that are necessarily accommodated to the limited capacities of human minds. They were understood by Demea theologians to be adequate for the purposes of religious life and practical living, while falling short of communicating a clear and distinct knowledge of 'God as God is in God's self'. To Whately's mind, humans must be humbly content with the representations of the divine that are given in the revelation of scripture — these being sufficient for all the practical purposes of religion. We must rest content with the limitations of our human capacities. After all, said Whately, 'it was the craving after forbidden knowledge which expelled our first parents from paradise.'[21]

For these Anglican Demea theologians it became methodologically important to observe the dissonance between humanly expressed representations of the divine, including those we find in scripture, and God's transcendent and absolute nature. The primacy accorded to faith over reason, in turn, generates a humble acknowledgment of the limitations of all rationalistic attempts to reach the divine using human reason and processes of inference. As in traditional negative theology, there is a gulf of the kind of which the Swiss theologian Karl Barth spoke in the first half of the twentieth century as an 'infinite qualitative difference' between created time and the eternity of God. Heaven is not just an extension of this world. It is essentially other, sublime, profoundly mysterious, ultimately incomprehensible.

Newman's regular defences of faith independent of rational arguments, and his many declarations concerning the practical usefulness of religious language, despite its acknowledged limitations, are unmistakable indications that his thinking was profoundly conditioned by the basic theological approach that King had enunciated over a century previously.[22] And it was as a consequence of his disenchantment with the rationalistic approach, again following the initial impulse of Demea, that he turned his attention to an acquaintance with the divine will through the moral dictates of conscience. His acquaintance with the Demea tradition thus opened the way for Newman to develop the fundamentals of a characteristic approach to God through the category of mystery, which he was able to marry with the insights of Joseph Butler about the inner dictates of conscience. This was regularly to flicker to life in his sermons and other writings.

The voice of Demea is consistently heard in Newman's work, almost from his very first theological reflections. At the beginning of his preaching ministry at Oxford Newman articulated a classic expression of the Demea tradition in one of his first sermons, which he delivered at St Clement's, Oxford, in 1824.[23] In this sermon he combined talk of the 'mysterious loftiness of God' with 'the frailness and weakness of the human mind':

> *While God is shrouded from my view in the obscurity of His incomprehensible essence, I may be told indeed and be convinced of His purity, wisdom and love, but such representations come with little force to my soul. I go forward — [and] — He is not there — and backward but I cannot perceive Him [Job 23]. The impression on my mind of His excellence is faint and weak — it is indistinct — He is so much above me that I cannot attain unto the knowledge of Him [Ps 139].*[24]

These same emphases were also expressed in a more sustained way in Newman's *University Sermons*. The clear voice of Demea may be heard, for example, in the assertion of a sermon of 1831 to the effect that 'Scripture communications ... are intended for religious purposes' rather than for the purpose of providing exact or scientific information or dealing with 'the determination of physical questions',[25] and that 'Reason' must not be allowed to become the 'judge of those truths which are subjected to another part of our nature, the moral sense'.[26] As he had said in another sermon: 'Conscience is the essential principle and sanction of Religion in the mind.'[27]

However, the significance of Newman's *University Sermons* is that they not only reveal Newman as a thinker who stands squarely in the

Demea tradition, but they also represent Newman's first attempts to make his own original contribution to the development of that tradition. In these sermons Newman was making his first forays towards providing a systematic exposition of the more fideistic approach to religious faith of Demea that Hume had left so undeveloped. Newman was convinced that it was as 'absurd to argue men, as to torture them, into believing'.[28] Instead of syllogistic processes, faith is based on 'antecedent probabilities' apprehended by the believer as a moral conviction of the will, rather than as something strictly proved by inference.[29] For Newman the decision of faith is not primarily the result of argument. Rather, as he was to contend in a sermon entitled 'The Nature of Faith in Relation to Reason', which he preached on 13 January 1839, 'Faith is the reasoning of a religious mind, or of what Scripture calls a right or renewed heart, which acts upon presumptions rather than evidence, which speculates and ventures on the future when it cannot make sure of it.'[30]

It is possible to observe the way Newman's thinking around this point clarified as he became more and more disenchanted with a rationalistic temper of mind, not just in relation to natural theology and the argument from design, but also in the approach to the understanding of the revelation of God in scripture.

Some of Newman's earliest sermons reveal that he had been attempting to integrate his inherited evangelicalism with the thought of Thomas Erskine, who wrote on the truth of revealed religion in 1823. These, in turn, he tried to marry with the insights of the Demea position of his Oxford theological mentors. Erskine had expounded the view that in Christ the divine is revealed and thus made manifestly clear in the sermon he preached at St Clements in 1824. Newman likewise affirmed that 'the high and lofty attributes of the divine mind' were by revelation 'brought down to the level of our understandings'. The revelation of God in Christ means that 'the rays of His glory, which would else blind us, are attempered to the weakness of our vision — the infinitude of His counsels are traced out in legible characters as on a small tablet'. In this way the otherwise mysterious attributes of God are made manifest to us at least to some degree.

In a sermon preached on 21 September 1828 we find a similar view, though expressed with a suggestion of caution:

> *We cannot, My Brethren, understand the movements of the Divine Mind, and have no name even to denote in Him what in the case of men we call virtue and goodness. Yet surely, if we may dare accommodate earthly language to so high a purpose, there is no exalted grace or virtuous feeling which man can conceive, which is not shadowed out to us in the doctrine of the Incarnation of the Son of God.*[31]

Christ in this way of thinking becomes, if not the clear and distinct manifestation of the divine, then an indication of the divine nature that is at least 'shadowed out', whereby the attributes of God are 'rendered more intelligible'.

However, by the time Newman came to publish his Tract 73 in 1836, he had purged his views of this original reliance on Erskine. In this Tract 'On the Introduction of Rationalistic Principles into Religion', he urged the forsaking of what he termed a theology of 'Manifestation' in favour of a more aggressive theology of 'Mystery'.[32] Newman had come to see that the difficulty with the idea of 'Manifestation' was that it made the infinite so clearly intelligible and humanly available and accessible as to allow humans to imagine that they could possess and have it on their own terms and even confidently stand in judgment on it. This for Newman already involved an overconfident reliance on human reason and was thus a step in the direction of rationalism and liberalism. He corrected the tendency for theology to drift in this direction by insisting that in his mediatorial role Christ actually always points away from himself and beyond himself, and that the divine mystery to which he points cannot really be reduced to the proportions of finite human mind. Instead of speaking uncritically of the clear manifestation of the divine in Christ, Newman thus came to argue more forcefully for the essential mystery of God even when revealed in Christ.

This led Newman to the firmly held conviction that an element of essential mystery remains even when God is revealed, and that this is what would save theology from speculative, overconfident rationalism.

Instead of thinking of Christ as the bearer of clear and distinct information concerning the divine, about which theologians can then confidently speculate and engage in further high-flown argument and system-building of a rationalistic kind, Newman came to see that doctrine is always 'mysterious, because our information is *incomplete*'. In this way he could argue that a respectful and reverential awe needs to be retained in the approach to God in faith.

This became the key point in taking issue with Thomas Erskine. In Newman's view, Erskine represented an all too matter-of-fact and rationalistic approach to the doing of theology, which turned the object of faith into a system of propositions and formulas. These formulas were to be believed, and became the objects of faith instead of God. The formulation of these abstract beliefs depended on belief in a very straightforward and matter-of-fact revelation of the divine in the person and work of Christ. Newman believed this was far too overreaching. Erskine had tended overconfidently to claim to have an answer to everything, including, as we shall see in Chapter 4, a far too simplistic and neat rationalistic explanation of the saving Atonement of Christ in terms of his punishment for human sinfulness — the penal substitutionary theory.

In Tract 73 (which I think is far more theologically interesting than the notorious Tract 90 which got Newman into trouble with the English bishops and led to his exit from the Church of England), Newman thus argued against Erskine over what Newman spoke of as 'the introduction of rationalistic principles into revealed religion'. For Newman it was a mistake to imagine that the divine became clearly manifest, as plain as the nose on your face as it were, at the time of the Incarnation. The revelation of God in Christ does not somehow bring the infinite and divine down to our finite level; rather, it invites us finite human beings up to contemplate the infinite, but the infinite remains unchangeably as it is, a surpassing mystery before which humans must respond in awe and wonder.

By 1836 Newman's grasp of the importance of the category of 'Mystery' and his awareness of the orthodox antecedents of this as an important fundamental commitment in traditional Christian theology were firm. 'Mystery' was boldly cited as 'the badge or emblem of orthodoxy'.[33] 'To preach this is to preach the Gospel; not to apprehend it, is to be destitute of living faith.'[34] A speculative rationalism in theology that 'would account for everything' was to be avoided at all costs, for 'The Rationalist makes himself his own centre, not his Maker.'

In this way Newman understood revelation not as making clear to human reason certain fundamental divine truths or secrets of a propositional kind — which could then be accommodated to 'existing systems of knowledge' and developed rationalistically into a systematic catalogue of beliefs and formulas. Rather, he thought of revelation in terms of human apprehension more than comprehension, an engagement with mystery rather than rational assent to propositional truths, a sense of encounter with the surpassing reality of the divine presence rather than something that could be plainly grasped and humanly controlled and manipulated in a rationalistic way.

Revelation was the ambiguous disclosure of something beyond human systems, which could not therefore be reduced to a form of complete, clear and distinct propositional knowledge. As Newman himself put it:

> No revelation can be complete and systematic, from the weakness of the human intellect; so far as it is not such, it is mysterious. When nothing is revealed, nothing is known, and there is nothing to contemplate or marvel at; but when something is revealed and only something, for all cannot be, there are forthwith difficulties and perplexities.[35]

Newman goes on to say:

> A Revelation is religious doctrine viewed on its illuminated side; a Mystery is the self-same doctrine viewed on the side unilluminated. Thus Religious Truth is neither light nor darkness, but both together; it is like the dim view of a countryside in the twilight, with forms half extricated from the darkness, with broken lines, and isolated masses. Revelation, in this way of considering it, is not a revealed system, but consists of a number of detached and incomplete truths belonging to a vast system unrevealed, of doctrines

and injunctions mysteriously connected together, that is connected by unknown media, and bearing upon unknown portions of the system.[36]

In the second half of the nineteenth century, Newman, who had long since become a Roman Catholic, recognised a theological soul friend in H. L. Mansel, whose 1858 Bampton Lectures were published in 1859 as *The Limits of Religious Thought*. Indeed, Mansel was the other really great nineteenth-century Anglican theologian of the Demea tradition. Newman found Mansel's work on the limits of religious knowledge very congenial, and even imagined that Mansel might have drawn some of his ideas from Newman's own *University Sermons*. This was not the case, but Newman's perception of similarities between his thought and that of Mansel is not surprising, since Mansel also encapsulated the high orthodoxy of the Demea position. As Mansel understood the purposes of God, 'He has given us truths which are designed to be regulative, rather than speculative; intended not to satisfy our reason, but to guide our practice; not to tell us what God is in His absolute nature, but how He wills that we should think of Him in our present finite state.'[37]

The insights of William King also provided the essential kernel of the developed thesis of Mansel. In a letter to Professor Goldwin Smith (another Oriel College fellow) in the course of public discussion of the thesis of the *Limits*, Mansel actually acknowledged his dependence on William King, though the footnotes of the work itself reveal a heavy reliance also on the work of King's contemporary, Peter Browne, another Irish bishop and theologian of the Demea tradition.[38] Generally speaking, while King was concerned to underline the differences between the terms of analogical discourse when used in reference to God, Browne was committed to securing the elements of similarity despite acknowledged differences between human and divine nature.[39] Either way, for Mansel the conclusion to be drawn in relation to any finite attempt to conceive the infinite was that, 'in consequence of the inadequacy of the conception to express completely the nature of the object', further adventures in speculative thinking were rendered precarious.[40] Mansel thus argued that the surpassing mystery and otherness of God must entail that all humanly formulated religious truths are 'regulative but not informative'.[41] They are sufficient for the practical purposes of worship and religious living; they are not to be regarded as a body of information of a sufficiently clear and distinct kind to ground further speculative system-building.

Interestingly enough, a dispute over essentially this very same matter (about which Newman had taken issue with Thomas Erskine in 1836) resumed when F. D. Maurice, who had been greatly influenced by Erskine, argued against Mansel following the publication of the *Limits* in 1859. On this occasion Maurice pursued the idea that the revelation of God in Christ made the divine nature and attributes manifestly clear, while Mansel affirmed his conviction, as a Demea theologian, of the infinite mystery of God, even when God is revealed in Christ. Erskine publicly supported Maurice in the face of the sublimely transcendent theology of Mansel. Understandably, Newman registered his fundamental agreement with Mansel.

Newman and Mansel thus stand together as the great paradigms in the nineteenth century of the high orthodoxy of Anglican Demea theology. Even when Newman became a Roman Catholic in 1845 his fundamental theological commitments did not change. Indeed, inspired by Mansel's work on the limits of religious knowledge, in 1859 Newman resumed serious theological writing, something he had not done since he departed Anglicanism in 1845. It was this reigniting of his former theological interests that eventually led to the publication of *An Essay in Aid of a Grammar of Assent* in 1870.

Throughout his life Newman consistently pursued these ideas as an alternative to a more inferential and rationalistic approach to God from design. Eventually his quest was to find expression in this mature theological work. For example, in a passage of the *Grammar of Assent* that is resonant of the character of Demea, Newman says of God that only 'dim shadows of his Presence' may be discerned 'in the affairs of men', and '…He is specially "a Hidden God", and with our best efforts we can only glean from the surface of the world some faint and fragmentary views of Him'.[42] The last section of the *Grammar of Assent* in turn picked up and developed the theme of conscience in a broad discussion of the realtionship between natural and revealed religion.[43]

† † †

For contemporary Anglicans who inherit and own the theological tradition of high orthodoxy that was brought to clear definition in Hume's *Dialogues* through the voice of Demea, there are some very significant implications and outcomes. One is that we dare not race in prematurely to pontificate where even angels fear to tread. In the doing of theology a certain reticence and reserve are dictated by the fact that the revelation of God remains mysterious, and is not the explaining of a secret so as to make it transparently and manifestly clear and distinct. The German New Testament scholar Günther Bornkamm provides us with a contemporary expression of this same truth in his entry for 'Mysterion' in Kittel's *Theological Dictionary of the New Testament*. He says: 'It is not as though the mystery were a presupposition of revelation which is set aside when this takes place. Rather, revelation discloses the mystery as such.'[44]

It is for this reason that many of us are suspicious of a speculative rationalism in theology that overconfidently and even arrogantly presumes to know too much. God's nature and character are *not* manifested to us in scripture in such a way that we are able to set aside their essential mystery to engage in what Newman described as an intentional subjecting of them 'in an intelligible shape to our minds, and nothing more'.[45]

It also follows that, when we in faith become aware of a disclosure of the divine presence, we also become humbly aware of our own human limitations. What is revealed is revealed as a mystery, for as Newman said, 'we see but the skirts of God's glory in it'.[46] Revelation is not to be understood as a gnostic knowledge of secrets. As Archbishop Rowan Williams put it, we are not to assume that our theological system-building provides us with a body of clear and distinct truth which we can use as an instrument of power to browbeat and bludgeon others.

All this means that, even when something of the infinite God is revealed to us, he is not to be reduced to the limited proportions of finite human understanding; rather, just the opposite: as a result of revelation our finite human minds are opened up to the surpassing mystery of the infinite in awe and wonder.

† † †

Now, I believe we have here an explanation for the stereotypical perception with which we began this chapter, that Anglicans are not big on dogma. In other words, the very orthodox belief in the surpassing mystery of God is the theological basis of a certain reticence in matters of doctrinal definition that is characteristic of the spirit of Anglicanism. It has nothing to do with the liberalism of the post-Enlightenment Western world which would leave all matters of belief and value to be decided by the autonomous individual. Indeed, the Church as a community, as against an aggregate of isolated individuals, entertains a shared set of convictions in relation to faith and morals which it thinks important to teach and pass on to each succeeding generation. At the same time it is suspicious of the overconfident use of reason that characterises liberalism in its quest to accommodate faith to the wisdom of this world.

Moreover, given Hume's acknowledgment that a commitment to the surpassing mystery of God characterised the 'soundest orthodox divines who ever treated of the subject', it should not come as a surprise to find that what was brought to clear definition in Demea may be historically discerned already in the actual historical tradition, going back to the early Church Fathers. In that tradition, which survives particularly in the Eastern Church, enormous emphasis is laid on apophatic theology to correct any tendency to reduce the transcendent God to the finite level of the mundane. Gregory of Nyssa provides one of the classic instances when he said that 'we know that He is, but deny not that we are ignorant of the definition of His essence'.[47]

In the Western Church in the Middle Ages, Thomas Aquinas developed an extended discussion of the analogical use of language in reference to things divine as the first premise of all genuinely orthodox theology. That the ineffable reality of God is beyond expression in an unequivocal use of words does not mean for Aquinas that we have nothing at all to say. But we have to be aware of the limitations of what we do say. Indeed, from Thomas Aquinas we learn the clear methodological principle of apophatic theology — that because it is only possible to refer to God in analogical terms, every positive affirmation we make about God must be qualified by a negative and qualifying statement. In theological discourse the *via positiva*, the way of positive affirmation about God, must be balanced by a statement of the *via negativa*, a statement of what God is not. The value of apophatic theology is that it corrects any false tendency to create God in our own image by insistently reminding us that God is infinite, immaterial, impassible, atemporal and immutable.

This same emphasis of Christian orthodoxy is found in the writings of Richard Hooker, over one hundred and fifty years before Hume wrote. Indeed, Hooker not only saw the importance for authentic faith of an acknowledgment of the transcendent mystery of God, but also drew out its methodological implications for the doing of Christian theology with the kind of cautious reserve that has become characteristic of Anglicanism:

> *Dangerous it were for the feeble brain of man to wade far into the doings of the Most High; whom although to know be life, and joy to make mention of his name; yet our soundest knowledge is to know him not as indeed He is, neither can know Him: and our safest eloquence concerning Him is our silence, when we confess without confession that His glory is inexpressible, His greatness above our capacity and reach. He is above and we are upon earth; therefore it behoveth our words to be wary and few.*[48]

A sense of the surpassing mystery of God also explains why Anglicanism is uncomfortable with claims of infallibility, whether the infallibility of the Pope or the infallibility of the Bible. Instead, we Anglicans are content to live with a measure of ambiguity and to keep a respectful silence in the face of a reality that at the end of the day is acknowledged to be beyond our understanding. That is why theology must give way to the impulse to worship: when we encounter the divine we do not reach for a notebook to record the experience; we take off our shoes, for we are on holy ground. We become humbly aware of our human limitations, and our appropriate first response is one of awe and wonder. This is the primary impulse to worship and it explains why Anglicans spend more time on producing prayer books than on defining doctrines.

This respect for the awesome mystery and transcendence of God and the resultant acknowledgment of the limits of human understanding mean, for those of us Anglicans who value and insistently uphold these things, that the Christian journey is not a matter of appearing before the world as though we have nothing to learn. Certainly we do not presume to suggest we possess clear and distinct answers to every conceivable question. We feel no pressure to correct every other attempt to express divine truth. We can live comfortably with diversity because we acknowledge that all attempts to express the divine will in some way fall short of absolute truth.

We do not approach the practice of religion, therefore, as though it involved having all the answers, because we do not see life primarily as a problem to be solved. Rather, we see ourselves as being on an open-ended journey into a future to which we are called by God, a journey in faith and hope, in which there is always something new to learn, a mind-set to be expanded, a perception of things to be stretched, a deeper wisdom to be discerned. This is what I mean by 'progressive orthodoxy'. We Anglicans are called into the future by the God of hope in the firm conviction that our God is always the God who is beyond our human attempts to have him on our own terms. Because our God is also a God who promises to make all things new, life is a constant entry into the deepening awareness of his surpassing mystery, and the mystery we are to ourselves, and to one another. In the Church we enter together into the awesome experience of the mystery of human relationality in our communion together in Christ — hence, progressive, or dynamic, orthodoxy.

CHAPTER 2

THE NATURE OF DOCTRINE

G iven the surpassing mystery of God and the requirement that we
acknowledge the limits of finite human understanding in relation
to ultimate things, it is important to register some tentative reflections
on the nature of Christian doctrine. We can begin where we left off in
the last chapter, by underlining the characteristic Anglican reserve in
relation to matters of speculative doctrine. By way of a concrete
example, it is possible to see this principle of reserve at work in the
religious thinking not of a professional theologian, but of a well-
informed lay Anglican — the nineteenth-century British Prime
Minister William Ewart Gladstone.

Gladstone, who, like Newman, was brought up in a very strict
evangelical household, also made the gradual transition to a more
expansive position as a 'Catholic evangelical', and to what he himself
called a more 'traditional Anglicanism', during the course of the late
1820s. This quite significant spiritual transition occurred only after
some very serious grappling with the theology of baptism, and
particularly with the question of whether baptism was to be
understood primarily in terms of repentance or of regeneration. The
outcome of his study led Gladstone to reject the prevailing
individualistic view of the time, which held that baptism was merely

an outward sign of repentance on the part of the believer. In this received evangelical understanding of things, the believer 'submitted to baptism' simply as a public sign of Christian profession. But Gladstone came to an appreciation of the regenerative power of the grace of God in baptism. Apart from repentance, which he interpreted strictly as a human 'turning' to God, Gladstone saw that baptism also involved the covenant pledge of God's own love and the ensuing promise of the divine grace of human transformation, whereby all the baptised, including children, could confidently be said to have been embraced by God. The embrace of God could not fail to have a positive regenerative or humanly enhancing effect.

At around the same time, Gladstone found himself also rejecting the doctrine of predestination then entertained by evangelicals of a more Calvinistic persuasion and enthusiastically promoted by their chief spokesperson of the time, Henry Bulteel, a man of extreme predestinarian views. Gladstone's own transitional thought processes can be tracked in a collection of 'Papers ... Chiefly Theological',[1] which he wrote at Oxford during the period from 1829 to 1831. These included a paper on Calvinism. In addition, three pages of his notes have been preserved from the same period on the related subject of predestination.[2]

We have already noted that the decade prior to Keble's famous Assize Sermon of 1833, which is generally reckoned to have triggered the Oxford Movement, was a period when Oxford scholars, including Newman, were appealing to the notion of divine mystery. This notion was regularly used to answer Calvinist views of predestination, which appeared to minimise human freewill in favour of a kind of determinism. As we saw in the last chapter, the argument was that, as an implication of the ultimate unknowability of God, no contradiction could be drawn between the idea of divine predestination and human freewill precisely because we do not know exactly what divine predestination involves in God. The possibility of thinking of predestination in terms of a kind of divine foreknowledge without committing to a strict determinism was commonplace at the time. Those who appreciated the fundamental importance of the mystery of God could see that no human being really has a sufficiently intimate access to the inner workings of the divine mind to pronounce on such things with any confidence. At the same time human freewill and moral responsibility seemed incontrovertible realities of ordinary human experience that dictated the need to revise thoroughgoing determinist theories.

Given the prevalence of these views in the theological atmosphere when Gladstone first went up to Oxford in 1828, it is no coincidence that Gladstone himself came under the influence of the same broad approach in dealing with the problem of predestination and freewill. In a classic expression of the position espoused by Demea theologians from William King onwards, Gladstone first affirmed the importance of not probing too far into the divine mystery. But he went further than just delivering a warning against overconfidently asserting the apparent inconsistency of belief in divine predestination and the human experience of freewill. He also expanded on this theme in a way that may well have been original. He seems to have perceived that the exercise of the predestining will of God could not be located in a moment of created time, for it belonged in the essentially timeless eternity of God. In relation to the human exercise of freewill this means that the very moment in which the human decision of faith is taken in historical time actually coincides with the essentially timeless moment of God's act of predestining. In other words, the moment of human decision *is* the moment of divine predestination. It is all a matter of trying to get one's mind around the relationship between God's eternity and created time. Gladstone wrote: 'Rest ... satisfied that as the foreknowledge and the decree are simultaneous in Him so are the predestination and the faith in us — and ... inquire no further — for now thou seest that it is ... *absolutely impossible* that the question should be answered ... since it goes to make *two* of things which are *essentially and therefore indivisibly one*'. Then, in a way that is unmistakably reminiscent of the theological tradition of Demea, Gladstone goes on: 'it is not pretended that the question is *solved* — no, far from it — by this reasoning — but something is done if it be shown that [it] is necessarily insoluble' and thus 'removed to the realm of "*mystery*"'.[3]

Gladstone's biographer Peter Jagger feels that Gladstone was at this point merely recognising the limitations of his appeal to insolubility in an apologetic kind of way. However, he was in fact confidently expressing the orthodoxy of those who, like Newman in the Oxford of the 1820s, had been influenced, whether consciously or unconsciously, by Coplestone and Whately on the basis of the original insights of William King. Certainly, the idea of the divine mystery and incomprehensibility was in the theological air at Oxford at the time. As Gladstone was to apply it, the apparent logical tension between the idea of divine predestination and the exercise of human freewill must be 'deposited in the bosom of God who alone has perfect knowledge'. Given, the inscrutable mystery of God, there was no alternative; from their limited perspective, mere humans must 'there let it rest'. And 'Let us implore the grace of God to keep us from troubling ourselves, or from being troubled by others upon it.'

It was not just that Gladstone had become disenchanted with the rationalistic speculations of the Calvinist party of his day so as to opt out of theological controversy in favour of a quieter life. Rather, he was expressing the then standard approach of orthodox Demea theology so as to disarm those who claimed an intimate but overconfident knowledge of the inner workings of the predestining mind of God in a way that minimised the role of human freewill. No doubt this was also conditioned by the commonsense need to defend the importance of freewill in the interest of protecting belief in human responsibility and practical morality.

We have already noted the roots of this interest in regulative rather than speculative truth in the high orthodoxy of the Demea tradition. It is of interest that Gladstone had by this stage already come into direct contact with Newman[4] and had almost certainly been exposed to his ideas concerning both the importance of the category of mystery and the resultant pragmatic orientation of doctrines. As Newman was to put it, revelation is for a practical purpose, that we might 'do better' rather than 'know more'. Newman argued that we 'are only informed so far on the subject, as bears upon *practical purposes*'.[5] In other words, scripture gives us sufficient knowledge to allow us to get on with the living of our religious and moral lives; it is 'sufficient unto salvation' in this sense, even if it is admitted that it does not tell us everything we might wish to know.

Similarly, some years later, in 1836, in a sermon preached a few months after the publication of Tract 73 (in which he had emphasised the importance of the category of mystery for the whole theological enterprise), Newman underlined the 'singular practical effects' on the believer of accepting the mysteriousness of the God. In his dealings with his creatures God is not obliged 'to take us into counsel, and explain to us the reason for everything ... There is nothing according as we are given to see and judge of things, which will make a greater difference in the temper, character, and habits of an individual, than the circumstance of his holding or not holding the Gospel to be mysterious.'[6] The emphasis of this approach to the articulation of Christian doctrine is on the importance of getting on with the practical business of Christian living in this world, rather than on a form of evangelical soul-saving involving assent to a catalogue of more speculative matters of belief as a kind of required passport to a heaven beyond this world. Though the ultimate heavenly destination of the believer is not of course denied, salvation in this view is concretely achieved by grace at the final end of a moral life of faithful obedience, rather than an automatic reward for believing abstract doctrines as tends to be suggested by the catchcry 'Believe and you will be saved.'

† † †

This pragmatic assessment of our limited religious insights and concepts had also been spelled out by Copleston. He noted, by way of analogy, that when humans speak of the sea they use such words as 'placid', 'as cleansing with a priestlike ablution', 'as now becoming restless, turbulent, furious, raging, and then abating in its anger — becoming peaceful, calm, tranquil, benign'. All this, said Copleston, is analogical discourse whereby the sea is understood by reference to ourselves; the mood of the sea is interpreted through a kind of imaginative anthropomorphism.[7] In meteorological terms this is inexact language, but it is important insofar as it leads to practical consequences. If one speaks of the sea as becoming restless, then one begins to take in the sails, check the moorings and batten down the hatches. Despite the inexact, imaginary and metaphorical nature of the language used when the sea is described as 'restless', it is sufficient to prompt us to action. Without explaining much about the connection of effects in the sea to imminent climatic change, or exactly why it is that a storm is about to break, the perception of what is described as its 'restlessness' is sufficient to guide our behaviour.

Copleston argued that Christian doctrine is of a similar nature. We also think of God in analogical terms. These are of limited value and may be relatively uninformative when it comes to transmitting an exact knowledge of 'God as God is in God's self' but they are pointers to an understanding of God's nature and, despite their limitations, are sufficient for the practical purposes of religious living.

It is not difficult to think of other mundane examples to illustrate the same point. One does not have to know all that there is to know about gravity in order to know the regulative truth that one must take care when standing close to the edge of a sixth-floor balcony with balustrades of doubtful reliability. We know enough about gravity to know that we must keep our feet firmly on the ground, without being able to explain the physics of the gravitational forces with scientific exactness.

Likewise, we may at first not know what the colour 'magenta' is in scientific terms. We can learn the meaning of the concept by ostensive definition, by being shown a magenta shirt. Or else we can have the colour described to us. We may be told, for example, that magenta is a kind of purple, a very specific tonal purple, a nuanced red-purple rather than a blue-purple. With this rough-and-ready description, and without knowing the exact proportions of red and blue pigment in its make-up, when we encounter somebody wearing a magenta shirt we can put two and two together and say, 'Aha, that is magenta!' When we have also learned that magenta shirts are regularly worn by bishops, this may even make it possible for us to go on to say identifyingly, 'Aha, this is a bishop!' We do not have to know all that there is to know about the concept 'magenta' in order to put it to good practical use.

Now, in the apophatic tradition of Christian orthodoxy, religious concepts work in the same kind of way. We do not have to know all there is to know about the being and nature of God in order to formulate doctrines that are of practical usefulness for religious and moral purposes. For example, in the present generation we have come to appreciate that what appears to many as the somewhat high-flown and abstract doctrine of the Trinity in fact has huge repercussions for the way human society is ordered. The idea of the equal status of the distinct and distinguishable persons of the Trinity, and the mutual exchange of love amongst them in the communion of one unity of being, actually have enormous practical implications. The doctrine of the Trinity operates as a kind of model for the way we are and how we behave in the Church as a diversity of distinct and distinguishable persons living in the unity of one communion by mutual self-gift. Indeed, the experience of the interpersonal communion known in the life of the Church gives us an experiential insight into the nature of the unity of God within complexity as three persons and one communion. This kind of interplay between doctrine and experience is illustrated in the seminal discourse on the Holy Spirit by Basil of Caesarea in 374 AD. In this it is clear that the communion of the Church, which is understood to have been established by the gift of the Holy Spirit, is also a pointer to the unity of God.

Likewise, the doctrine of the Incarnation of the God who entered into this material world in human form reverberates through the life of the Church in a number of practical ways. Without being able to explain exactly how both divine and human natures are present in the person of Jesus Christ, and in the face of a variety of christological models that historically have attempted to do this, the doctrine is of enormous practical importance in Christian approaches to the natural world. The doctrine of the Incarnation of God in Christ inclines us to an appreciation of the essential goodness of material things, for example. This incarnational principle, in turn, informs our sacramental thinking about the way loaf and cup can be understood as signs to communicate spiritual realities at the Eucharist. The doctrine of the Incarnation of God also informs a sensitive response to the problem of the degradation of the natural environment. In other words, the doctrine of the Incarnation of God in Christ, the gathering into one of things earthly and heavenly, has enormous implications for matters of attitude and practical behaviour. All this is what is meant by affirming that doctrine is intended for a regulative rather than an exclusively speculative and informative purpose.

† † †

This brings us to the point where we may profitably pause to analyse the nature of doctrine in a little more detail. A contemporary North American Lutheran theologian, George Lindbeck, has argued in a book entitled *The Nature of Doctrine*[8] that there are three identifiable ways of approaching an understanding of the nature of Christian doctrine and the way it relates to faith and experience. I do not recognise the position of regulative and non-speculative truth in any of them, so I shall be suggesting a fourth option. Nevertheless, Lindbeck's clarifying analysis is a helpful way of approaching this subject.

Lindbeck's first category is what he terms the *descriptive or propositionalist* view of Christian doctrine. This might also be referred to as the traditionalist or naively realist model. It suggests that faith is a matter of assenting to the truth of certain abstract propositions about God and about the way in which God and humanity go together. Doctrines are straightforwardly descriptive and referential. They are believed to map onto the divine realities they describe in a one-to-one kind of way. Doctrine in this sense is fundamentally and exclusively informative.

Secondly, Lindbeck speaks of the *experiential-expressivist* view of doctrine. This is the view of liberal theological movements, which tend to think of doctrine not as descriptive of God as a religious object, but as the expression of the experience of the religious subject. They are anti-realist, in the sense that they do not map onto any objective reality in a clearly descriptive way. Rather, verbal expressions of doctrinal belief are to be understood much more as a way of talking about a non-cognitive and subjective religious experience. There is no claim of having to do with a religiously significant objective reality; rather, doctrines are simply ways of expressing subjective experience. Religious belief is a self-contained activity, like holding one's breath.

Thirdly, there is the *linguistic-cultural* view. This view has developed a 'rule' theory of doctrine. It places doctrine within the linguistic activity of a community, where it operates to guide belief and behaviour without necessarily claiming to describe objective realities. Doctrines operate in the context of specific communities like a set of grammatical rules, which allow some things to be said and done while others are either forbidden or at least ruled out of order. Of Lindbeck's three types, this may at first sight be the closest to the pragmatic and less speculative or less rationalistic view of doctrine for which I have been arguing. However, I shall also be arguing that doctrine is an index to objective reality and that religious experience can be an experience *of something*, and not just a self-contained activity.

We can unpack the main differences between Lindbeck's three approaches to doctrine by starting with the second of them, which I think is the least appealing. Even though this liberal view of things may today in fact be the most prevalent and popular within much contemporary Christianity, I think it is the least satisfactory.

The experiential-expressivist model notes, and indeed makes a virtue out of, the diversity of contemporary theological systems. For example, it is well known that in the early Church there were different and, to some extent, competing doctrines of the Trinity. Contrasting doctrines were found respectively in the East and in the West. Briefly put, in the East God the Father was understood to be the eternal source of the divine Son, who was said to have been 'begotten by the Father'. Likewise, the Father was the source of the divinity also of the Holy Spirit, who was understood to have 'proceeded from the Father'. The divinity of the second and third persons of the Trinity thus flowed from the divinity of the Father, in whom they both had their eternal origin. The Father was thus always the first person of the Trinity. The co-inherence of the distinct persons by mutual self-gift was then worked out so as to produce the so-called social understanding of the Trinity of three persons in one unity of being, or three persons in one communion of love.

By contrast, in the West the beginning point was not the originative divinity of the Father, but the idea of divine substance in which each of the three persons of the Trinity equally shared. This shared divine substance was what gave unity to the persons, who thus might all be said to be 'equal in divinity'. They were all equally divine because they all shared equally in the one eternal divine substance.

Clearly in the history of Christian doctrine there have been two different approaches to the understanding of the Trinity, broadly speaking, one Eastern and the other Western. At some points mishearing between the East and the West led to controversy, as with the dispute about the *filioque* ('and the Son') clause, which the Western Church added to the credal affirmation about the Holy Spirit's proceeding from the Father (see the Prologue). This was offensive in the East, not just because it was added in an unauthorised way to a universally agreed conciliar definition, but also because of the standing commitment in the East to the originative divinity of the Father alone with respect to the other two divine persons.

This diversity of doctrinal viewpoints concerning the Trinity suggests a more general truth about the nature of doctrine. For, while there may have been one common experience of the three-ness of God in the working out of salvation in practice, through participation in the divine life and love of God the Holy Trinity, when it came to expressing that experience abstractly in words different models emerged. The human experience of the three-ness of God may have been the same, but the words employed to describe the unity within the diversity of divine persons varied. Different communities of thought used different vocabularies and arrived at different doctrinal conceptualisations. Variety of expression, in other words, arises out of a unity of experience. But the patent fact that there have been different doctrinal attempts to explain the Trinity could mean that no single form of expression can claim to be an exact description of the divine mystery of the inner nature of God.

The doctrine of the presence of Christ at the Eucharist has also been expressed differently by different groups of Christians at different periods in history. For Christians living in Europe in the fourteenth century it involved the belief known as 'transubstantiation'. For Lutherans in the sixteenth century it was a matter of consubstantiation. For Christians living in Belgium in the mid-1960s it involved talk of 'transignification'. Clearly the language has been different but, so the experiential-expressivist theory of doctrine would have it, this arises out of a common Eucharistic experience of encounter with the presence of Christ in the sharing of loaf and cup.

If this kind of doctrinal diversity can emerge within Christianity, it perhaps also provides us with a way of understanding the differences between Christianity and other religions — at least theistic religions. Perhaps Christianity, Judaism and Islam, all of which are monotheistic religions, arise out of a fundamentally common experience of God, for example. It could be contended that amongst the adherents of these three great religious traditions there are different doctrinal formulations, but they all have a common point of origin in the shared experience of the one God. They use different sets of concepts, and a different basket of stories to illustrate those concepts, but all express a single human experience of God. Indeed, perhaps Hinduism and Zen Buddhism also arise out of the same fundamental encounter with God, even if each formulates a different approach to expressing it.

Those who favour the experiential-expressivist understanding of religious doctrine locate ultimately significant contact with whatever is finally important for religion in the pre-reflective experiential depths of the individual self. Friedrich Schleiermacher's 'feeling of absolute dependence' on something other than oneself would be a good example of this approach to theology, and may indeed be its historical origin. As 'the father of modern theology' Schleiermacher oriented all subsequent liberal approaches to theology towards the religious subject. Christian doctrine is then understood to express the subject's experience but does not necessarily seek to describe a religious object in an exact kind of way.

The experiential-expressivist model is thus the liberal approach to the understanding of doctrine. It entails that a variety of verbal formulations may be tolerated, because none of them will claim exclusively to be the only one-to-one description of what is the case. Rather, the verbal formulation is simply an attempt, using human words and symbols, to express how a particular inner experience strikes a specific individual. It is thus rightly said to be a non-cognitive, even anti-realist, approach to the understanding of doctrine, in the sense that it does not necessarily make claims to the knowledge of an object in a propositional way. Rather, the existence of an object is at best inferred on the basis of some kind of vague inner apprehension: God is indirectly detected in the depths of the subjective soul's experience.

According to this account of religious doctrine, the various world religions, no less than the various doctrinal systems within Christianity, could be regarded as diverse symbolisations of one and the same core experience of the ultimate. They must therefore tolerate and respect one another and perhaps even reciprocally enrich one another without ever really being in direct competition with one another. In some degree even the Roman Catholic theologian Karl Rahner moves in the direction of this approach when he speaks of the adherents of other religions or of no religion as 'anonymous Christians' — people who do not claim to be Christians, and do not use a Christian vocabulary, but who share the fundamental experience of God of which Christians speak in their doctrines. Christians may make a better fist of verbalising it, but the core experience is available to everyone.

In direct contrast with this approach to the understanding of Christian doctrine, what Lindbeck calls the descriptive or propositionalist approach makes the claim that doctrine does more than just expressing how an experience might appear to a subjective believer. Doctrine also involves claims as to what is in fact the case; it seeks to describe a religiously significant object or state of affairs in a clear and distinct kind of way. Doctrines are descriptive and referential, and therefore embody cognitive claims, rather than merely being expressive of a subjective religious experience or feeling. They embody truth claims about objective realities or states of affairs of an indisputably informative kind.

The crucial difference between this propositionalist view and the experiential-expressivist view is that while the latter can tolerate a number of apparently different and perhaps competing alternative ways of expressing a religious experience, the propositionalist view can really tolerate only one formulation, for only one form of words will correspond to or map onto what is actually the case. The most hard-nosed and uncompromising form of this view would hold that only one doctrine will accurately describe the objective reality or state of affairs to which it relates. Alternatively, a more moderate view might hold that one doctrine will at least be held to be a more accurate description than others and will therefore be preferred to them.

In the case of the linguistic-cultural approach, doctrine provides us with 'communally authoritative rules of discourse, attitude and action'. Lindbeck argues that doctrine operates as a set of rules within a specific linguistic and faith community. He draws an analogy with traffic rules. For example, some countries work with the rule 'Drive on the right', while others use 'Drive on the left.' Just as such rules guide and thus regulate behaviour in a way that is specific to a particular context, so Christian doctrine can be understood to give us rules to guide what we can legitimately say and appropriately do relative to the particular context. And just as traffic rules are not descriptive of some universal state of affairs or of some objective reality, nor expressive of universal human experience, but operate by legal convention within different cultures and are relative to those specific cultures, so doctrines must be understood from within the culture in which they properly operate. Different traffic rules operate to guide behaviour in the specific cultures of Australia and America, for example, in different ways. They do not claim to express a truth of a cognitive kind that is valid for everyone, nor do they express some kind of shared experience that is common to all motor vehicle drivers, but in different ways. It is not that we have equally valid but different verbal expressions that arise out of the universal experience of driving a motor vehicle. Rather, doctrines operate to regulate life within a particular ecclesiastical community context.

These different ways of understanding doctrine involve different attitudes to truth-seeking. In the case of the propositionalist model, opposing doctrines are necessarily in competition with one another and one must be judged to be true and the others false or inadequate. Moreover, if a doctrine is understood to map onto an object or religious state of affairs so as to describe it accurately, it will be held to be immutably true. There will be little room for change in this view of doctrine. Pluralism will be ruled out in a way that it is not in the experiential-expressivist approach. In the experiential-expressivist model all doctrines are more or less equally valid ways of expressing experience so long as they are sincere. In the case of Lindbeck's linguistic-cultural model, the apparent opposition between doctrines can be resolved in large part by reference to the cultural context within which each specifically belongs and operates. The opposition between them is not resolved by declaring one to be correct and the others wrong. Nor is there any need to alter them to bring them into conformity with one another. All are valid, but in different contexts.

Using this model, for example, it could be said that in the Middle Ages the doctrine of transubstantiation guided the Church's talk about the real presence of Christ in the Eucharist. This was in the context of an intellectual culture within which the Aristotelian concept of 'substance' was already familiar. Since the Second Vatican Council the concept of transignification has operated in some places to achieve something similar — but in a different kind of culture which has long since lost its attachment to Aristotelian categories of thought. In a single culture, if both doctrines were appealed to at the same time, they might almost certainly come into collision. But placed within the respective cultures to which they belong, they remain meaningful and useful. The potential conflict between them can therefore be harmonised by putting them in the context from which they come.

Likewise, a complex doctrinal statement such as the Nicene Creed could be said not simply to report what is the case in a propositional or purely descriptive form, but instead to operate as a rule of belief in such a way as to exclude alternative and conflicting statements, while permitting others. The statement that Christ is 'of one Being with the Father' in its original form was intended to exclude the teaching of Arius about Christ as a created being and therefore as separate from, and lower than or subordinate to, the Father. The modern phrase 'of one Being with the Father' does not set out to tell us about the precise way in which the Father and Son are one. Its purpose is not so much to describe as to operate as a rule to help orthodox Christians distinguish themselves from Unitarians,[9] but it does not specify in positive and exact terms what is to be affirmed about the unity of the

Father and the Son. Indeed, today we are in the position of asking what exactly can be meant by the phrase 'of one Being'. However, while the expression 'of one Being with the Father' may be rather vague and imprecise language that needs further theological unpacking, it at least helps prevent people from abandoning belief in the divine nature of the Son and in his equal status with the Father.

† † †

Now, while the three ways of understanding doctrine in Lindbeck's analysis may clarify things, I do not recognise my own understanding of the nature of doctrine in any of them. I therefore wish to propose a further option to his three, which is really a combination of aspects of all of them. Instead of regarding these three approaches to the understanding of doctrine as mutually exclusive and competitive, I find it more helpful to see them as each illuminating a different aspect of doctrine. Like a smorgasbord, it is a matter of taking 'a bit of everything'.

The *pragmatic or regulative* view of doctrine that I wish to uphold is to some degree similar to both the experiential-expressivist and the linguistic-cultural models, but without denying that doctrinal statements also attempt to signify what is the case, as in the traditional propositionalist view. While admitting that revelation is only ever the partial disclosure of a God who remains essentially mysterious, and that doctrinal statements can therefore only 'point towards' the truth they seek to express, they do seek to tell us something. Just as to perceive the restless sea in Copleston's analogy is to know at least something about the behaviour of the sea without being able to explain the precise meteorological details that account for it, so doctrine does set out to tell us something about objective realities that are religiously significant, or about religiously significant states of affairs. Moreover, while we readily admit that we are not privy to everything that might be said about the inner make-up of the divine, which therefore remains a mystery, the something we do perceive is sufficient to move us to action.

One of the purposes of theology is to systematise and order the various images that are used to refer to God, from the somewhat crude image of a rock or a wind, for example, to the more sophisticated view that God is a loving father or shepherd. By arranging images of God in a kind of hierarchy and by balancing one against the other, it is possible to construct a conceptual edifice that has a certain directionality about it. While admitting the fundamental deficiencies of this kind of exercise, since ultimately the divine mystery is beyond all our conceptions of God, when taken together these descriptions are nevertheless sufficient to allow us some inkling of the divine nature. We perceive something of the being of God and therefore claim to know and to communicate something, without being foolish enough to claim to know everything. But this has a pragmatic rather than a purely descriptive or informative purpose: what is thereby communicated is sufficient to allow us to get on with the practical business of worship and religious living.

On the other hand, to agree that doctrine arises out of religious experience does not automatically rule out the possibility that it is an experience *of* something, rather than being a purely subjective expression of a person's inner feelings, detached from what is the case in the realm of objective reality. In insisting that religious experience may take the form of encounter with a reality that is external to the believer, we may wisely avoid the naive realism of the strictly propositionalist view. Instead we can adopt a critical realism which admits that what we claim to know is also to some degree conditioned by the categories available for handling it within a specific linguistic community and culture. Doctrines are always subject to the limitations of finite minds and are necessarily culturally conditioned, for in articulating them we have no alternative but to employ the language of a particular time and place. We can therefore also accept the fact that doctrines are put to a practical use as the grammar or rules that guide religious belief and behaviour within a specific linguistic and cultural community. We can see that Lindbeck's three categories are not necessarily mutually exclusive; it is possible to combine elements drawn from all of them. We can acknowledge that doctrines arise out of and are thus expressive of human religious experience, without necessarily thinking in terms of self-contained subjective experience. If a religious experience can be an experience *of* something, it is important to say that this reality can be known not just abstractly by description, but also concretely by acquaintance. To affirm that doctrines seek to indicate a state of affairs in which God is to be understood as a religious object is not to deny that human beings are capable of the experience of at least a partial knowing of him.

The doctrine of the love of God is a case in point. We refer to his love when we talk descriptively about it as a generously wasteful and overflowing grace that flows to us unconditionally and moves amongst us in the communion (*koinonia*) of the Church. But the love of God is not something entirely abstract and theoretical that is to be approached in an entirely rationalistic way; rather, it is something Christians intuitively encounter and identify in their actual experience of communion together. This happens both definitively in the fellowship of the Church and outside this fellowship in hints and glimpses as Christian people live their lives in the world. Apart from asserting something important about God's nature, to which we might assent in a rationalistic kind of way, and claim to know *about*, the doctrine also provides us with the concept of the love of God and rules for its use, which enable us to use it identifyingly in concrete human experience. When we encounter it concretely in living experience, the doctrine operates as a kind of grammar of God that allows us to say in the judgment of faith: 'Aha! This is what they were talking about.' The judgment of faith is not just an intellectual assent to belief in the existence of the God of love abstractly conceived and independent of our experience of God. In addition to affirming that the Christian God is a God of love, we can therefore by ostensive definition point to a reality of our experience in the *koinonia* of the Church. We can affirm in faith: 'This is nothing less than the love of God!' The doctrine thus makes it possible for Christians to claim to know the love of God identifyingly in concrete experience.

While doctrine may connect with religious experience in this practical kind of way, it is important to acknowledge that it is not the verbal outcome of some kind of general or universal religious experience which can be expressed in any form of words or equally in a whole range of alternative religious discourses. What is identified as the object of faith in Christian experience is a highly specific kind of reality, such as was uniquely revealed in the person and work of Jesus Christ, and which demands quite specific language and rules for its use.

Like Lindbeck's propositionalist view, a regulative non-speculative view of doctrine seeks to signify the nature of divine reality, while admitting that because of the limitations of human reason and the fact that only part of a greater whole is revealed, our knowledge will necessarily be partial and incomplete. The surpassing mystery of God dictates that we admit the inadequacy of our feeble attempts to express him. In the language of modern structuralist thought, we have to 'defer' a final and ultimate statement of truth until the full revealing of God at the eschaton (end of the world), but that does not deter us in the present from saying at least something. Nor does it prevent us from truth-seeking in the present. Like Lindbeck's propositionalist view, our doctrine will seek to say at least something about the God who has revealed something of himself to us. As Wittgenstein once said, 'a nothing would be as good as a something about which nothing could be said'. But because something has been revealed, at least something can be said. In fact, sufficient is revealed for the practical purpose of allowing people of faith to identify a spiritual presence or a religiously significant state of affairs and then get on with the practical business of the living of their lives in relation to such realities.

This is what is meant by the *regulative* as against a purely *speculative* understanding of doctrine. It is sufficient for the purposes of religious living, but it may not be anywhere near sufficient to ground further overconfident ventures of speculative thought.

This does not rule out, however, the fact that doctrine may also be understood to warrant rule-guided discourse and behaviour, as in Lindbeck's linguistic-cultural view. Amongst other things a statement of doctrine allows us to exclude incompatible expressions of belief. While we do not claim to say everything, what we do affirm is sufficient to exclude logical competitors.

† † †

Now, this assessment of the complex and diverse nature of religious doctrine may help those of us who view Sydney Anglicanism from the outside to observe that one of its identifying characteristics appears to be a tendency to overconcentrate on a deceptively clear and distinct propositionalist or descriptivist view of doctrine at the expense of religious experience. The following historical example illustrates this in a particularly telling way.

On 18 September 1956 the then Archbishop of Sydney, Howard Mowll, wrote to the Principal of Moore Theological College, Dr Broughton Knox, about the architectural propriety of placing large crosses on the east walls of churches above the holy table or altar. Apart from declaring such practices to be illegal,[10] Dr Knox argued that such crosses were 'liable to be used for superstitious purposes'. He then went on to outline the theological reasoning that he believed warranted this judgment. He explained to Mowll that idolatry is not the worship of a statue instead of God so much as the worship even of the true God by means of materialistic representations. While the first commandment forbids the worship of other gods, the second commandment, he said, 'forbids the worship of the true God by the aid of unauthorised sensuous media'. Even the use of a cross for a devotional rather than a merely decorative purpose falls under this condemnation.

What is of enormous interest in the letter is Dr Knox's use of the word 'sensuous', for this has a clearly perjorative moral sense. He might have more accurately used the word 'sensory' to connote the bringing into play of the senses, or he might have spoken in a morally neutral way of the involvement of sensory experiences as an aid to the worship of God. However, the negative moral colouring imported by the use of 'sensuous' appears to be quite deliberate.[11] He goes on:

> If we persistently worship God with the aid of material media, our religious life will be confined to the lowest element in our soul, the sensuous, and we will never truly know God. God is a Spirit and must be worshipped spiritually. His worship is hindered when we multiply to ourselves materialistic aids in our approach to Him. True Faith is evoked by the promise of God entering our understanding.

Clearly, we have here a paradigm statement of the propositionalist-descriptivist approach to faith and doctrine. Faith is an intellectual assent to abstract doctrinal truths, rather than a response of a more affective and experiential kind to the perceived presence of God. Indeed, there are indicators of an alarming dualism in Dr Knox's statements, insofar as he draws an unfortunate gnostic dichotomy between the spiritual and the material. Faith is said to be a response of the understanding to abstract propositions, rather than a response of the whole person involving 'tender feeling, sentiment, and emotion' which the worshipper, says Knox, 'may and in my opinion often does, mistake for one's faith'. These responses are said to be 'nothing more than refined sensuous feelings and do not bring him into fellowship truly with God'.

Any sense that the Christian believer might employ doctrines in order to be led towards a concrete experience of the holy, or to a deepening engagement with the communion of God, is missing. Likewise, the idea that the doctrine of the love of God might point the believer towards an awareness of an incarnational reality that might be experienced with the aid of aesthetic, symbolic or sacramental aids to worship is ruled out of court. Such an understanding of things is dismissed as 'a constant desire of fallen man to worship God with the aid of sensuous media'. St Paul's statement that 'God's love has been poured into our hearts by the Holy Spirit that has been given to us' (Romans 5:5) might lead most of us to think of the activity of the Spirit as a form of the presence of God's love that can be humanly experienced in and through the texture of the life and worship of the community of faith, for example. However, for Knox the Spirit is intellectualised so that its role is confined to illumination of the individual's understanding.

This goes a long way to helping us understand that it does not come naturally to Sydney Anglicanism to dwell upon aesthetic and symbolic aspects of the Church's sacramental system that appeal to sight, hearing and touch. Indeed, even music might be proscribed as an aid to worship if Knox's dislike of 'sensuous media' were taken to its logical conclusion. In other words, there is nothing in our relationship with God to echo St Augustine's observation that 'reciprocated love uses such semaphorings — a smile, a glance, a thousand winning acts — to fuse separate sparks into a single glow, no longer many souls, but one'.[12] The idea that love as the bond of society and definition of God might be known in a concrete empirical way in and through the material texture of human relationality, through signs and symbols, the kiss of peace, the handshake, the breaking of bread together, does not bulk large. Indeed, it does not really feature at all.

Significantly, Dr Knox was hugely influential on generations of theological students in the Diocese of Sydney. It is understandable that he established a firm theological mind-set. His views are certainly not isolated. Essentially the same ideas were echoed by Donald Robinson, Knox's teaching colleague at Moore College and later Archbishop of Sydney, who also recoiled from the use of a visible symbol as a mistaken 'instinct of fallen man'. Identical views may also be found in an article written by the Reverend Graham Goldsworthy and published in the *Australian Church Record* on 16 June 1966: crosses 'fixed to the east end of church buildings become objects for contemplation which cannot convey truth without also conveying error ... Cross images only appeal to sentiment, but the Word challenges the heart.'[13] Certainly, this helps us to understand the roots of the rationalistic approach to faith and doctrine that today prevails amongst Sydney Anglicans.

This also helps us to account for the characteristic Sydney approach to the Eucharist, which involves concentrating not so much on a deeper entry together into a sacramental presence as upon a bringing to mind of the more abstract belief *that* Christ died for our sins upon the Cross. This kind of emphasis also shows itself in a disinterest in the aesthetics of liturgical worship as an aid to consciousness of the presence of God. By contrast, an overriding interest in the preaching of the Word comes to dominance, a style of preaching in which communication of a body of information is the main concern, with faith being understood as a kind of assent to the truth of abstract propositions.

† † †

There is another sense in which the approach to religious doctrine as represented by Sydney Anglicans seems more clearly questionable and certainly troublesome to many. This has to do with the status that appears to be arbitrarily accorded to particular doctrines over others, even to the point of elevating some doctrines to the level of required beliefs equal to the affirmations of the dogmatically defined Christian Creeds. This leads to a propensity to condem those who fail to pass the test of assent to them as 'unorthodox' or even 'heretical'. The propensity to require assent to a particular subset of beliefs or a particular theological stance, in turn, tends to move the Church in a confessional direction which, historically speaking, has been foreign to mainstream Anglicanism. In order to understand this aspect of Sydney Anglicanism it is necessary to examine some additional features of the nature of doctrine.

To this point I have argued that a non-speculative turn of mind that acknowledges the limitations of human understanding and appreciates the transcendent mystery of God is important for the understanding of Anglicanism. It is precisely because of a respect for the awe and mystery of God that Anglicans tend to put more effort into the expression of faith in forms of worship, rather than following the Roman Catholic emphasis on dogmatic formulas and definitions. This is something that I think is undeniably characteristic of Anglicanism and an important index to Anglican identity: as stated earlier, our energies focus on the painstaking production of liturgical texts rather than on definitions of doctrine and moral directives. If there is a kernel of truth to the stereotypical view that we are not big on dogma, it is equally true that we are known for being big on worship. For us Anglicans doctrine is expressed in the context of worship in words addressed to God.

Of course, this is not the exclusive preserve of Anglicans. In the classical Christian theology of the undivided Church in the first five centuries after Christ, an approach to the expression of belief through worship was defined on the principle of *lex orandi, lex credendi* — the law or rule of prayer is the rule of faith. This maxim is usually attributed to Prosper of Aquitaine, the deacon secretary of Pope Leo I in fifth-century Rome. Prosper of Aquitaine wrote against Eutyches' exposition of the uniqueness of Jesus and the way it undervalued or minimised his true humanity. Prosper also worked with Hilary of Poitiers to mount a case against John Cassian, whose approach to grace was in conflict with that of Augustine. He pointed out that Augustine (in *De Correptione et Gracia*) had argued that perseverance is as much a gift of God as faith is, and in doing so quoted the support of Cyprian's commentary on the Lord's Prayer.[14] In other words, he argued that Augustine had appealed to prayer to prove a theological point.

Prosper of Aquitaine developed this precedent into a theological principle: *lex supplicandi legem statuat credendi*. This maxim means that the practice of normative prayer sets up, establishes, founds and constitutes the norms of belief. But the norms of prayer also transcend and subordinate the norms of belief. Just as the Creeds are recited in the context of prayer and worship, so they must be understood from within this context, for Christians do not worship because they believe, but rather believe because they worship. In response to the initiative of God they first respond in faith and trust, and find themselves both addressing God as Father and thinking of themselves as God's children. Only then do they begin to reflect upon, and express in abstract doctrinal form, what is grounded in their concrete experience.

The Roman Catholic liturgical scholar Aidan Kavanagh therefore argues that, if God takes the initiative and calls his people to himself and promises to be with them always, it follows that the *lex credendi* (belief) is subordinated to the *lex supplicandi* (prayer), 'because both standards exist and function only within the worshipping assembly's own subordination of itself to its ever-present Judge, Savior, and unifying Spirit'.[15] Kavanagh expresses the interrelationship between prayer and doctrinal belief as follows:

> *In this view,* lex supplicandi *and* lex credendi *are not detachable or opposite laws but subtly correlative, the first founding the second, the second affecting (although not founding) the first. Each law functions in concert with the other within the discourse of primary theology.*[16]

The response of faith is an acknowledgment in awe and wonder of the mystery of God, who is met in the act of communal worship. In the context of worship some attempt is made to express and describe the religiously significant reality that the worshipper encounters. The implication of this venerable theological tradition in its Anglican incarnation is to emphasise the importance of the response of worship, and to spend a good deal of time fine-tuning the language of liturgical texts to ensure that they express the best doctrine of which we are humanly capable, and then to counsel prudence in relation to further purely speculative matters.

This means, once again, that it is not the case that Anglicans do not believe anything much and believe nothing in particular. Rather, if anybody wants to know what Anglicans believe they will in the first instance find it enshrined and expressed in a prayer book. We express what we believe in liturgical texts because our theological thinking is done in the context of a prayerful response to the awesome mystery of God. This is one of our fundamental starting points, and it entails that our primary theological affirmations are essentially doxological or glorificatory in nature.

This is why the Anglican Church is a liturgical and non-confessional Church. It gathers around a liturgical text rather than around a confession of faith formulated by some founding father and his preferred way of doing theology. Historically speaking, Anglicans appear to have been content to live with mystery and ambiguity, and this has meant that Anglicanism has not involved confessional definitions in its approach to Christianity. The Anglican Church did not begin with a specific set of doctrinal teachings articulated by a founding father, a Luther or a John Calvin, or even a Thomas Aquinas. The Church did not begin, historically speaking, with a written confession of faith, such as the Lutheran Augsburg Confession, or the Presbyterian Westminster Confession of Faith — a foundational statement of belief that is intended to define a version of the Christian faith preferred to other confessional statements. As Richard Hooker said in the statement already quoted in the previous chapter, 'we confess without confession'. Even the Thirty-nine Articles of Religion to which we give assent as a key document of our Anglican history were intended at the time of the Elizabethan Settlement not so much to exclude alternative confessional viewpoints as to include as wide a range of beliefs as possible. Indeed, even to this day what Anglican clergy are sworn to uphold is 'the Catholic and Apostolic Faith *expressed in* the Prayer Book, the Ordinal and the Thirty-nine Articles' (my emphasis). This is to be contrasted with the giving of assent in a legalistic way to a surface reading of these texts, as though the texts themselves were a confession of faith. What Anglican clergy are sworn to uphold is the catholic and apostolic faith of the ancient undivided Church, contained in those key documents of Anglican history, not a version of faith with a spin put on it by a particular theologian or theological tradition.

† † †

Already implicit in what I have been saying about the nature of doctrine is a basic distinction, which is easily missed, between dogma, doctrine and theological reflection of a more general kind. If we think of a dartboard with a bull's-eye at the centre, the bull's-eye may be taken to represent the core beliefs of Christianity as defined in the ancient councils of the undivided Church, the ancient Creeds: such matters as the Trinity, the definitive revelation of God in the person and work of Jesus Christ, the ongoing activity of the Holy Spirit, and so on, may be placed at the core. These are the dogmatically defined truths of the catholic and apostolic faith, grounded in scripture and expressed in the credal and liturgical texts of our prayer books.

Then there are various doctrines of a less definitive kind: the doctrine that seeks to explain the presence of Christ when people gather for the breaking and sharing of the bread of the Eucharist, for example, or the doctrine of divine grace which affirms that we do not save ourselves by pulling ourselves up by our own bootstraps. Then further out from the centre are the reflections of various theologians through the ages, who have sought to expound and systematise the central dogmas and doctrines commonly held in the Church. Thomas Aquinas's view of the precise way in which Christ is present in the Eucharist in the doctrine of transubstantiation and Luther's alternative doctrine of consubstantiation, for example, or Anselm's penal substititutionary theology of the Atonement would be examples. These are items of theological reflection which, mercifully, have never been dogmatically defined.

Sometimes within Anglicanism this kind of distinction between the central dogmas and doctrines, and theological reflection of a more general and peripheral kind, is expressed by speaking of the fundamentals to which all Christians give assent. Such fundamentals as the love of God, or the two natures — divine and human — of Christ, or the belief that salvation for us is a matter of relationality in love, such as we know through the Trinity, can be found in scripture or can be proved by appeal to scripture, and are required belief. These core beliefs may be placed in the bull's-eye of dogma and in the next circle of Church doctrine around the bull's-eye.

But then there are those less fundamental things to which we may give assent as a matter of commonsense, that are at least not contrary to scripture even if not explicitly defined in scripture, and about which views may differ. These less important things are beliefs to which we can afford to stand more loosely; we can accept that in relation to them there is more variety of opinion. To use the more modern idea of the Second Vatican Council of the Roman Catholic Church, we work with a hierarchy of truths. Some things are regarded as being more important than others.

This does not mean that Anglicans do not believe anything in particular, or are free to believe just anything. Rather, we simply wish to distinguish the fundamentals from other less important things, to require assent to the fundamentals and leave more freedom in relation to the rest. Thus, rather than not believing anything much, we affirm and uphold the basic dogmas and doctrines of the catholic and apostolic Church through the ages as essentials, and allow more flexibility in relation to the more peripheral matters.

However, we must beware not to fall victim to the fallacy of moving items from the periphery of theological reflection into the dogmatic centre by a kind of theological sleight of hand. This is, unfortunately, what I believe some Sydney Anglicans tend to do with the penal theory of the Atonement. This twelfth-century theory of St Anselm has never been dogmatically defined by the Church. Indeed, no theory or doctrine of the Atonement has been dogmatically defined by the Church in such a way as to exclude all alternatives. To elevate this one historically conditioned theory to the status of a requirement of authentic Christian belonging, with the same importance as the dogmatic affirmations of the Christian Creeds, is entirely arbitrary and illegitimate. It has the effect of turning Anglicanism into a kind of confessional Church.

† † †

This means that Anglicans are able to celebrate and cherish all true theological insights of the Christian tradition and inheritance in an eclectic kind of way, whatever their source, provided they are congruent with the norms of scripture. It seems also implicit in this fundamental non-confessional posture of the Anglican Church that Anglicanism is open to God's truth wherever it may lead. Because we do not begin with a limiting confession of faith that excludes alternatives and then has to be defended at all costs, Anglicans are free to pursue and entertain all theological insights whose truth commends them. Certainly, the Anglican Communion is not committed to a particular and historically conditioned confessional expression of the faith simply because it is thought to be what gives the Church its identity, even in the face of the theological pressure of truth to lead elsewhere.

Apart from our recognition of the ultimate mystery of God and of our human limitations when it comes to the expression of our faith in words, we acknowledge in the spirit of the New Testament that it is only at the end time, at the eschaton, that 'we shall know even as we are known' (I John 3:2). Until then we live by faith and not by sight, knowing that the revelation of Christ belongs to the future (I Peter I: 6–9). The future ultimate revelation of the returning Christ relativises everything that we have received to date through historical processes and gives us a sense of the ambiguity and provisionality of what has been revealed, even in the life, death and resurrection of Jesus. This is once again most clearly expressed by St Paul when he declared that for the time being we see partially, through a glass darkly, not face-to-face (I Corinthians 13:12). The clarity of face-to-face encounter belongs essentially to the future.

But to be open to the discovery of new ways of expressing traditional truths and further insights is, of course, quite a different thing from not believing anything, or from the contention that as individuals we may believe anything we happen to choose. That is why, when I am asked if I am a liberal, I usually answer, 'No. I'm progressive orthodox.' One aspect of progressive or dynamic orthodoxy is that we live out of the apostolic tradition of Christian faith that is common to all Christians but, in receiving that tradition in the present and making it our own, we leave our own fingerprints on it. The receiving of the tradition necessarily entails the reinterpreting of it for our own day in our own language and in the light of current scholarly perceptions of truth. For all our Anglican reticence about definitions of new doctrines, we may own that, as we hand on the received faith of the Church, it almost automatically undergoes a process of development. The expression of faith as we pass it on to the next generation is therefore unavoidably one we have a hand in fashioning. We are thus not just receivers of the tradition but makers of it as well. We live into the tradition as much as out of it.

However, the unavoidable development of doctrine in the process of receiving it and handing it on to the next generation raises a problem about its continuity through change. Since Charles Darwin, we have all become more conscious of evolution — including evolution of thought and of its conditioning by its cultural context. However, if we believe we are grappling with an essentially modern problem I think we are mistaken. My assessment is that questions relating to the engagement of doctrine with culture are much older than we imagine.

I think, for example, of Newman's 1845 *Essay on the Development of Doctrine*. Historically, interest in the *Essay on Development* has tended to focus on its autobiographical insights into the processes that led to Newman's conversion. The *Essay* was apparently intended to explain how Newman came to the conviction that he could only retain the full truth of the Christian faith by submitting to the authority of the Church of Rome.

For the contemporary believer, as against the historian, the more interesting question posed by the *Essay* is: if the doctrine of the Church has been subject to a process of development, how is the

Church to distinguish necessary or legitimate developments from corruptions or perversions of the faith?

Newman could see that what he called 'great ideas' are many-sided truths that cannot be grasped by our finite and limited human minds all at once on the occasion of their first introduction or discovery. As we seek to apprehend them, or better, as we seek to comprehend them over time, a succession of formulations with increasing insight will surface, each more adequate and exact than its predecessor. Newman also noted that 'if Christianity be an universal religion, suited not to one locality or period, but to all times and places, it cannot but vary in its relations and dealings towards the world around it, that is, it will develop'.[17] He came to the conviction that if development is inevitable, we cannot halt the process at Nicaea, Constantinople or Chalcedon. Development continues beyond the world of the early Fathers. It follows that there will be a possibility that misapprehensions and outright wrong interpretations will emerge that will require correction. J. B. Mozley, in his critique of Newman's *Essay on Development*, was particularly concerned about the need to check exaggerated developments. Newman conceded that this was a problem that he had not adequately treated, and he tried to address this in the 1878 edition of the *Essay*.

The question this raises for us today is: how is it that faith and doctrine can be conditioned by, and relevative to, the culture out of which they come, yet perceived to retain some kind of continuity with the 'original Idea' (Newman)? Or again, how do culturally conditioned expressions of faith and doctrine retain continuity with the original insights of scriptural revelation, so that we can judge them to be authentic rather than inauthentic?

Newman came to see that culturally conditioned developments dictated the need for an authority to test developments. He spoke of it as the need for a 'developing authority', but he clearly means in the first instance an authority to test developments — some instrument to maintain the essential truth of the original revelation. For Newman the Roman Catholic Church possessed consistency, permanence and the claim to infallible authority. No rival system could be discerned anywhere else. It has to be noted that Newman lived at a time when the Church of England's decision-making Convocations of Canterbury and York were in suspension (and had been since 1717!) and the modern development of synodical government as an Anglican instrument of authoritative decision-making both at a diocesan and at a national level had yet to emerge.

Apart from the need for the Church to have some kind of instrument for decision-making and for expressing its mind, and particularly for distinguishing authentic from inauthentic developments within the life of the Church in relation to faith and order as well as morals, Newman came up with his famous seven tests for distinguishing legitimate developments from corruptions:

1. Preservation of Type or Idea
2. Continuity of Principles
3. Power of Assimilation
4. Early Anticipation
5. Logical Sequence
6. Preservative Addition
7. Chronic Continuance

Of these, the second and third are perhaps the most important for us as we think of faith and culture. When Newman speaks of the continuity of principles — or continuity of general character — the emphasis is on general character as contrasted with preservation of specific verbal formulations of doctrines and moral precepts. For example, the incarnational principle is embodied not only in Christology but in ecclesiology (the Church as the extension of the incarnation). It can also be discerned in the doctrine of sacraments (outward and visible/inward and spiritual), or expressed in the relationship between matter and spirit in the development of an ethical approach to the sustainability of the environment.

Given that the Christian faith must come to terms with culture, and will naturally be affected by the social and economic environment, just how does Christianity assimilate to these without losing its own distinctiveness and integrity? Can assimilation for the purpose of communication avoid the excesses of liberalism, which surrenders faith's distinctiveness and integrity? Can the Church adapt faith to the environment without surrending its prophetic voice, without ceasing to be the salt of the world? In other words, can it absorb but also transform and transmute? These are all questions that have to be kept in mind as we acknowledge the inevitable conditioning of faith and doctrine at the hands of successive cultures.

In the present context, it is sufficient to acknowledge the inevitability of the development of doctrine and its historical conditioning in our own self-understanding and self-identity as Christians. I think at the very least we must see ourselves as a pilgrim people, a people on the move, open to an ever fuller appreciation of the meaning and truth of God. This means that Anglicans affirm the ancient defining dogmas of the apostolic and catholic faith, and that we receive and appreciate the theological insights of the historical past, but we are not constrained by them. When modern science leads us to the view that the world came into being in an evolutionary way over millions and millions of years, as evidenced by the fossil record, then we are open to revision of the traditional doctrine of the Creation of the universe by God in seven days. This does not entail that we abandon truth-seeking when it comes to the belief that God created the natural order. It does mean, however, that the Church must be prepared to bury its dead from time to time. It must be prepared frankly and candidly to acknowledge that occasionally it will be necessary to set aside inadequate expressions or perhaps mistaken theological views of the past. The need to be open to change while seeking to retain the essentials of apostolic faith and practice explains why it is appropriate to speak of a 'dynamic' or 'progressive' orthodoxy.

† † †

We cannot leave even a preliminary discussion of the nature of doctrine such as this without addressing the contention, often expressed in Anglican writings of the last generation, that what gives Anglicanism its unique or essential identity is not a body of theological teaching (such as from a Luther or Calvin) so much as a method, a way of theologising, a style of theological reflection.[18] Moreover, it is regularly said that this basic style of doing theology goes back to the Elizabethan theologian Richard Hooker, insofar as he articulated a way of sorting out the fundamentals from less important articles of belief and behaviour by appealing to the threefold authority of *scripture, tradition* and *reason*.

In other words, it is contended that a distinctively Anglican way of doing theology is signalled by this threefold appeal. Thus while we respect the authority of *scripture* as the foundational expression of the revelation of God though history, and particularly in the person and work of Jesus Christ, scripture does not just stand alone. While nothing is to be required of anybody as necessary for salvation other than what is contained in scripture or can be proved thereby, scripture is not just picked up and read cold, as it were, but understood from within the context of Church *tradition*. It is read and interpreted from with the historical context of faith and worship. The scriptures are the Church's documents, written by inspired believers and interpreted from within the ongoing life of faith. So both scripture and doctrinal tradition, as this is expressed in Creeds and liturgical texts, are important in the process of the discernment of meaning and the judgment of truth.

Hooker is also credited with highlighting the importance for Anglicans of the commonsense dictates of *reason*. Given that reason is God's gift to us and distinguishes humans from all the other animals, Hooker argued that it is a legitimate medium through which God's truth may be discerned, and is a court of appeal for judging both what is to be believed and how life is to be lived. One example he gives is of the rightness of men wearing garlands of flowers around their necks in church on festival days. This practice was challenged in his time by the Puritans on the grounds that there was nothing explicit in scripture to warrant it. Hooker's reply was that it was not to be judged contrary to the will of God, nevertheless, because it was not unreasonable.

The difficulty with talk of a distinctive Anglican theological method expressed in the catchcry 'scripture, tradition and reason' is that Roman Catholic and Greek Orthodox theologians, or Lutheran or Uniting Church theologians, would probably also agree, not to mention Christians of many other denominational traditions. Therefore I do not see that there is anything distinctively or uniquely

Anglican about the method of doing theology using this threefold court of appeal.

Instead of a distinctive method or style of doing theology, what is distinctive for Anglicanism is a method of authoritative decision-making that appeals to the evidences of scripture read in the historical light of the Christian dogmatic, doctrinal, theological and liturgical tradition and using human reason. This way of expressing the faith of the Church and articulating a moral viewpoint comes to focus in the gathering of the Bishop-in-Synod. The distinctively Anglican development of synodical government is a product of the need in the mid-nineteenth century to provide for a way of decision-making in the scattered national and regional Churches of colonial expansion. As it happens, the chief architect of Anglican synodical tradition was the same William Gladstone whose theological reflections on mystery provided us with the launching pad for this chapter. Gladstone provided a legislative model for the colonial churches, which at the end of the day was not accepted by the House of Commons but which served to guide the colonial development of autonomous synodical structures. What was distinctively Anglican about this model was that it provided for the inclusion of the laity in synods and a method of voting on contentious issues by bishop, clergy and laity in separate houses. Gladstone's proposals allowed a kind of veto by the bishop, because important measures have to pass in all houses, and the diocesan bishop is the sole member of the House of Bishops.

At the time when Gladstone originally made these proposals there was a significant discussion about whether the laity should have a role in the determination of matters of doctrine. Some leaders of the Oxford Movement, such as E. B. Pusey, resisted such a development while being prepared to allow lay people a role in temporal matters affecting the life of the Church. (From the sidelines even John Henry Newman contributed in an oblique way to this debate in his 'On Consulting the Faithful in Matters of Doctrine' of 1859.[19])

While this is really another story, the important thing for us to note is that it is not a distinctive method of doing theology, employing the various sources of scripture, tradition and reason, but the living mechanism of bringing material from those sources together and coming to an authoritative determination in the forum of the Bishop-in-Synod that is most characteristic of Anglicanism. In this way the Church as a whole plays a determinative role in the Anglican expression of doctrinal, theological and moral viewpoints.

Meanwhile, the settled dogmatic nucleus upon which Anglicans rely for the expression of the fundamentals of faith, and for the determination of the grammar and the boundaries of all subsequent theological reflection, is found in the credal determinations of the great ecumenical councils of the ancient Church. These have a quality of irreversibility about them that historically formulated doctrines do not enjoy. At these councils, often as a result of controversy, a determination was agreed upon to say one thing rather than another in relation to some specific disputed topics, which committed the Church thenceforward to a particular tradition of thought. All subsequent authentic doctrine and theological reflection will take account of both scripture and this defined tradition of dogmatic thought. The theological reflection of a particular theologian or school has a more fluid and thus much less secure status.

This is why the contention of some Sydney Anglicans that Anselm's doctrine of the penal substitution theory of the Atonement is a required belief, even to the point where it is made into a test of Christian orthodoxy, is entirely untenable. This has the effect of moving an item of passing theological reflection of a specific theologian and his followers from the theological periphery to the Church's dogmatic centre. Even if a version of this teaching enjoyed a period of popularity, notably under the formidable influence of John Calvin, it cannot today be placed at the dogmatic centre of faith. The Church has never defined this theory of the Atonement. Indeed, as we shall see in Chapter 4, biblical reflection on the saving significance of the Cross is more heavily weighted in the direction of the controlling concept of sacrifice and the self-offering of Christ as an expression of the obedience of love, than on an explanation of the meaning of the Cross worked out in terms of punishment. But it has been the wisdom of the Church to leave the matter of the saving efficacy of the Cross an undefined mystery and thus open to a range of theological reflections. For this reason assent to a particular speculative explanation of the saving efficacy of the Cross quite simply cannot be elevated into a dogmatic test of Christian orthodoxy. Anglicans would be wise to continue to exercise a little cautious reticence in relation to such matters.

CHAPTER 3

SCRIPTURE

On overseas trips I have regularly been asked about what is often spoken of as 'Sydney fundamentalism'. Usually those who ask have only a second-hand acquaintance with the Anglican Diocese of Sydney through press reports, though in some cases articles by Sydney clergy have been consulted through the Internet on the Sydney Diocesan website. Indeed, sometimes one has the sense that the Sydney website is regularly consulted by those who imagine they are logging on to the most extreme and idiosyncratic Anglican theological position.

I usually find myself pointing out that the Anglican Diocese of Sydney is not nearly so monochrome as many people around the world imagine. Like most Anglican dioceses the world over, its parishes range from those that are clearly and uncompromisingly evangelical, through to some with a mildly charismatic flavour, to more clearly recognisable, middle-of-the-road Anglican parishes. A few are distinctively and unmistakably Anglo-Catholic; indeed, one or two of these are possibly amongst the most exotic of their kind to be found anywhere in the world. While the predominant style of the diocese may exhibit a distinctive kind of evangelical colouring, not all parishes conform to this stereotype.

This diversity may be illustrated by the fact that, whenever some elements within the Diocese of Sydney enthusiastically pursue the idea of legislating in the diocesan synod to sanction lay presidency at the Eucharist, or threaten to sever their association with traditional Anglicanism, it is often reported that up to fifty Sydney parishes might consider approaching the college of Australian bishops to seek a form of 'alternative episcopal oversight'. Alternatively, it is sometimes conjectured that a group of parishes might seek to challenge the validity of the proposed legislation and part company with the main body of supporters of lay presidency in a formal or legal way so as to remain loyal to the rest of the Anglican Communion. In this circumstance the first divide would not be between the Diocese of Sydney and other dioceses of the Anglican Church of Australia, or Sydney and the worldwide Anglican Communion, but internally within the Diocese of Sydney itself. So my point is that it is a huge mistake to think of Sydney as a monochrome diocese in which everybody thinks and worships and behaves in an identical manner. The Diocese of Sydney contains as much diversity of thought as most other Anglican dioceses, even if it is to be frankly admitted that a distinct and characteristic kind of evangelicalism predominates as the presenting face of the diocese. Within other dioceses of the Anglican Church of Australia pockets of the same mind-set are also discernible; indeed, most metropolitan dioceses have a few parishes that exhibit this likeness.

As we seek to come to terms with the defining characteristics of 'Sydney Anglicanism' it is clear that a quite distinctive approach to scripture is of enormous importance. Whether Sydney Anglicans are rightly to be understood as 'fundamentalists' or not is less important than trying to discern the material sense in which the approach of Sydney Anglicans to the reading of scripture differs from the mainstream, not only of Anglicans, but probably of other denominations of the Christian Church as well. Some examination of the phenomenon of Christian fundamentalism and its characteristic commitments is, however, a useful point of entry in this pursuit.

As a teenager in the 1950s I lived and worshipped in a typical suburban parish of the Diocese of Sydney, at least until I felt the need of more substantial fare which prompted me therefore to change parishes. At that time the term 'fundamentalist' was not just used by others in reference to Sydney Anglicanism, but owned by many Sydney Anglicans themselves as a code word for identifying Sydney's own distinctive style of evangelicalism. This was particularly the case following the publication by Dr James Packer of *Fundamentalism and the Word of God*[1] in 1958, a book which was widely read and frequently quoted by Sydney Anglicans. Indeed, James Packer has been a very influential voice over the last half of the twentieth century in the Diocese of Sydney. The present archbishop, Dr Peter Jensen, has rightly identified Packer as an important formative influence.[2] Interestingly enough, although Packer himself registered a preference for the term 'Evangelical' and thought 'Fundamentalist' had reached its shelf life, he claimed that by the word 'Fundamentalist' he simply meant 'Evangelical'.[3] I will return to Packer's views presently. For the moment, it is sufficient to note that the term 'Fundamentalist', while not being the preferred term, was once in common use and was not originally used in any sinister sense.

In recent times, however, there have been signs of some discomfort with the term. Archbishop Jensen, for example, finds the term unpalatable. Indeed, in addressing the 2002 Sydney Synod he said he was concerned to distinguish 'classical, orthodox Christianity from fundamentalism'. This is almost certainly because, over the last generation, most world religions have had to contend with the phenomenon of an aggressive, uncompromising, even obscurantist fundamentalism. The fundamentalism of other religious traditions has been regularly associated with the most rigid of views and even violent behaviour. Today, we thus hear of Muslim fundamentalists and Hindu fundamentalists, no less than Christian fundamentalists. It is understandable that those Christians who formerly thought of themselves as 'fundamentalists' now no longer wish to be tarred with that brush. Nobody wants to be thought of as the Christian Taliban. In this vein, following the controversy surrounding my *Bulletin* article, the Victorian Branch of the Evangelical Fellowship in the Anglican Communion (EFAC) wrote to me on 25 May 2000 asking a number of clarificatory theological questions. These might have been thought to arise out of a fairly fundamentalist point of view, but they were very keen to say, 'We strongly object to the use of the pejorative designation "fundamentalist" to describe our position, which if used to describe us, misunderstands our position entirely.'[4] I am not privy to any of the detailed thinking of the Victorian members of EFAC and have no cause to refer to it using any term at all, but it is noteworthy that people who are prepared to describe themselves as conservative evangelicals certainly do not wish to be understood to be 'fundamentalists'.

Current discomfort with the nomenclature notwithstanding, the historical connections of 'Sydney Anglicanism' with the Christian fundamentalist movement of the early twentieth century, particularly via the influential writings of James Packer, seem undeniable. The term was first applied to the position taken in a series of booklets entitled *The Fundamentals*, which began to appear on the world stage in 1909. These were paperbacks of one hundred and twenty-eight pages each, published by an unincorporated company called the Testimony Publishing Company of Chicago, Illinois. The booklets were distributed free of charge with 'the compliments of two Christian laymen' to 'every pastor, evangelist, missionary, theological professor, theological student, Sunday-school superintendent, YMCA and YWCA secretary in the English-speaking world, so far as the addresses of all these can be obtained'. It is said that the two laymen were wealthy men from California. There were twelve booklets on different subjects, which appeared between 1909 and 1915. Three million booklets were distributed in all.

For our present purposes we can summarise the basic thrust of these publications under two headings: what they rejected and what they sought to defend.

What was rejected was any inclination or preparedness to adopt scientific and critical-historical theories which delivered results that appeared to be inconsistent with faith in God's revelation, where revelation was understood in a propositional way as a compendium of all the truths found in scripture. In essence, the fundamentalist movement was an attempt to fend off the advances of liberalism — understood as a mood or cast of mind that was prepared to admit that the scientific discoveries of human reason might call in question hitherto unquestioned biblical beliefs. One obvious concern of the original fundamentalists, though it is far less threatening to Christians today, was the need to resist revision of the doctrine of Creation in seven days in the light of evolutionary theories of the emergence of life on this planet over millions and millions of years.

The critical-historical examination of the biblical texts in the second half of the nineteenth century, which also coincided with the rise of modern historiography, also called into question the traditional authorship of many of the biblical books. This too sent tremors through the churches. The subsequent reaction to liberalism in the first decades of the twentieth century cut right across denominational divisions. For example, just two years before *The Fundamentals* began to appear, the Pope issued the encyclical *Pascendi Gregis* and the syllabus of errors entitled *Lamentabili,* which condemned all critical theories about the dates and origin of the biblical books. The original American fundamentalists likewise sought to resist essentially the same modernising forces within the churches of the Reformation and their more contemporary derivatives.

Given a clear view of the enemy, the primary task was therefore seen as the defence of what were understood to be the fundamentals of Christian belief. The General Assembly of the Northern Presbyterian Church in the United States of America in 1910 specified five items as 'the fundamentals of faith and of evangelical Christianity'. These were to become the five most commonly held defining characteristics of fundamentalist belief:

1. The inspiration and infallibility of scripture
2. The deity of Christ
3. His virgin birth and miracles
4. His penal death for our sins
5. His physical resurrection and personal return

The World Christian Fundamentals Association, which formed in 1919, adopted these five fundamentals as its basic confessional platform. These were the basic doctrines that those who became known as 'fundamentalists' were dedicated to defend. We may note in passing that already in this list the penal substitutionary view of the Atonement was being viewed as a basic confessional requirement of fundamentalist belief.

The focus of the debate moved across the Atlantic from America to Britain in the mid-1950s. In Britain in August of 1955 the issue flared up in a series of letters to the editor which were published in the London *Times*. At that time a mood of anti-fundamentalism was abroad, and evangelical Christians began responding to a perceived general hostility which had brought the movement into disrepute. Thus the Reverend J. R. W. Stott, the then rector of All Souls, Langham Place, in London, pointed out in a letter of 25 August 1955 that 'fundamentalism' had become 'a term of opprobrium'. It is almost a symbol, he wrote, 'of obscurantism'. He complained that 'It is used to describe the bigoted rejection of all biblical criticism, a mechanical view of inspiration, and an excessively literalist interpretation of Scripture.' Though a conservative evangelical himself, Stott wished to be dissociated from the term.

Following upon the subsequent round of correspondence a substantial discussion of the issues was promoted by Father Gabriel Hebert of the Society of the Sacred Mission, who came from England to Australia to teach theology at St Michael's House at Crafers in Adelaide. Hebert published a thoroughgoing critique of fundamentalism in *Fundamentalism and the Church of God* in 1957.[5] Its chief problem, as he saw it, was to undervalue the human element in the production of the biblical texts. His view was that inspired theological and doctrinal truth and time-bound and culturally conditioned human perceptions, and even human errors in some matters of fact, are to be found in a kind of amalgam within the pages of scripture. While the fundamentalist tended to accord every word of scripture a divine status, he contended, others have been content to regard the truths of God that are to be discerned in the biblical texts as treasures in an earthen vessel. The human authors' contribution to the scriptural text is not incidental to the communication of divine truth, but necessary to it, and must be studied with the seriousness due to it and with all the critical skills that modern historical and exegetical scholarship can muster.

It was as an attempt to answer Gabriel Hebert that Dr James Packer published *Fundamentalism and the Word of God* in 1958. At the time Packer also acknowledged that 'fundamentalism' had become a dirty word — 'a theological swearword', but his book was nevertheless an attempt to rehabilitate and defend the substance of what the fundamentalists had sought to affirm and promote. 'Fundamentalism' is not, he said, 'a name for a modern movement of reaction'. It is 'just a twentieth-century name for historic Evangelicalism', though he added that he did not regard it as a very good or useful name.[6] Hence, for Packer 'fundamentalism' may be used as a synonym for 'evangelicalism'.

The essence of evangelicalism is said by Packer to be founded on the belief that Jesus Christ constituted Christianity as a religion of biblical authority because Jesus himself submitted to the authority of the Old Testament, and our submission to Jesus Christ means submission to scripture. A more docile submission to the text as it stands, or a surface reading of the text, thus tends to be contrasted with a critical-historical examination of the text. It is clear that, for Packer, the five fundamentals of the doctrinal platform of the 1910 formulation by the Northern Presbyterian Church General Assembly are basic essential elements in evangelical Christianity. The effect of Packer's understanding of the authority of the scriptures was to regard critical-historical work on the texts of scripture with suspicion as an unwelcome intrusion of human reason which implicitly challenged the authority of the scriptural texts. Indeed, anything short of unconditional submission to scripture is a kind of impertinence. Packer goes so far as to say that any view that submits the written Word of God to the opinions and pronouncements of men 'involves unbelief and disloyalty towards Christ'.[7]

For Packer, scripture was as a 'self-contained, self-interpreting revelation from God'.[8] His understanding of the inspiration of scripture by God led to belief in its infallibility: 'What Scripture says, God says; and what God says in Scripture is to be the rule of faith and life in His Church.'[9] Elsewhere Packer contended that God's inspiration of scripture was 'word for word', for the authors wrote 'word for word what God intended'[10] and this was primarily what Packer believed fundamentalism/evangelicalism was concerned to maintain.[11]

It seems incontrovertible that, though Packer disliked the use of the word 'fundamentalism' because it had become a term of opprobrium, and preferred instead the term 'evangelicalism', in terms of substantial belief content there is really little difference. It is a matter of not owning the name, but eating the fundamentalist cake.

This is not the place to submit Packer's work to detailed critical analysis. However, we may say in passing that it is not a work that can be accorded high marks for logical coherence. For example, while Packer regards the divine inspiration of scripture to be 'word for word', he even so denies that this entails a commitment to a literal reading of the story of the seven-day Creation. This suggests that while God is said by him to have inspired the biblical authors so that they got things right word for word, and not in some more general sense which might allow for a human element to creep in and open the way for a kind of critical-historical assessment, he is obliged to admit that God nevertheless allowed the biblical writers to get a good deal of its apparently factual information wrong. Packer is wary of dictation theories of biblical inspiration because they suggest a mechanical kind of operation which does not take account of the conscious input of the human author, and yet he is able to affirm that God 'was well able to prepare, equip and over-rule sinful human writers so that they wrote nothing but what he intended'.[12]

Certainly, Packer seeks to head off the possibility of talking about variant readings and interpretations of the biblical texts by speaking of an alleged 'proper' or 'natural' reading of the text.[13] According to him, this is the understanding of those to whom the text was originally addressed — the original hearers of it. Packer seems to think that he somehow knows what the original audience many thousands of years ago heard the texts to mean, but just how he might know this is not canvassed. A little later, however, he says with regard to the Creation story in Genesis that this is, of course, not to be taken literally. Indeed, he says that there is a good deal of 'highly symbolic' material in the early chapters of Genesis. Yet we are urged to read the texts in their 'proper, natural sense', and this is defined as 'the intended sense of the writer'[14] and the sense in which the original readers understood them! Judging from the controversies surrounding Galileo and Copernicus, and the drastic suggestion that the sun and not the earth might be the centre of the universe, or the controversy following the publication by Charles Darwin of the *Origin of Species* in 1859, it is a little hard to believe that the authors and first hearers of the early chapters of Genesis understood them in the non-literal or purely symbolic way in which Packer is apparently now constrained to interpret them. In other words, despite the furor caused by Charles Darwin's theory of evolution which so traumatically disturbed those who up to that time had read the story of the seven-day Creation as literally and historically factual, we are urged to believe that an anonymous audience of first hearers did not hear the story in a literal kind of way but understood it symbolically, roughly in the way we understand it today! Special pleading of this kind is found throughout *Fundamentalism and the Word of God*.

Logical consistency is not a big point in Packer's book. Indeed, while he insists that a critical-historical reading of the biblical texts by appealing to human reason is an impertinent questioning of their authority, in a chicken-and-egg pirouette of reasoning he himself appeals to arguments of reason to try to defend his own approach to the biblical texts. Packer advances reasons to support the view that Jesus accepted the Old Testament texts without submitting them to any critical examination, for example, and argues that we should adopt a similar attitude with regard to the New Testament texts as well.

Fundamentalism and the Word of God is a highly tendentious and propagandist piece of writing, not the kind of work that can really claim a place in the world of serious academical theology. Nevertheless, there is no doubting its influence in fashioning the mind-set of Sydney Anglicans over the last fifty years.

† † †

Clearly, different assessments of both the inspiration and authority of scripture will make for a quite different outcome in the way the biblical texts are handled and interpreted. If one tends to shun critical-historical research on these texts on the basis that they are inspired word for word by God, and that such work is therefore an intrusive impertinence, and another believes a critical-historical approach to the texts to be not just appropriate but absolutely necessary for the discernment of the divine truths contained within them — because anything less would be a dishonouring of the texts — then we are bound to end with quite different and logically competing outcomes.

It must be said that Sydney Anglicans are not fundamentalists in the sense of regarding every word of the scriptural text as true in a literal sense, or as historically or scientifically factual. Indeed, people generally are probably well able these days to discern the poetry of the Book of Psalms from the historical writings of the Books of Kings, for example, or the more legendary material of the first chapters of Genesis from a modern scientific attempt to describe the evolutionary origins of the universe and of the various forms of life on earth. Differences of genre within the body of biblical literature are well appreciated. Nevertheless, a conservatively minded or fundamentalist Christian is more likely than not to gloss over differences in the scriptural texts and to claim historical accuracy and even inerrancy for biblical stories as an inspired and reliable index — at least with respect to what Jesus is actually portrayed as doing and saying in the Gospels.

The conservative or fundamental Christian will also probably propose that the 'will of God' is plainly and straightforwardly manifest in the pages of scripture, and will tend to understand revelation as a body of doctrinal and historical information found in scripture. This kind of commitment will not allow too much consideration to the contributions of the human authors who were open to the conditioning of the cultural norms of the time in which they lived and wrote. Such considerations can only undermine confidence in the revealed text. This makes the fundamentalist Christian uncomfortable with an emphasis on the literary contribution of the respective human authors. A residual commitment to the inspiration and infallibility of scripture continues to govern the general approach to the texts, so whether we are speaking of fundamentalists, or conservative evangelicals, or simply Bible-believing Christians, there will be a family likeness of approach to the biblical texts. This explains why Packer, while he had a preference for one label rather than the other, frankly admitted that fundamentalism and classic evangelicalism are really the same thing.

How, then, can we begin to outline in broad terms the alternative approach to scripture followed by most other Australian Anglicans, which allows for the development of a community of theological endeavour which is self-consciously 'different from Sydney' and in which sadly Sydney scholars by and large do not even participate?

Many of us, while seeing God as the ultimate author of scripture, in the sense that he wills the Church with the inspired scriptures and intends us to be formed, sustained, challenged and judged by them, do not rule out that a positive contribution has inevitably been made to the texts by the human authors themselves in the actual writing process. A critical, scientific and historical reading of the texts designed to uncover the theological perspectives that respective authors themselves contribute to the overall design of their work, as against the oral traditions they received, is important to us in the quest to discern their meaning.

Many of us are more than willing to accept that the theological commitments of particular biblical writers and their specific insights, inform and thus condition the editing of the traditional material that they received. By comparing the various Gospel traditions, particularly of the synoptic Gospels (Mark, Matthew and Luke), and noting the inclusion of some material and the deletion of other material by a particular Gospel writer, as well as their locating of a story in one place rather than another, it is possible to discern something of a particular Gospel writer's distinctive theological perspective. All this becomes part of the complex processes involved in the discernment of a writer's specific assessment of the meaning and unique significance of Jesus in relation to the ultimate purposes of God.

A commitment to the transcendent mystery of God and the awareness of the limitations of finite human understanding also dictates a certain attitude of humility with regard to the interpretation of scripture amongst those of us who do not see ourselves as fundamentalists. With a less than absolute confidence in any form of words brought to the work of interpreting the nature and purposes of God, and an acknowledgment in humility of the limitations of human knowledge in relation to these things, we shy away from extravagant claims about the plain meaning of the biblical texts. Biblical texts continue to be regarded as normative but not infallible or inerrant. From the fundamentalist perspective this alternative appears to be a kind of liberalism that does not take the scriptural text seriously. The irony is that those of us who are committed to a critical-historical reading of the texts believe we are taking the texts of scripture more seriously not less so. A surface or uncritical reading of the text is for us what fails to accord it the honour which is its due.

Some of us also prefer to see the text of scripture as the attempt of the witness of the first generation or two of Christians to express in words something of the mystery of the actual experience of the revelation of God, particularly as they came to terms with something of the humanly transcending Spirit that was outpoured in their lives. One statement of Packer's with which I heartily agree is that 'all the great biblical doctrines — the Trinity, the incarnation, the Atonement, the work of the Spirit in man, the resurrection of the body and the renewal of the Creation — are partly mysterious, and raise problems for our minds that are at present insoluble'.[15] I also agree with Packer when he says that 'God gave the Scriptures for a practical purpose'.[16] Packer does not follow through on the logical implications of these statements, however, in his more general rationalistic quest for 'accuracy', 'certainty', and 'matter-of-factness'. Indeed, philosophically speaking his understanding of the divine revelation in clear and distinct propositions strikes me as an echo of the philosophy of Descartes. By way of contrast, the revelation of God as I understand it, in terms of acquaintance rather than in abstract propositions, might be said to be rather more Kantian in epistemological structure. Instead of giving the text absolute status as the revealed and inerrant 'Word of God', many of us receive and handle it as a verbal record of the historical revelation in more concrete interpersonal terms. We see it as a bearing of witness to the incarnate Word of God revealed in the person and work of Jesus Christ, who both points beyond himself to his transcendent heavenly Father and at the same time makes both himself and the Father at least partially (though ambiguously) known in the continuing work of the Spirit.

In this understanding, the texts of scripture are also seen as the instruments through which the Word of God continues to be heard today, as a living word of address. Hence, in liturgical worship, at the end of a scriptural reading, instead of saying 'This *is* the Word of God' we prefer to say 'Hear the Word of God', for the living word is heard in and through the reading of the words of the text rather than being identical with the static text itself.

✝ ✝ ✝

Perhaps the best way to illustrate a contemporary critical-historical reading of the scriptural text in contrast with fundamentalism's surface reading of the text-as-it-stands would be by way of example. There is a manageable example in a comparative reading of the Gospels of Matthew and Mark, both of which include an incident in which Jesus is said to have come upon a fig tree. This is found in Matthew 21:18–22 and in Mark 11:13–21. While the general outline of the story is the same in both Gospels, there are some significant discrepancies that emerge as soon as the two texts are critically compared. In relation to these the fundamentalist Christian, who is pre-committed to an uncritical reading of the text itself as the infallible and inerrant Word of God, is unlikely to pay any attention. He or she will be prone to pass these off as only minor and incidental discrepancies. Karl Barth, writing in the first half of the twentieth century, adopted a similar approach to the text of scripture as the written Word of God, shunning what he regarded as an over-interest in critical issues in favour of a more general or 'middle distance' reading of the text, which simply did not focus on what he thought of as minor discrepancies in matters of detail. But those who read the texts with a more critical eye are inclined to detect important nuances of meaning as being of great significance for discerning the good purposes of God, by openly acknowledging discrepancies and attending carefully to them. Indeed, alleged minor discrepancies of detail between the narratives of different Gospel writers are exactly the clues to what is often theologically significant in what they respectively have to say.

For example, in Mark's version of this story Jesus finds that the fig tree was without fruit and, somewhat uncharacteristically he curses the fig tree (verses 12–14). Its fate is to wither up and die (verse 21). But in between these two elements of the fig tree story Mark places the story of Jesus going into the Temple where he overthrows the money changers (verses 15–18). It is on his way from the Temple after this incident that the fig tree is found to be withered.

Matthew has essentially the same story. But there is a significant difference. In Matthew the completed story of Jesus' encounter with the fig tree, including its withering up and dying, follows the story of Jesus' entry into Jerusalem where he overturned the tables of the money changers and drove out those who sold doves from the Temple (verses 12–17). The two discrete stories are simply narrated end-on by Matthew, one following the other. By contrast, instead of narrating the two incidents in simple sequential order, Mark takes the fig tree story and editorially slices it in half in a typical cut-and-paste exercise, and then inserts the Temple episode in the middle. In a sense he makes a kind of literary sandwich out of it, with the Temple episode (verses 15–18) sandwiched between the two halves of the fig tree story (verses 12–14 and verses 19–21). In terms of the actual narrative this means that Jesus curses the fig tree, then goes into the Temple and deals with its abuse, and then, only when he leaves Jerusalem, he comes across the fig tree once again, but this time he finds that it is withered.

These stories could be read as nothing more than historically factual accounts of incidents in Jesus' life. But both cannot be historically accurate and factual. Alternatively, the action of Jesus with respect to the fig tree could be understood to have provided the first Christians with a graphic commentary on the fate of Israel, as they processed what had happened amongst them. Given Israel's perceived failure, as the first Christians saw it, to fulfil their divine vocation, they concluded that Israel was to be superseded by a new order. All this is communicated in the symbolism of the fig tree and its fate: as unfruitful trees which do not serve their intended purpose are cut down and cast aside, so a similar fate can be anticipated to befall Israel. It is as though Mark is using the fig tree story as a heuristic device to provide the interpretative clue for understanding Jesus' action in cleansing the Temple.

Any suggestion that these are two discrete episodes, with one happening to follow the other chronologically, such as we might conclude from Matthew's account, is ruled out by Mark. At his hands the theological point is clearly made that Israel has fallen short of its vocation under God by failing in the stakes of fruitfulness, and is to be condemned to wither up and die for not bearing good fruit.

Moreover, a critical comparison of the texts will show, that over and above this piece of cut-and-paste editing, Mark also adds a very significant phrase to his text, a phrase that Matthew does not have. After Jesus' words 'My house shall be called a house of prayer', Mark adds the very important words 'for all the nations'. This is the meat in Mark's sandwich, if you like. It makes the nature of Israel's failure at the very centre of Temple worship even more specific. Israel has lived to itself and become exclusive of others instead of being true to its calling to minister to all nations. Israel, in this understanding of things, is destined to wither up because of its exclusiveness and consequent failure to further the mission of God to the world. Mark's editorial handling of the material is thus the clue which is used to make a specific theological point about the fate to befall Israel given that it has lived to itself and forsaken its vocation.

The contrasting inclusiveness of Jesus' new mission to all nations is underscored by Mark. Elsewhere in his Gospel he has an eye for accounting for the Church's mission to the Gentiles, such as in his presentation of such stories as the Syro-Phoenician woman who, even as a social and racial outsider, demanded that her daughter be healed and fed from the table crumbs; and the Roman soldier of foreign occupation at the foot of the Cross who, significantly, is the first to declare that Jesus was 'truly the Son of God'.

The making of this theological point, that Israel and its Temple would be superseded or even replaced by the new Israel, appears to override any interest on the part of Mark in simply narrating a theologically neutral sequence of historical events; indeed, little attention appears to be paid by Mark to the niceties of historical accuracy. His chief concern appears to be theological rather than historical. The historical episode becomes for him more clearly an acted-out parable to make a specific theological point. While to many of us this seems a perfectly legitimate way of reading the relevant texts, James Packer seems to rule it out methodologically as an impertinent submitting of the text to critical reason, which for him amounts to a questioning of the authority of scripture!

By contrast with this way of handling the obvious discrepancies between the Marcan and Matthean versions of these stories, Packer would insist that the 'apparent contradictions' of scripture should be harmonised for 'God's revealed truth is a consistent unity, and any disharmony between part and part is only apparent, not real.'[17] In the case of material that cannot be harmonised, Packer's advice is frankly to admit 'that in our present state of knowledge we do not see how these apparent discrepancies should be resolved'.[18] But what we may not do is in any way engage in a critical-historical reading of the Bible which might account for and explain the discrepancies, for this would be to admit that they are not simply apparent but real. Indeed, Packer even goes so far as to say that 'The fact that Scripture records events is sufficient proof that they happened ...'![19] How the events reported by both Matthew and Mark concerning the fig tree and the ejection of the money changers from the Temple can have happened in the alternative ways they are said to have happened cannot therefore be explained. Rather, according to the logic of Packer's argument, the historical occurrence of both accounts must be said to be proved simply by virtue of their inclusion in the deposit of scripture. Surely this defies all reason.

Curiously, Luke does not narrate the fig tree story as an incident in Jesus' historical life at all. Rather, he includes a parable about a fig tree which Jesus is said to have told (Luke 13:6–9). In this case, when it is suggested that the unproductive tree should be cut down, the reply is that with further time, plus an additional application of fertiliser, the fig tree might even yet bear fruit. Biblical commentators note that Luke writes with a more expansive sense of time and without the sense of urgency of the kind that accompanied the early belief that the end of the world was imminent, such as we find in the theology of Mark and Paul. By contrast, in Luke's day the world had not come to an end and the Church was beginning to pursue its historical mission as the Spirit-bearing community in a world that showed every indication of having a protracted historical future. For Luke the eschaton is delayed and understood to be some way off. For Paul the presence of the Spirit is a down-payment or sign of the imminence of the end. For Luke the Spirit becomes a kind of substitute for the delay of the end. Clearly, despite the passage of time, Israel had not withered up and died. Luke's theological point in his handling of the fig tree parable seems to be that in the good purposes of God there is yet time, with a little patient and tender care, for this tree, the symbol of Israel, to bear fruit.

The same editorial device of sandwiching one story within another, such as we noted in Mark 11, is also used by Mark is his handling of the two feeding stories: the feeding of the five thousand and the four thousand. These two stories contain clear similarities, despite different numbers of baskets of crumbs that are said to remain over. In one case there are twelve baskets of crumbs over — sufficient for all of the twelve tribes of Israel. In the second case there are seven baskets of crumbs over — in Jewish terms a complete number. In both cases the abundance of left-over food signals the active presence of the God who created the world in seven days and who has sufficient resources to feed not just Israel but the Gentile world as well. In this example of Mark's editing method, the story of the Syro-phoenician woman is sandwiched between the two feeding stories. In this story, the woman is said to have come to Jesus seeking healing for her possessed daughter. Jesus somewhat harshly turns her away but she persistently demands, significantly, to be fed from crumbs from his table. Nor is it insignificant that she is a foreigner as well as a woman, perhaps even a prostitute. Once again Mark's point seems to have to do with the question of the inclusiveness of God — this time the God who is able to feed large numbers of Jews but with enough crumbs over for those yet needing to be fed, including Gentiles and the socially disadvantaged. By the end of the story the woman's daughter has had her demon possession dealt with, and, very importantly, she is reclining at table in the place of honour!

The chief theological point being made here is of a piece with Mark's concern about the inclusiveness of the mission of God to people of every race and social situation, but it is only really picked up through the critical work of noting Mark's editorial efforts with the traditional material.

A critical reading of the texts will thus be alert to the different voices of the respective evangelists in this kind of way. It will avoid any tendency to gloss over differences and discrepancies to produce a kind of homogenised harmony of the texts. And it will seek out the nuances of the various versions of the same story, which Packer would pronounce an impious and faithless challenge to scriptural authority, and thus gain further insight into God's word.

† † †

We have therefore to note the differences of theological emphasis between the Gospel writers so as to begin to discern the rich and diverse freight of meaning carried by the respective texts. It is important to note that our contemporary awareness of the diversity of theological viewpoint within scripture is not just the outcome of postmodern literary theory with its general celebration of unavoidable diversity in the interpretation of literary texts. This is not just a matter of the celebration of *différance* and the abandonment of the quest for a more absolute and single expression of truth. That postmodern insight has to do with differences of interpretation that arise out of a single text, given that it will be read and heard differently by different readers. That, too, is an unavoidable challenge to fundamentalism, with its pre-critical commitment to thinking in terms of a single or 'plain' reading of the text. We will come to that in a moment. Here the concern is with differences *between* the various texts of the New Testament canon.

As early as the 1950s the great German biblical exegete Ernst Käsemann pointed out that the fact that we have four Gospels and not just one already points to the truth that there is an irreconcilable diversity of viewpoint amongst the Gospel writers in presenting the good news of Jesus and his saving significance.[20] The confession that is common to all the evangelists — that Jesus is the Son of God — is differently explicated, apparently in response to differing needs of the intended audiences for whom they were produced. And it is proclaimed with the help of culturally conditioned concepts and ideas assimilated from different contemporary environments. Disparate theological treatments by the evangelists of essentially the same Gospel stories thus eventuate. Käsemann noted, for example, that Matthew appears to take offence at the way in which the healing of the woman with the issue of blood is treated by Mark (Mark 5:27f). The idea that the garment of a miracle worker 'imparts divine power which is transmitted by touch and has healing properties is a popular Hellenistic conception', says Käsemann. In other words, this is a motif that is 'at home' in a specific kind of cultural context. In scripture it occurs again in accounts of Peter's healing shadow and Paul's miraculous handkerchief (Acts 5:15; 19:12), and Käsemann observes that this tradition may be at the root of the cult of relics in later ages. But Matthew corrects any suggestion of a quasi-magical outlook by omitting the detail of the story which suggests that Jesus' healing was made effective through contact with his garment; in Matthew it is more clearly effected through Jesus' word of power (Matthew 9:22). Subtle differences of this kind between the various Gospel narratives abound in the scriptural text.

Käsemann went on to say that other clear doctrinal differences could also be discerned within the New Testament, between St Paul and St Luke or St Paul and the writer of the Epistle of James, for example, or between St Paul and the author of the Pastoral Epistles (I and 2 Timothy and Titus). Also, Luke's treatment of Paul's apostleship in Acts makes assumptions which Paul himself passionately contests in Galatians I, and Luther appears to have been right in judging that the Pauline doctrine of justification by faith is in tension with the views of the Epistle of James on the importance of good works. Käsemann therefore came to the conviction that, even though the sixteenth-century Reformers imagined that scripture could be used as a relatively straightforward court of appeal for settling doctrinal disputes, scripture itself is the ground of doctrinal diversity in the Church.[21] This poses a very considerable problem for those who fondly think that scripture delivers a single clear, distinct and entirely harmonious set of theological and historical propositions to which unquestioning assent is to be given.

Sydney Anglicans are uneasy about being thought of as fundamentalists, and have expressed a preference for the alternative label 'Bible-believing Christians'. It is easy to speak of 'Bible-believing Christians', but the question is exactly which interpretation of the Bible is to be believed? To claim that only those who promiscuously skate over differences and discrepancies in the texts can really be regarded as 'Bible-believing' is offensive to those who believe that the true message of the Bible can only be discerned, not by following the letter, but with the help of the Spirit, as the Word of God is discerned in and through the diversity of the faith perspectives found within the canon of scripture. Indeed, many of us believe that to refuse to acknowledge the diversity of faith perspectives and differences in ways of presenting the Gospel within the pages of the New Testament would leave us open to the charge of rank dishonesty.

† † †

Both the conservatively minded evangelical Christian and the biblical fundamentalist have over the last twenty-five years also had to contend with an even greater challenge posed by contemporary approaches to textual meaning that are usually grouped together under the banner of postmodernism. Not least amongst these challenges is that posed by contemporary reader response theory, which has now made us well aware that what the reader brings to a text in the form of his or her basic presuppositions, and the precise questions that are put to it, will condition what it is heard to say.

Any so-called 'simple' or 'plain' reading of scripture becomes a sheer impossibility in the face of obvious differences that inevitably arise amongst different people in the reading of a single text. Reader response theory has invited us to be alert to the fact that it is not just the discrepancies *between* New Testament texts, but different contemporary readings of a single text that call in question the idea that there is a straightforward meaning to be discerned. In the interpretation of biblical texts this can happen with respect to a single isolated paragraph or story, or with respect to a whole book and what is discerned to be its fundamental theme. Hence, the seemingly neverending production of successive commentaries on the biblical books. But the unavoidable multiplicity of interpretations raises difficulties for those who fondly continue to speak of '*the* plain meaning of scripture'.

Sometimes, in response to the postmodern challenge of contemporary reading theory, it has been argued that it is nevertheless possible to discern one particular interpretation of a text that is that intended by the author. This indeed was Packer's view, long before the more recent postmodernist turn. This meaning is often spoken of as the 'authorial intent' behind the texts, which may be discerned in a 'plain', 'proper' or 'natural' reading of the text. The problem is, in the absence of authors who are no longer with us, that there is no way of asking them if we have their intentions exactly right, and what we imagine to be the so-called 'authorial intent' is often precisely that — something imagined. It quite simply cannot be verified in any incontrovertible sense.

One reason why we cannot be quite sure of an author's precise meaning and intent is because there is always what we might call a 'surplus of meaning' in relation to the interpretation of a text. In other words, authors always reveal more than they actually intend, unwittingly disclosing more about their time and circumstance than they are aware of doing.

Also, new emphases and nuances of meaning constantly come to light. Sometimes nuances of meaning can be read from a text by associating it with other texts that resonate with it and that are known to the reader, but that could have been entirely unknown to the original author. In other words, we have to be alert to the dynamic of intertextuality which adds to the meaning of a text as it may have been originally intended. Indeed, the original author may have had another text in mind when producing his or her own, which is unknown to a contemporary reader who will thus read the text differently from how it was intended.

Often it is some change of contemporary historical circumstance that sends the reader back to the scriptural texts and triggers fresh understandings of them. Take, for example, Anglican openness during the last generation to hearing a new appreciation of St Paul's statement of Galatians 3:28, that in Christ (as a consequence of baptism into the Christian community), there is neither Jew nor Greek, bond nor free, male nor female. This has helped us to see with new clarity that in Christ humanly erected barriers of race or social class or *gender* should no longer hold sway. In turn, this is one of the things that has allowed us, even obliged us, to embrace the ordination of women in the Churches of the Anglican Communion. This renewed grasp of the Pauline truth that we are all one in Christ, people of equal dignity and status, despite our obvious differences of race, class and gender, is what impels us to reassess our previous more clearly patriarchal readings of the New Testament texts. In much the same way, Christians of the eighteenth and nineteenth centuries found it necessary to read again those texts which they had imagined warranted the practice of slavery. It is a new reading of the same texts that requires us to rethink inherited, historically conditioned practices and procedures.

We are also today alert to what we might call 'the fallacy of direct transference'. When an ancient text produced in the context of a particular culture and circumstance is picked up and transported through the centuries and dropped down in a different context, it will inevitably be heard differently. For example, the Creation story of Genesis will obviously be heard differently today in the light of an evolutionary understanding of the universe and its origins millions of years ago from the way it would have been heard just two centuries ago. Likewise, human nature will be understood differently from the way Aristotle thought of it, in the light of the findings of modern psychology and the human genome project. If the Church were to say exactly the same thing in different cultural contexts it would be heard differently. Indeed, even as individuals and members of different cultures and subcultures of the same period, we all bring our own specific baggage of presuppositions and interests to the reading of texts, a pre-understanding of things, which will condition the precise way we hear and how we interpret them.

One classic example of this was brought to the attention of bishops of the Anglican Church of Australia at the national bishops meeting at Gilbulla in 2001 by the Adelaide theologian Dr Alan Cadwallader. It relates to B. F. Westcott, one of the really great New Testament scholars of the late nineteenth century. In his exposition of the miracle of the changing of the water into wine at the end of the marriage feast of Cana in Galilee (John 2), when people had drunk well and the wine ran out, Westcott noted the large quantity of water in the six jars that were turned into wine — each jar contained twenty or thirty gallons! Today the huge supply might well be taken as a sign of the over-abundant generosity of God, who provides for his people in good measure, pressed down and running over. But Westcott held that Our Lord would only have changed a small amount of the available water into wine, so that what the guests received was a kind of small medicine glass full, like a small glass of port at the end of a dinner. When we ask why it is that Westcott so innocently imagined things to be this way at Cana, Dr Cadwallader's explanation is not by way of the after-dinner port of his Cambridge College, but by the fact that Wescott wrote at the height of the late nineteenth-century temperance movement! Even the greatest of New Testament scholars is not immune from the unconscious conditioning of his own time and place in the handling of texts.

I also think it is helpful to work with the distinction between the manifest and the latent meaning of a text. If there is almost always a surplus meaning of a text, then there is more than one can pick up on a first reading or reading at its face value. Texts have a capacity to yield a deeper meaning than just the surface reading, the superficial or manifest meaning. That Jesus himself was aware of this deeper or latent meaning of a text is implicit in his own teaching in parables: parables allow for a certain freedom in interpretation — it is possible to have eyes to see but not see, and ears to hear, but not hear and understand the full meaning. Scripture itself also indicates that in the reading of texts the difference between the Spirit and the letter has to be observed by the discerning person; for the letter kills but the Spirit gives life. Thus, the point is that the very same text is capable of being read in entirely different ways. This illustrates the truth that, whatever the intention of the author, the outlook of the reader in very large part determines what a specific text is heard to say. It is not possible to speak of the 'proper', 'plain', or 'natural' meaning of a text, for these terms beg too many questions.

Given the undeniable diversity of possible interpretations of biblical texts, many of us are these days less inclined than conservative evangelical, fundamentalist, or so-called Bible-believing Christians to imagine that a single preferred finite human understanding of things can itself be made absolute. As any teacher of English literature will know, there is no one definitive reading of any literary text. There is no one interpretation of *Hamlet*, for example, only the received or predominant reading amongst readers of a particular time or culture. Scripture is the same; it is open to a wide variety of interpretations. Many of the optional readings will be non-competitive, and this means that the question of truth will not be raised in the way it would if interpretations were radically opposed and competing. Whether any one reading can claim a monopoly on truth, however, is very doubtful, given that different readings of the scriptural texts are inevitable. There is, quite simply, no such things as *the* so-called 'plain' reading of scripture. These hermeneutical insights are now well appreciated by modern literary theorists; they are even par for the course for secondary school students of English literature who must shake their heads whenever they hear pulpit talk of 'the plain meaning of scripture'.

This, of course, is very challenging, and probably very disturbing to those who think of the scriptures as a clear and distinct revelation of the mind of God, or as a compendium of answers to religious questions, which can be called upon not just to guide but to direct human behaviour — and this with a degree of absolute certainty. If that were so there would be only one set of biblical commentaries instead of the neverending plethora of commentaries that continue to be produced by earnest scholars in the quest to expound the rich depth of meaning to be found in the scriptures.

All this means that, as Anglicans most of us are not generally biblical fundamentalists. In our reading of the texts, it is not the manifest or superficial as distinct from the latent meaning of the text that is regarded as the only one to live by. Indeed, we note that for the fundamentalist, it is usually very much *his or her* own reading of scripture that is imagined to be *the* meaning of scripture. This then becomes the only one, which the fundamentalist seeks to enforce on others. But one has to ask whether this approach to scripture reduces the revelation of the mystery of God to a gnostic knowledge of secrets.

† † †

The unavoidable diversity of meanings that derive from the biblical texts underpins some of the most hotly contested debates around the Anglican Communion today. One topical example is the contemporary difference of opinion in many parts of the Church in relation to the question of homosexuality. Differences in the reading of the relevant biblical texts condition attitudes as to whether long-term committed relationships amongst people of the same gender might one day be sanctioned, and whether people in such relationships might even be admitted to ordained ministry.

At the General Synod of the Anglican Church of Australia held in Brisbane in July 2001, a report on human sexuality and the Church's approach to issues relating to homosexuality, in particular, was received and commended to the Church at large for continuing study. The report, consisting of a collection of essays, was entitled *Faithfulness in Fellowship*.[22]

I was myself the Chairperson of the Doctrine Panel which produced this report on what is certainly a very difficult and sensitive issue. While members of the panel represented a wide diversity of viewpoint, I think all of us learned a huge amount from one another as we worked together, and despite some media reports to the contrary, we worked together in exemplary harmony. It was a delight to be a member of such a hard-working group of congenial if somewhat unlikeminded people.

Faithfulness in Fellowship came to the General Synod of 2001 for its initial consideration with the recommendation that it be commended to the Church at large for ongoing study. In a sense, however, this horse had already bolted, given that the publication of the report had already triggered very widespread discussion and debate in the community at large. It is important, however, that such complex and sensitive issues be studied by direct acquaintance with the contents of the report itself and not just on the basis of selective media reporting. Study materials have therefore been produced to assist parish communities in this process.

But firstly, it may well be asked, why are we today involved in this exercise at all? I think there are both historical and pastoral reasons.

As is well known, the definition of what we speak of today as 'exclusively homosexual orientation' was determined in the middle of the nineteenth century, just on one hundred and fifty years ago. Since then the entire Western world has been struggling to come to terms with it. First, it was the question of the criminalising and then the decriminalising of homosexual behaviour; more recently in the community there seems to be a growing degree of acceptance of homosexual orientation, with the possibility of the legalising of same gender domestic partnerships in some kind of way, and so on. Inevitably, we Christians live in a world in which we have to face this reality and bring the norms of scripture to bear upon it. This set of issues is not going to go way. As a Church we have to engage in the work of determining what our moral responses will be.

Secondly, all parties in this Church debate agree about the authority of scripture, and there are clearly some key biblical texts which must be taken into account. But, as the discussion of those texts by our biblical scholars in *Faithfulness in Fellowship* amply demonstrates, they are by no means simple texts to interpret. In a sense, because differences of viewpoint emerge in the reading of them, scripture itself triggers the current debate and is the ground of diversity of outcome; scripture itself does not settle the debate.

One basic reason why we are currently engaged in discussion and debate rather than basking in the comfort of a settled and decided mind is epistemological. We still have to face the basic problem posed by the undisputed fact that the concept of 'exclusively homosexual orientation' is a nineteenth-century development and was not previously in use. We cannot read a modern understanding of things anachronistically, back into the minds of first century authors of New Testament scripture. We quite simply have to face up to the implications for us of the Kantian epistemological dictum that 'intuitions without concepts are blind; concepts without intuitions are empty'. What Kant meant by 'intuitions' was roughly 'the deliverances of sense experience'. When applied to the present problem, this dictum means that without the concept of 'homosexual orientation' any intuition or sense experience of a person of whom we might speak of today as a person of homosexual orientation would have been blind to its existence. In just the same way, people were blind to the existence of oxygen, even though they certainly experienced it, until somebody discovered oxygen and brought it under the concept 'oxygen'. Prior to the discovery and naming of oxygen, people could not make claims to a knowledge of it, and it is the same with the discovery and naming in the nineteenth century of 'homosexual orientation'. Conversely, according to Kant's dictum, if somebody were to coin the concept of 'homosexual orientation' in a world where there were no homosexually orientated persons it would simply be an empty concept. Objects of sensory experience thus fill concepts which would otherwise be empty.

This explains why it is that the key biblical texts all presuppose an approach to human sexuality which does not differentiate heterosexual and homosexual orientation. The concept of a 'homosexually orientated person' was not part of the mental make-up of the biblical writers. If anything they presuppose what we might call an undifferentiated heterosexuality. This, for example, is implicit in Lot's offer of his *daughters* an as appropriate substitute for the angel visitors whom the people of Sodom demanded to be sent out to them 'that we might know them'. (Genesis 19:5). An undifferentiated heterosexuality is also implicit in Leviticus' prohibition on lying with a man '*as you do with a woman*' (Leviticus 18:22), and in St Paul's explicit mention of abandoning wives and going off with other men (Romans 1:27). Clearly, while these texts may refer to what we would call today homosexual behaviour, none of these texts is explicitly and specifically about what we call today homosexually orientated persons, and certainly not homosexual persons in long-term committed relationships. Even to speak of 'bisexual orientation' would be an anachronism in relation to the biblical mentality. There are overtones of faithless promiscuity in all of the key biblical texts, which is understandable given the Bible's broad teaching on the importance of faithfulness in human relationships, which properly should reflect the steadfast love and faithfulness of God. What this teaching has to say about faithful, long-term homosexual relationships is an open question. Certainly, we can understand why this difficult issue is currently on the Church's agenda.

Nevertheless, a quite fundamental difficulty is posed by the fact that the concept of a 'homosexually orientated person' is a modern discovery which, in epistemological terms, cannot have been in the minds of the biblical writers, unless of course we are prepared to reduce biblical truth to a kind of non-rational gnostic secret knowledge, and somehow infer that it was in the minds of the biblical authors even if there is no explicit evidence to provide support for this. The biblical texts as we have them have therefore to be pressed into service on the essentially modern question of homosexual orientation, and then persons of homosexual orientation in long-term committed relationships.

All Anglicans agree with respect to the normative and authoratative place of scripture within the Christian tradition, but face significant problems with regard to its interpretation and application. It is because of the lack of specificity in the biblical texts with regard to many modern questions that the Church and the world at large are involved in seemingly endless discussion and debate. In other words, the biblical texts trigger the discussion; they do not settle it.

If it is imagined from the outset that scripture is basically a body of teaching in the sense of a compendium of answers to theological questions, or a boxed set of moral directives for living, or indeed the 'standing orders' for Christians to follow and live by, as Archbishop Peter Jensen has put it, then the reader will concentrate on the discernment of its meaning as a straightforward index to the sovereign will of God as a way of settling questions. But, if the message of scripture is understood not so much as a set of directives, but as a call to discipleship, an invitation to have to do with God himself, rather than just to assent in a rationalistic sense to a set of propositions or formulas, it will be read differently. One can begin to explore scripture for indications of what God has in store by way of promises for humanity's fulfilment, and then respond in obedient discipleship. The question will then be: is the Word of God essentially a Word of a directive kind or of a promissory kind? Depending on how one approaches it, the answer will be different. Moreover, if the Word of God is not understood primarily in terms of 'standing orders' or directives, but in the first instance in terms of the covenant promise to be with his people as they make their way in the world, they may have to wrestle to discern moral and doctrinal truth in the context of today. This is the perspective of 'progressive orthodoxy'. The reading of scripture does not somehow eliminate the categories of ambiguity and mystery by making everything clearly manifest; rather, the scriptural text calls us out of our mundane and matter-of-fact world and opens us up to transcendent mystery.

CHAPTER 4

CROSS AND
RESURRECTION

When St Paul expounds the meaning of Resurrection faith in his most extended treatment of this theme, I Corinthians Chapter 15, he resorts to the concept of mystery: 'Listen, I will tell you a mystery! We will not all die, but we will all be changed, in a moment, in the twinkling of an eye, at the last trumpet' (I Corinthians 15:51–52). Paul is therefore in the position of having to seek to penetrate the mystery and reduce it to a measure of manageability in the best way he can. This means that when he tries in the same chapter to explain what the Resurrection body might be like, he naturally finds himself appealing to an analogy. This is inevitable. Given that the resurrection of the dead has already been identified by Paul as surpassing our ordinary human experience it must thus tax both our understanding and our linguistic capacities of expression.

St Paul's appeal is to the analogy of a botanical seed, such as wheat or some other grain, which is inert and lifeless, until it is buried in the ground and dies. Nevertheless, miraculously, in the good purposes of the God of all creation, new life springs from it. This is a life that has continuity with the original seed while in another sense being a genuinely new creation. In this way the generation of new life from the burial of a seed is used by Paul to illustrate the mysterious possibility of human resurrection to new life beyond the grave.

As a pharisee, St Paul believed in the resurrection of the dead prior to his Christian conversion. He already entertained the hope of the general resurrection at the eschatological end time when it was anticipated that the trumpet would sound to announce the final purposes of God. This is the essential eschatological hope of the Kingdom of God and the consummation of all things of which Christians still speak today as the Last Judgment. The significance of the Gospel of the Resurrection of Christ for Paul, which he proclaimed with such dedication and vigour after his Christian conversion, was that the resurrection to new life of the living and the dead (those who sleep and those who were yet to die) had already in a sense begun with the Resurrection of Christ — the first born of the dead. Christ's Resurrection is thus the promise of the general resurrection of all the living and the dead, and the ground of our specifically Christian hope. Thus, reaffirming his inherited pharisaic belief, Paul says: 'if there is no resurrection of the dead, then Christ has not been raised'; but, conversely, drawing on his newfound experience of Christian conversion, he declares 'if Christ has not been raised, then our proclamation has been in vain' (I Corinthians 15:13–14).

In I Corinthians 15 he therefore begins his discourse on the theme of the resurrection of the dead by reminding the Corinthians of the original good news of the Resurrection of Christ, which he had proclaimed to them on his first visit to their city. This is found in I Corinthians 15:3–8. Furthermore, he says that this was in fact a tradition that he himself had earlier received. We can be quite certain of the authenticity of the original Easter tradition which Paul said he had handed on to the Corinthians as something that he had himself received, for this is verified by the fact that the substantive kernel of his proclamation actually contains some language that is not characteristically Pauline.[1] This attests to the very primitive antecedents of this Easter proclamation.

The Gospels are, of course, later than Paul's epistles. The earliest Gospel, St Mark's, is usually dated to around 65 AD, whereas Paul wrote I Corinthians over a decade prior to this, probably around 52 AD. Furthermore, if the original proclamation of which Paul reminds the Corinthians had been passed on to them when he first visited them, this visit would have been around 49 AD. Given that he identifies the kernel of the Gospel he had proclaimed at that early time as something he had himself received even earlier, this passage commends itself, methodologically speaking, as the correct point of entry into the New Testament for understanding the resurrection good news. It is right to begin with this earliest known report of the Easter proclamation.

It is important to note that this original Easter proclamation of Paul to the Corinthians, which is now found in I Corinthians 15:3–8, focused upon the evidence of the first reported appearances of the Raised Christ as the foundation of faith. Paul lists the appearances in temporal sequence, beginning with the appearance *first* to Peter, and *then* to the Twelve, *then* to over 500 on one occasion, *then* to James and *then* to all the Apostles, and *finally* to Paul himself. Curiously, there is in this list, which concentrates on the reports of the first experiences of the appearance of the Raised Christ, no explicit mention of the empty tomb tradition which bulks so large in the later Gospel traditions. Rather, the earliest coming to faith is said to be based, not inferentially on the negative evidence of the empty tomb, but on the more positive tradition of the reports of the appearances.

Just what these experiences were like is as hard for us to envisage as it is to imagine our own resurrection beyond death. It is also hard for us to match this list of reported appearances with the actual descriptions of first appearances found in the later Gospels. In the Gospel stories Mary Magdalene features very centrally, though in Paul's list of first appearances she does not feature at all. Paul's tradition of the first appearance to Peter is at least corroborated insofar as Luke recounts the story of the appearance to disciples on the way to Emmaus upon which they immediately returned to Jerusalem where it was already being declared that 'Jesus was risen, indeed, and that he had appeared to Peter' (Luke 24:34). Other than this it is hard to match up the list of first appearances of the Pauline tradition with the Gospel stories.

What is clear is that there is no suggestion in the list of appearances in I Corinthians 15 that Paul understood that his own experience of the appearance of the Raised Christ on the Damascus Road was qualitatively different from those mentioned earlier in the same list. Indeed, Paul jealously defends his own status as an Apostle, equal to all the others, and this is based on his claim that he too, like the other Apostles, 'had seen the Raised Christ' (I Corinthians 9:1).

In the accounts of Paul's own Damascus Road experience in the Acts of the Apostles, it is clear that this was some kind of visionary experience of the Raised Christ 'from heaven' as it were.[2] Likewise, in his resurrection discourse in I Corinthians 15 Paul speaks of the resurrection body as a 'spiritual body' appropriate to a heavenly or celestial state, as distinct from a purely or straightforwardly physical or earthly body, the terrestrial body. Clearly, Paul is grappling with the problem of having to work with the tension between continuity and change which is also present in his talk of the burial of the seed and the genuinely new life that bursts from it.

Some inkling of what Paul intends to convey by this highly suggestive but admittedly elusive language can be discerned from another idea in the key passage of I Corinthians 15. This is the declaration that the Raised Christ has become 'a life-giving Spirit' (I Corinthians 15:45). This reference to the life-giving Spirit of Christ the new Adam clearly resonates with similar Pauline statements found elsewhere. At the beginning of the Epistle to the Romans he says, for example, that Christ, though 'descended from David according to the flesh', was 'declared to be Son of God with power according to the Spirit of holiness by his resurrection from the dead' (Romans 1:3–4). In 2 Corinthians 3:17 Paul says more starkly and quite simply that 'the Lord is the Spirit', and in Romans 8 the term 'Spirit of Christ' is used together with 'Holy Spirit' and 'Spirit of God', apparently without differentiation of referent.

It is also apparently the Raised Christ's presence as the animating Spirit of the community of faith that makes it possible for Paul to speak of that community as Christ's Body. Indeed, it is both significant and consistent with Paul's emphasis on the positive experiences of the first appearances rather than the empty tomb that when Paul speaks of Christ's Body he does not just speak negatively of its absence from the tomb, but more positively of its whereabouts: the Body of Christ is said to be located in two places — on the altar and around the altar, as it were. For the bread of the Eucharist is now said to be the Body of Christ and the community that shares it is said also to be the Body of Christ. Thus, St Paul says that a second tradition which he had received and passed on to the Corinthians related to the Holy Eucharist (I Corinthians 11:23–26) and it is on the basis of this tradition that we understand his words: 'The bread that we break, is it not a sharing in the body of Christ?... we who are many are one body, for we all partake of the one bread' (I Corinthians 10:16–17). Once again, it is significant that in handling the extended meaning of the Easter mystery and the continuing presence of Christ with his people, Paul is again resorting to the language of analogy and metaphor. The community which shares the Eucharistic Body of Christ and which is fed and sustained by it, is said also to be the Body of Christ. To find the Body of Christ we are not directed by Paul to go to a tomb, not even an empty tomb, for it is not the absence of the body from the tomb that is of interest for St Paul; rather, it is the new location of the Body of Christ that is important.

If we understand the human body in an instrumental sense in the context of human relationality it can be defined as that which gives us access to a person. Conversely, the bodily absence of a person denies us access to that person. If this is the kind of thing Paul has in mind in his body talk, then the Body of Christ of the Eucharist and the ecclesial Body of Christ can be understood as giving us a means of access to the Raised Jesus himself.[3] For Paul 'somebody's "body" is simply the person him or herself insofar as this person is available to other persons ...'[4]

It is certainly clear enough that St Paul is struggling to express something of the mystery of his Resurrection faith with a variety of linguistic tools: he points both back to the first reports of the appearances of the Raised Christ, including his own experience on the Road to Damascus, and to the present, to the continuing experience of the Spirit of Christ in the life and worship of the Christian community. However, like the nature and being of God himself, the Resurrection as the central mystery of the Christian revelation cannot be captured within the net of a few clear and distinct concepts. This is because the Resurrection of Christ is not to be placed along with the ordinary events of human history in a field of like occurrences; it remains an utterly unique event. Indeed, it is a uniquely transcendent event, the pivotal act of God for the redemption of humankind that inevitably surpasses our limited human capacities of understanding. This should alert us to the folly of reductionist attempts to express it in a few literal and prosaic concepts, as though the appearance or presence of Christ were the kind of thing that could be photographed. As the supreme moment of the revelation of God in Christ, the composite event of Cross and Resurrection essentially involves the disclosure of a mystery that transcends our human capacity to express in mere words.

In my book *The Structure of Resurrection Belief*, published in 1987,[5] I acknowledged that the Resurrection of Christ is to be understood at the outset as a transcendental and eschatological event, and took account of this in order to articulate a primary methodological principle of Resurrection theology: that in talking about the Resurrection of Christ we necessarily have to employ a number of different avenues of approach to what, by definition, is beyond words and which will remain a transcendent mystery until the eschaton. This means that different theological models have to be employed, each of which helps to penetrate the essential mystery of the Resurrection of Christ without any of them being entirely satisfactory when taken separately. Indeed, *The Structure of Resurrection Belief* can be understood as the attempt of Demea-type theology to come to terms with the Resurrection without surrendering its essential mystery by reducing it to a simple historical happening of the mundane order. If we think we can reduce the magnitude of the Resurrection down to proportions understandable by our finite minds, and so contain and thus have the Raised Christ within the net of our limited human understanding, we may be surprised to find that he, passing through the midst of it, will go his way.

† † †

What then are we to say of the empty tomb traditions of the four Gospels? These certainly appear to be of a piece with the historical reports of any other occurrence of the human past. An appearance of the Raised Christ or some kind of post-mortem encounter with him as Spirit may be difficult to describe. But an empty grave can certainly be spoken of in clear, matter-of-fact terms, and the reports which we have of it can be submitted to historical examination. However, it is exactly at this point that we begin to run into difficulties. For a start, there are discrepancies in the Gospel stories of the empty tomb. The lists of women's names differ from Gospel to Gospel; Mary Magdalene is the only name common to all accounts. (It may therefore be that the original tradition is preserved in St John's Gospel, where Mary Magdalene is said to have encountered Jesus alone in the Garden.) The accounts of the appearance either of a 'young man' as in Mark or of angels in Matthew and Luke also vary. In Mark a single person acts as messenger to direct the women to go and tell the Apostles to go into Galilee to rendezvous with the Raised Christ there. In Matthew an angel becomes an active agent in the story; the angel rolls away the stone and there is an earthquake, and so on. These accounts appear to have to some degree grown in the telling of them over time to meet the need of different circumstances. In Matthew guards are placed at the tomb, a device that may have arisen to combat a charge that Jesus' body had been stolen away.

Given the absence of references to the empty tomb tradition in Paul's letters, some scholars conjecture that the entire story is a later development, and that its lateness is alluded to in Mark's statement that, though commanded to tell what they had witnessed to the others, the women told nobody, 'for they were afraid' (Mark 16:8). Others conjecture that the empty tomb story is not the basis of Easter faith but a way of expressing it. This was the view of the late twentieth-century German New Testament scholar Rudolf Bultmann. At two thousand years' remove, and with no possibility of cross examining the women who were said to be its witnesses, it is not possible to come to an incontrovertible historical conclusion.

Indeed, even more important than the all too obvious discrepancies in the various versions of the story, any attempt to try to prove the Resurrection on the basis of the empty tomb tradition runs into the problem that an empty tomb can be rationally explained in a variety of different ways. The tradition may have arisen because the grief-stricken women originally went to the wrong tomb. Alternatively, by the time the Easter proclamation based on appearances in Galilee had reached Jerusalem the exact location of the tomb may have been difficult to identify. But there are also indications in the empty tomb story itself that it did not ground Easter faith: Mary Magdalene is reported to have concluded that they had taken Jesus away — 'we know not where they have laid him'. Peter departs the scene 'wondering at that which had come to pass'. And the reaction of those on the way to Emmaus was that they were 'amazed at what had happened' (Luke 24:12). Clearly, the empty tomb is not even portrayed in the Gospel traditions as triggering Easter faith. It is rather a cause of perplexity. By contrast, it is the more positive, if somewhat elusive and mystical, tradition of the apprehension of the presence of the Raised Christ, both in the Pauline list and in the Gospel stories of his various appearances, that triggers the response of faith.[6]

The unavoidable historical inconclusiveness of the empty tomb story is why in the tradition of orthodox Christian theology, at least from Thomas Aquinas onwards, the empty tomb has been regarded as a *sign* but not a *proof* of the Resurrection. The real basis of Easter faith is found in the more positive evidence of reports of appearances, corroborated by the continuing experience of the Spirit of Christ within the ongoing communion of the Christian fellowship. Paul well knew this. In this sense, the experiential basis of Resurrection faith, both as Paul understands it and as we still receive it today, has two poles. One is historical and expresses a tradition of reports going back in time to the original tradition of apostolic appearances; and the other the more immediate encounter with the presence of Christ 'from heaven', from the radical hiddenness of God's timeless eternity through the medium of the Spirit. Another way to say this is to say that one pole is diachronic, stretching back through time; and the other synchronic, belonging to the present moment. Faith is not just a rationalistic assent to the truth of reports without supporting evidence of an experiential kind. Rather, the Raised Christ is known in the response of faith, not just by description but by acquaintance.

It is characteristic of the more rationalistic, less experiential bent of mind — such of that of Sydney Anglicans — however, to avoid talk of encounter with the presence of the Raised Christ or of the real presence of Christ and to stress the diachronic pole of faith as a more exclusively propositional, past-centred form of assent to the abstract belief *that* Jesus was raised from the tomb two thousand years ago. The reliance on the Gospel traditions also entails a fairly matter-of-fact and descriptive understanding of what actually happened. The many discrepancies notwithstanding, this means that there is no alternative to picturing the event in a very physical, naturalistic way. As a consequence the Resurrection of Christ is inevitably assimilated to events of the mundane order. This leads to a diminishing of the uniquely transcendental nature of the event.

The original fundamentalists also felt the need to defend a purely physical understanding of what happened on Easter Day. One of the so-called original five points of fundamentalism was belief in the physical Resurrection of Jesus from the grave. The fundamentalists therefore became committed to defending the historical factuality of the empty tomb as the basis of faith. They were clearly uncomfortable with any suggestion that Christ's Resurrection might be removed from the realm of the purely visual and matter-of-fact for, as soon as it is treated as something more mysterious or transcendental, an appearance of the Raised Christ from the radical hiddenness of God's heaven, the Resurrection becomes an object of faith rather than of sight. As such it is removed from the arena of scientific historical investigation.

Fundamentalists also tend to overlook the fact that even the Gospel stories contain elements that suggest that the appearances were more visionary than simply visual. Despite the fact that in some of the later Gospels the Raised Jesus is said to have eaten a piece of fish, or to have had his wounds actually touched by Thomas the Doubter, in all of the accounts the Raised Christ actually appears somewhat mysteriously to the Apostles. For a start they are explicitly said to have been assembled in a room behind closed doors that a resuscitated material body of flesh and bones would not normally be able to penetrate. Likewise, on the way to Emmaus the Raised Jesus is apparently so changed that he is only recognised when bread is broken and shared, and then he as quickly and mysteriously disappears. This perhaps explains why Luke makes it plain in the Book of Acts that Jesus appeared, not in such a way as to be available to everybody with eyes to see but only to selected witnesses. The Easter appearances are much more in the nature of a revelatory disclosure than a simple being around for inspection by anybody who might care to look.

This is made clear by St John. In reporting Jesus' farewell discourse with his disciples just prior to his death and Resurrection, John has Jesus say: 'A little while and you will not see me, and again, a little while and you will see me' (John 16:16). The interesting thing about his passage is the use of two different Greek words for 'see'. In the first case, in which Jesus says he will in a little while not be seen, the sense appears to indicate that a purely visual seeing is in mind. The statement has the sense of 'In a little while you will not be able to scrutinise or look at me.' Then, in the case of Jesus' promise of a future Easter seeing, an altogether different word is used. This happens to be a cognate of the word used in I Corinthians 15 when St Paul says that the Raised Christ 'appeared to' or 'was seen by' the first Apostles. Those who seek to reduce the Easter appearances to an ordinary visual seeing as against a more mysterious heavenly appearance or visionary encounter must at least explain the change of verbs in this statement which appears to signal that different ways of seeing and perceiving are being referred to.

† † †

It is, of course, impossible for us to describe the actual event of the Resurrection inside of the tomb. This is not just because at two thousand years' remove we cannot garner the evidence of the witnesses, but because nobody was actually present when Jesus was raised from the dead. If nobody was present in the tomb when the Resurrection occurred, nobody witnessed it. Rather, it occurred, as St Ignatius of Antioch once said, 'in the silence of God'. We can only therefore imagine what might have happened in the darkness of the tomb.

There are two basic ways of imagining the Resurrection of Christ in the tomb. One way describes an event in literal terms, as plain as the nose on your face. Put baldly, it suggests that Jesus simply resuscitated and woke up. Had anybody been there the event would have looked like a kind of an awaking from the sleep of death — perhaps first signalled by an emotionally moving flickering of the eyelids. This is the kind of event suggested by those who want to underscore the physical materiality of Jesus' raised body. It is what the original fundamentalists sought to defend insofar as they insisted on Christ's *physical* Resurrection from the dead. Curiously, at this point the fundamentalists occupied the same ground as the nineteenth-century liberal rationalists whose theories and ideas they found most challenging. For example, early in the nineteenth century the liberal German scholar H. E. G. Paulus portrayed the Resurrection as an event essentially of this physical kind, and went on to fill in the details of what happened next.[7] After unwrapping the winding sheet, the resuscitated Jesus, he said, made his way out of the tomb and borrowed the gardener's clothes. This explained for Paulus the otherwise strange fact that Mary Magdalene mistook him for the gardener.

The trouble with this kind of reconstruction of the Resurrection event as a purely physical occurrence is that the more realistic and physical it is made to appear, the more the reality of the actual death of Jesus is called into question. A person like Mary Magdalene, bumping into a Jesus resuscitated and restored to life in this world, and recognising him in the garden despite the gardener's overalls, would logically have concluded: 'Oh, we thought you were dead. But clearly you are not. You have been resuscitated and restored to us again.' In other words, the more realistic and purely physical the account of the post-Resurrection body, and the more simply visual and less visionary the appearance is said to be, then the more the reality of the death is called into question. The Resurrection is reduced to a mere physical resuscitation. Thus, Paulus himself concluded that Jesus revived in the tomb physically, because of its coolness, and because of the effect of the spices, which, operating like smelling salts, resulted in the reactivation of the physical processes of his body, and set lungs breathing and heart pumping again. This is clearly a very rationalistic explanation of the Easter story. And is an example of the Liberal Protestantism which, in fact, triggered the rise of fundamentalism throughout the later half of the nineteenth century. But curiously the fundamentalists in their attempt to counter it actually occupied the same ground. In both cases the Raised Christ is understood to have appeared in a way that was clearly manifest to anybody with eyes to see.

Those who come to the Gospel story from a different, less rationalistic perspective informed by the Pauline tradition, however, will work much more with the concept of mystery of which St Paul himself speaks. It is clear from what Paul has to say that Jesus is not to be understood just to have been physically resuscitated and restored to this world, but as one who was translated to a new and more heavenly plane of existence. In the Pauline tradition Jesus' Resurrection body, while enjoying a continuity with the former earthly body, is not a body of flesh and bones simply restored to life *in this world*, but a changed body, a body now transformed and glorified, for 'flesh and blood cannot inherit the Kingdom of God' (I Corinthians 15:50). Weak and vulnerable humanity has to be transformed and reinvigorated by the Spirit of holiness. This is why he can say that we are to think of the body of the Resurrection, not so much as a physical body, but as a 'spiritual body', a celestial body rather than a terrestrial body. It is a transformed and glorified body which has 'put on immortality'. Unlike the resuscitated Lazarus, the Raised Christ is 'never to die again' (Romans 6:9).

In this more mysterious way of looking at things, the Raised and glorified Jesus appears as a transcendent, other worldly reality, 'from heaven', as it were — from the radical hiddenness of God. In the more rationalistic and mundane way of looking at things, one has the impression, as the North American Lutheran theologian Robert Jenson puts it, that Jesus was restored to life in this world and was holed up between appearances somewhere in the Jerusalem caravan park. And when he disappeared from the company of the disciples on the way to Emmaus, perhaps he merely slipped out as somebody might today slip quietly out of a room for a smoke. N. T. Wright, in

The Resurrection of the Son of God,[8] even goes so far as to suggest that when John says that Jesus appeared behind doors that were 'locked', he meant literally that Jesus opened locked doors. Perhaps the key was under the doormat. Or perhaps he said 'Can I come in?' In his attempt to portray the narratives as basically historical, and the 'robustly bodily' nature of the Raised Christ, Wright coins the term 'transphysical'. But the element of transformation tends to be reduced to mean only that the earthly body avoided the normal physical corruption of post-mortem disintegration and decay of the tomb. It is as though God the Father operated with respect to Jesus' resurrection body in a way analogous to the newly discovered Nanog gene within human stem cells.[9] This gene, under the right conditions, triggers the process of endless reproduction of biological immortality. This is the disastrous outcome of milking the narratives of the element of mystery by making them historically matter-of-fact.

I think it is clear that there are two essentially different imaginative accounts of what happened in the garden on Easter Day. One is in terms of a clear and distinct 'manifestation'; the other in terms of 'mystery'. Given that nobody was there to witness the actual event, and that nobody has left us an account of exactly what happened in the darkness and silence of the tomb, we can only conjecture. There is no indisputably reliable account of what happened between Jesus' burial and the reports of his Easter appearances. We have to make the most that we can of the fragmentary evidence and open our minds in awe and reverence to the theological imagination.

Certainly, the Pauline tradition persuades me to imagine the Easter event not just as an event of the mundane order, an emotionally moving flickering of the eyelids, so much as essentially a uniquely transcendental event. Rather than being a happening that can be reduced to and contained within an ordinary finite human description, it is a huge and cataclysmic act of God for our salvation which surpasses our understanding. Theologian Karl Barth once said that the empty tomb is like a great crater left after a massive explosion. I find myself thinking not so much of a mere historical event, essentially like any other humanly observable occurrence that might be in principle open to inspection by anybody with eyes to see, but in terms of a great explosion of blinding light to be known by faith. As a transcendental and revelatory event that is absolutely unique, and therefore quite unlike the events of mundane human history, it is one to be perceived by faith rather than simply by sight. This is why an over-concentration on a purely historical or literal reading of the empty tomb traditions I find wanting.

I outlined these alternative approaches to imagining what happened in the tomb on Easter morning in a sermon in St John's Cathedral, Brisbane, on the day the General Synod was to be convened, 22 July 2001. This happened to be Mary Magdalene's Day and the readings invited some comment on the Easter experience she is reported to have had. Curiously, it was deemed necessary by Anglican Media Sydney to post a response to the sermon on its website in faraway Sydney! The response was prepared by Glenn Davies, who is now the regional bishop in North Sydney. He had been asked to prepare it for the 'Sydney constituency'. In registering his disagreement with an approach to an understanding of the Resurrection from the point of view of transcendent mystery, he appeared to support a more straightforwardly physical view similar to that of the nineteenth-century liberal Paulus, of which I had been critical. He failed to address the problem posed by the fact that the more realistic and simply physical the portrayal of a resuscitated body is made, the more Jesus is restored simply to this world and the more the reality of Jesus' death is called in question. But the really perplexing question that occurred to me at the time was why it was thought necessary that Sydney people should be in need of protection from views that might be new to them ... and expressed in a sermon far away. The need for what appears to be a brand of 'thought policing' so as to try to confirm people in a more conservative position tells us a great deal about the nervously defensive mentality of some 'Sydney Anglicans'.

† † †

When we come to reflect on what the death of Christ upon the Cross might mean for us at the beginning of a new millennium of Christian history, we approach it with an inherited language which includes a number of interpretative images and metaphors mostly drawn from the Old Testament. The New Testament traditions indicate, for example, that when the first Christians sought to express something of the effect of Cross and Resurrection in their lives, they said it was as though a 'ransom' had been paid to release them from bondage to sin.[10] Alternatively, they said that their liberation had been 'purchased' at the price of Christ's blood.[11] Sometimes they spoke as though they had been 'transported' with Christ to heavenly places.[12] We must not fail to note the metaphorical nature of this imagery of 'ransom', 'purchase' and 'transportation'. These concepts derive from the arenas of recovering prisoners of war, or the world of commerce, and even of travel.

But by far the most sustained interpretative concept on which the first generation of Christians relied to describe their newfound experience of both liberation from the oppressive burden of sin and of sheer joy of reconciliation and communion with God, was the concept of sacrifice. Just as the Old Testament language of Isaiah 53 came to their lips to describe Jesus as a suffering servant who, like a 'lamb led to the slaughter', was silent before his oppressors and did not defend himself, so the Old Testament motif of sacrifice easily and naturally suggested itself to describe their own newfound experience of peace with God as a result of Christ's death on the Cross. The idea of sacrifice was a commonplace of the world of religious thought which the new Christians inhabited, and its early popularity as a heuristic concept to interpret the meaning of Christ's Cross may be measured by the fact that it is found across the whole spectrum of New Testament writings.[13] It is by far the most sustained motif for interpreting the meaning of the Cross in the New Testament. Apart from allusions to sacrifice in the accounts of the Last Supper and the Passion in the Gospels, the concept is explicitly used regularly in the writings of St Paul and also, notably, in the Epistle to the Hebrews, where Christ's sacrifice is understood to have superseded the Temple sacrifices of bulls and goats and rendered them no longer necessary. Once again, it is clear that the Cross is interpreted as a means of neutralising the alienating effects of human sin and of achieving reconciliation with God.

Today, however, we come to an understanding of the Cross with a collection of more extensive explanations and developed theories which have accrued to it during the course of the Christian centuries. Given that these theoretical explanations are later developments and were not items of the mental make-up of the first believers, we might well be wise not to try to reduce any of the metaphors and analogies originally used to express the meaning of the Cross to a more prosaic specification, and still wiser not to base further speculative theorising on them. Indeed, at this point we would do well to follow the example of the Christian Creeds, insofar as in the Creeds of orthodox Christianity the Atonement simply does not feature. Instead, the occurrence of the crucifixion and death of Christ, and of the Resurrection and Ascension, are simply affirmed as being 'for us humans and our salvation'. This is why, as I pointed out in Chapter 2, all theories of the Atonement that seek to explain the efficacy of the Cross must be located in the outer circle of the Church's theological speculation, rather than as a central article of defined truth in the inner circle of dogma. Certainly, the indisputable fact of the silence of the Christian Creeds when it comes to theories of the Atonement is itself significant. It is something with which those Christians who are ardently and exclusively wedded to a single theory must come to terms.

One of the difficulties with which attempts to explain just how the sacrificial death of Christ had an eternal reconciling effect have had to grapple is the fact that most of the subsequent theological work of the Church has taken place away from the original religio-cultural context in which sacrifices had their place. The destruction of the Temple in Jerusalem in 70 AD meant that the Jewish cult of sacrifices disappeared overnight. Subsequent Christian reflection on the meaning of sacrifice has therefore not had the benefit of a living sacrificial system against which to measure attempts to understand its precise significance. On the other hand, the Church's dogmatic reticence in relation to theories of the Atonement is almost certainly because deep down it has sensed that all theological attempts to explain the meaning of the Cross have been halting and feeble, historically and culturally conditioned, and, at the end of the day, inadequate to probe a mystery that ultimately passes human understanding. Words cannot pretend to plumb the depths of meaning of so momentous an event and its revelatory and saving significance. This should not surprise us. Long ago the Psalmist cautioned that any overconfident, simplistic explanation of the transcendent acts of God is bound to fail: 'Who can express the mighty acts of the Lord: or fully voice his praise?' (Psalm 106:2). At the very least, these cautionary words of the Psalmist should prevent us from rushing in where even angels fear to tread. At the end of the day, we shall have to concede that the Cross of Christ is an event too full of meaning to be reduced to a mere theory or formula. As the twentieth-century North American New Testament scholar John Knox once put it, there is a sense in which the death of Christ upon the Cross is shrouded in darkness:

> ...it has always been remembered as a moment of strange and awful pregnancy, significant beyond our understanding, pointing us towards heights incalculably beyond our reach and making us aware of the depths in our existence which we know we shall never sound or probe. No wonder the sun was hidden 'from the sixth hour ... until the ninth'. It is significant that, according to the Gospels, both the death of Christ and the Resurrection took place in darkness — events too sacred to be gazed upon, too full of portent to be plainly seen.[14]

Despite cautionary words of this kind, it has to be admitted that an often overconfident rationalistic claim to know the details of exactly how the Cross effected human reconciliation with God has been a recurrent feature of much Christian thought. In a sense this is understandable. The human quest to know and explain, and the psychological need to be confident and certain, and the propensity, then, even to use knowledge to dominate and put down others in apologetic debate, are indicators that it is often difficult for people to relax into a more humble and docile acknowledgment of the limitations of human reason. For better or worse, the outcome is that in the history of the Church a range of theories have been devised in an attempt to explain just how the Cross of Christ achieved its result.

Of all the theories that have been brought forward, perhaps the most popular has been that known as the penal substitutionary theory which has frequently entered the discussion to this point. As we have noted, it was originally articulated by St Anselm in the twelfth century in a work called *Cur Deus Homo* (Why God Became Man). The theory was not known before Anselm's time; for its first thousand years, Christian reflection on the redemptive meaning of the Cross had got on perfectly well without it.[15] It was never popular in the East, and in the West since Anselm's day it has been the churches of the Reformation more than the Roman Catholic Church that has made most use of it.

Briefly put, this theory seeks to work out exactly how the sacrifice of Christ upon the Cross overcame the alienating effect of sin and achieved human reconciliation with God by appealing to the concept of retributive justice. After first focusing on the basic idea of God's justice, the theory argues that a debt had to be paid for human sin and disobedience in order to satisfy God's demands of justice. This is what made Christ's death upon the Cross necessary: somebody *had* to pay the debt to the God of justice and all righteousness for human sin and rebelliousness. In his great love for us, Christ is therefore said to have taken the punishment deserved by all humanity upon himself. In other words, even though he was himself sinless, Christ is said to have suffered a humiliating penalty instead of, or as a substitute for, sinful humanity — hence the *penal* substitutionary theory.

This deceptively simple doctrine of human redemption, couched in terms of a clear and distinct manifestation of God's justice in the form of the imposition of the death penalty, is of a piece with the very simple and even naturalistic understanding of Christ's Resurrection reduced to a mere physical revival or resuscitation. Some of the more popular and crude expositions of this theory of redemption even seem to suggest that it involves an overreaching knowledge of a mythic behind-the-scenes transaction between God the Father and the Son, of the 'you do this and I'll do that' variety. Crudely put: you suffer a horrible fate and I'll forgive the sins of the world. Indeed, it even seems to be suggested in some popular preaching that God views the additional outrageous crime of Pontius Pilate and the Jerusalem mob as satisfaction of his own need to be placated for the sins of the world! Measured by the Bible's own standards such views generate an uncomfortably dubious picture of God.

The inadequacies of the theory are today all too apparent. It is not hard to see why many people are uncomfortable with it. Given the alleged necessity of Christ's death in order that the demands of justice might be satisfied, there is a basic moral question about what kind of justice it is that gets manifested in the punishment of the innocent for the guilty? By today's standards this rates as a gross miscarriage of justice. Why should God's justice conform to this arbitrary and rough-and-ready standard?

Then there is the problem that the theory projects, if not an uncomfortably angry and even tyrannical God, a God who, like a character in a Greek tragedy, becomes a victim of his own system of justice. For, despite the biblical teaching about the virtue of turning the other cheek, and about the abundant generosity of a forgiveness that forgives not just seven times but seventy times seven, or simply receives a repentant sinner in the warmth of a fatherly embrace as in the parable of the Prodigal Son, it suggests that God himself cannot for some reason forgive sinful humanity without the prior operation of such a mechanism of punishment. It is as though God were somehow entangled, however reluctantly, in a justice system that he himself has put in place. Indeed, it suggests that God could not freely exercise forgiveness without the fulfilment of its requirements!

This was one of John Henry Newman's complaints about the theology of Thomas Erskine. In Tract 73, to which reference has already been made in Chapter I, Newman questioned the kind of justice that was said to be manifested in Erskine's deceptively simplistic and reductionist understanding of the surpassing meaning of the Cross. Newman noted parallels in the classical story of Zaleucus, prince of the Locrians. In that story Zaleucus is said to have decreed that the penalty for adultery throughout his kingdom should be that those found guilty have two eyes put out. In order to show his abhorrence of adultery along with his steadfast determination to execute the law he had himself enacted, Zaleucus was obliged to condemn his own son. Therefore, in order to satisfy the needs of the system of justice that he had put in place, and at the same time to manifest his love for his son who had been convicted of the crime, Zaleucus willingly submitted to lose one of his own eyes, and ordered at the same time that one of his son's eyes be put out. In this way the demands of justice were satisfied because the penalty of putting out two eyes was exacted, but the father's love is manifested by the putting out of only one of Zaleucus's eyes.

But Newman's question is this: how is this arbitrary punishment of putting out two eyes for adultery really justice? Whose justice and what kind of justice? How is this anything more than the very rough-and-ready justice of this world? Our contemporary question is the same: does this not involve a gross and arbitrary penalty, like chopping off hands of those convicted of theft in Islamic societies today? Where is the justice of God in the punishment of the Son to fulfil his own laws? Clearly, to presume to define God's justice in a manifestly clear way, even if to the modern mind it appears to be a miscarriage of justice, and to claim this as an article of certain knowledge about the mind and will of the infinite God goes well beyond the warrant of the biblical revelation. The former Bishop of Ely, Stephen Sykes, notes: 'Contemporary defenders of the penal satisfaction theory rightly now speak of the language as metaphorical.' Interestingly enough he has in mind James Packer! Sykes goes on: 'This important concession is bound to imply that, in certain respects, the application of the theory of specific penal exchange to the death of Christ is not appropriate to the Atonement, and that there remains a dimension of mystery.'[16] This was precisely Newman's point back in 1835–1836.

As we have seen, despite difficulties of this kind, and indeed, even in the face of them, one of the so-called 'fundamentals' of the early twentieth-century movement of fundamentalism was the spirited defence of this particular approach to the understanding of the Atonement. Indeed, this theory was urged upon other Christians not just as a preferred option amongst a range of other possible contending Atonement theories but as the *only* legitimate one that could possibly be entertained. This was made clear from the manifesto of 1910 onwards, one of the key five points of early twentieth-century fundamentalism being 'the penal death of Christ upon the

Cross'. In the subsequent literature of the movement concentration of attention upon the defence of the penal substitutionary theory has meant that it has almost become the essential content of the Gospel, the *sine qua non* of authentic Christian teaching and the test of Christian orthodoxy. The corpus of hostile correspondence from people who identified themselves as 'Sydney Anglicans' that I received following the publication of my *Bulletin* article about the meaning of Easter in April 2000 indicated this position is alive and well. Indeed, it is more than likely that this is but the tip of an iceberg. Many contemporary Christians across the spectrum of the denominations appear to have been led into following the original fundamentalists by making the penal substitutionary theory of the Atonement so central to their preaching that it has become almost synonymous with the Gospel: to preach the penal substitutionary theory of the efficacy of the Cross is therefore to preach the Gospel; to stand loosely to it or to dare to enter into a critique of its logical coherence triggers a hostile defensiveness because of what is thought to be a departure from 'the Gospel'. This explains the Reverend Philip Jensen's complaint in his Sydney website response to my original *Bulletin* article charging that my omission of explicit adherence to substitutionary theory of the Atonement was the root cause of the article's alleged shortcomings. Subsequent correspondence with members of the New Cranmer Society in the Diocese of Melbourne has indicated that they are likewise wedded, somewhat nervously, to the defence of essentially the same Atonement theory. Archbishop Peter Jensen is much more confident and categorical:

> *It is because evangelicals have always been conscious of the power and the penalty of sin that their gospel has always majored on the atoning sacrifice of Christ on the cross, through which pardon comes ... Whatever else we may and must say about the cross of Christ, for evangelicals the central feature of its effective power lies in the sin-bearing penal substitution of the Saviour.*

The emphasis is thus on the 'just punishment of God' and the 'penal substitutionary work of Christ' to save us from it.[17]

† † †

Originally, the fundamentalists of the first decades of the twentieth century felt that this particular theory of the Atonement had to be defended against the challenge of liberal Protestantism. Liberal critiques of the theory had, in fact, been building through the nineteenth century. Amongst these, perhaps the most trenchant was Albrecht Ritschl, whose three-volume work *The Christian Doctrine of Justification and Reconciliation* was published in 1882–83. In this monumental work, Ritschl questioned the apparently vindictive justice of a God who demanded the death of his own Son as unworthy of the God of the biblical revelation. Apart from the difficulties we have already noted of suggesting that God cannot show mercy without satisfying an abstract idea of justice, and that it was a strange kind of justice in which the innocent victim was said to have suffered punishment for the guilty, Ritschl also discerned a more serious defect. Insofar as a punishment is said to have been exacted from one person of the Trinity in satisfaction of another, it appeared to fracture the perfect unity of the Godhead by pitting one person of the Trinity against the other. In other words, the idea of punishment is in tension with the idea of the perfect unity of the Trinitarian life established by mutual self-gift.

An uncritical adoption of Calvinist teaching, rather than the original formulation of the doctrine at the hands of St Anselm, was probably behind what tended to be interpreted in the early twentieth century as the only correct doctrine of the Atonement amongst the fundamentalists. Certainly, much fundamentalist language reflects Calvin's heavy talk of a Christ 'who took the punishment upon himself' in place of humans who are 'accursed and condemned' by a God who is 'hostile to us' and 'our enemy'.[18] Calvin even speaks of the 'transfer' of God's punishment from humans to Christ. Despite the reliance of the original fundamentalists on John Calvin, however, we can better grasp an understanding of the penal substitutionary theory by considering its original formulation by Anselm in the context of the medieval cultural environment out of which it came.

Anselm, apparently following Radulphus Ardens, appealed to the idea of 'satisfaction' to explain exactly how the sacrifice of Christ upon the

Cross had its beneficial effect for all humanity. This aspect of Anselm's explanation is very much a product of an age that was dominated by feudal religio-social conventions. Some scholars have sought the origin of the idea of satisfaction in the Germanic custom of 'Wergeld', whereby compensation had to be paid by a person convicted of homicide to the victim's clan. The payment of a penalty thus exempted an offender from further responsibility. Alternatively, in the highly stratified society of medieval feudalism, in which contractual relationships secured by oaths of fealty were so important an element of social cohesion, an offence committed against a person of higher social status called for the redressing of his slighted honour by the performance of a public token of atonement in order to make satisfaction. A verbal apology was not enough. Rather, in this case, the satisfaction offered, let us say by a vassal to a lord, operated in the public arena as a required payment of what was justly due. Thus Richard Southern observes that 'Anselm's favourite image of the relations between God and Man was that of a lord and his vassals.'[19] In the context of this feudal relationship, the violation of God's honour constitutes the essential sin of disobedience: 'He who does not render to God His due honour, takes from God what is His, and dishonours (exhonorat) God; and this is sin.'[20] A principle of justice dictated that a penalty had to be exacted in order to appease the slighted honour of the lord and thus to allow for the restoration of proper relationships and right public order. Against this religio-social background it is understandable that St Anselm might see that the slighted honour of God because of the rebellious sinfulness and disobedience of humanity could be redressed or satisfied by the perfect sacrificial offering of his Son.

The concept of satisfaction also featured in a genre of literature of St Anselm's day known as the penitentiary. The medieval penitentiary outlined the appropriate kinds of penance to be done in satisfaction of a kind of grocery list of specific sins. These came to include the temporal punishment that might be imposed by ecclesiastical authorities, as distinct from the eternal punishment that a sinner might meet from God beyond death. In the case of the commission of a very public outrage, particularly by a person of superior social status, including even kings and rulers, the most public and extravagant satisfaction might be required. This was particularly so when a notable penitent returned after his excommunication. It was not sufficient that he should privately express his repentance, or even plead for forgiveness with elaborate protestations of sincerity and contriteness of heart in a public apology. Along with a promise in future to do better, it was often necessary to demonstrate contrition by making a full public and visible expression of remorse. Particularly if he wished to be reinstated in his former station in life, with his properties and former rights and privileges restored, a much more public satisfaction had to be exacted. Hence, the view that the temporal demands of justice sometimes required a punishment by public humiliation and chastisement.

In the jostling for power between medieval Church and State, particularly as the Church increased its hold on power after the Investitures Contest of 1075, this became a regular sport. In 1075 Pope Gregory VII (Hildebrand) challenged the Emperor's customary prerogative of investing bishops with the symbols of their administrative and pastoral office — the ring and pastoral staff. This in effect made bishops officers of State. The skirmish that followed ended with the spectacle of the Emperor Henry IV on his knees in the snow at Canossa, pleading for the forgiveness of the Pope. From this time on kings and rulers had regularly to submit to a public humiliation in order to avoid the penalty of excommunication, and the deprivation of their royal property and privileges that this entailed. One of the most celebrated episodes of the time, which became well known right across Europe, was the story of King Henry II of England publicly doing penance on his knees along the pilgrims' way to Canterbury for the involvement of his knights in the martyrdom of Thomas Becket.

Throughout the thirteenth century this kind of thing was commonplace. For example, on 18 June 1209 at the beginning of the Albigensian Crusade against the Cathar heresy, Count Raymond VI of Toulouse underwent a public scourging at the hands of the papal legate Milo on the steps of St Gilles in his native Languedoc, for the crime of tolerating the Cathar heresy as well as allowing Jews to occupy high public positions. Similarly, some twenty years later, on 12 April 1229, Raymond's son, Raymond VII, found himself having to consent to a public scourging at the hands of the papal legate Cardinal Romano before the facade of Nôtre Dame in Paris. This public spectacle went on in the presence of the regent, Blanche of Castille, and the very pious young future king, Louis. Throngs of thrillseekers jammed the stoops, windows and rooftops to witness the exalted brought low as Raymond, barefoot and clad only in shirt and breeches, underwent a degrading lashing also for his tardiness in pursuing and exterminating the Cathar heretics in Languedoc. Raymond's scourging was the high-profile public price that had to be paid in order to wring a peace from both Church and Crown.[21] Part of the deal was that some of Raymond's property was restored but, henceforth, Toulouse and the surrounding area of Languedoc became a part of France. Following this the Albigensian Crusade gradually came to an end. For the counts of Toulouse, public obloquy was almost a family tradition; only so could they retain at least some of their lands and secure peace and the possibility of future prosperity for their people. Such public displays as a way of making satisfaction for past sin were part and parcel of the culture.

It may therefore be argued that Anselm, without thinking twice as it were, naturally projected this kind of social and ecclesiastical commonplace of the medieval world onto a heavenly stage in his attempt to explain the need for Christ to make satisfaction to God for the sins of the world. Indeed, when logic was at an end Anselm resorted to a feudal image: The work of redemption was compared with the act of a king whose people had all, except one, been guilty of a crime worthy of death. The one innocent man offered to perform a service on behalf of others greater than that demanded by the offence of all his fellow subjects put together. The king accepted this service and agreed to pardon all who wished for it on the condition that they presented themselves in court on the day this unique service was performed.[22] Anselm does not try to explain the logic of the need to attend the court on conditions laid down by the lord. It is simply part of the story. But such acts of the renewal of homage and fealty were a regular part of Anselm's world. In relation to God it was natural for him to argue that justice demanded a full and sufficient satisfaction that would be appropriate to redress the sins of the whole world.

Given that Anselm chose to think of sin as an abstraction and in quantitative terms, he argued that the sheer amount of human sin demanded an infinite offering. In other words, adequate satisfaction for such a huge amount of sin could only be made by the infinite giving of life, and that meant the life of God's own Son. Unfortunately, there is a logical flaw in the theory even here. The sin of all humanity abstractly conceived obviously adds up to a huge amount. For the theory to work, satisfaction had therefore to be made for an exceedingly large amount. But the sin of humanity, though of enormous proportions, is not really an infinite amount. Yet the death of God's Son offered an infinite life and carried an infinite worth. The Anglican scholar R. C. Moberly pointed out in his magisterial *Atonement and Personality* in 1901[23] that there is a sense in which this theory was therefore doomed from the start, and that the mathematical categories presupposed by Anselm already pointed to its failure.

† † †

There is yet much more to be said in criticism of the penal substitutionary theory. But before we move on it is important to pause to unpack just a little more of the meaning of the concept of satisfaction. We have noted that the idea of punishment and chastisement for sinful disobedience accrued to the idea of making satisfaction through the Middle Ages, particularly as a consequence of the Church's administration of temporal punishment for perceived sin. At the time of the Reformation this idea emerged in a fearsomely unrestrained way in the theology of John Calvin, who, from this perspective, must be classed as a late medieval thinker. From Calvin it then passed into the mentality of twentieth-century fundamentalism. Almost as certainly, it is from Calvin that it has uncritically passed into the minds of generations of students of Moore Theological College in Sydney. Certainly, it now appears to be domiciled in the mentality of 'Sydney Anglicans'.

Interestingly enough, a starkly penal interpretation of the concept of making satisfaction is not the only way the idea of satisfaction may be understood and handled. An earlier use of the concept of satisfaction than the one that came to predominate in the medieval era did not necessarily resort to the associated idea of temporal punishment for sin at all. Rather, amongst the early Fathers the concept was used in a much more benign sense. In the era of the Church Fathers (in a more clearly ecclesiastical and liturgical but less political context), the making of satisfaction was understood simply as a third element, following confession and contrition, in the Church's rite of the reconciliation of a penitent. Indeed, in this sense, the idea of satisfaction featured in the almost day-to-day lives of faithful Christian people. In this context, the idea related not so much to the notion of imposing a punishment to satisfy the demands of justice, or to coax further virtue out of the penitent by his or her chastisement, but to a softer idea of the 'doing of a penance'. In this case the penance or satisfaction was not a punishment for sin so much as a token of sincerity and good faith on the part of the penitent. This meaning of the term, as it had been used by the early Fathers, also survived into the medieval era as an element in the Church's penitential rites, though confused with the idea of the imposition of a punishment.

In contrast with Calvin's heavy talk of the anger of God and the need for the punishment of human sinfulness, this earlier patristic and less political sense of the making of satisfaction after confession and contrition was taken up within Reformed Anglicanism. For example, Richard Hooker, commenting on Tertullian, points out that 'repentance and the works thereof are termed satisfactory, not for that so much is thereby done as the justice of God can exact, but because ... they draw the pity of God towards us *illices divinae misericordiae* (Tertullian, *De Poenitentia*, 9).[24] Hooker goes on: 'Satisfaction as a part [of repentance, i.e. — as distinct from confession and contrition] comprehends only that which the Baptist meant by *works worthy of repentance*' (Luke 3:8).[25] Clearly, the occurrence of the word 'satisfaction' was sustained in this late sixteenth-century Anglican usage as a remnant survival of the language of the medieval penitentiary, but its meaning was basically the same as the patristic sense: it meant a 'penance', an outward token of repentance and inward contrition, not a punishment inflicted in the name of God's justice. Thus, Hooker says: 'The name of Satisfaction, as the ancient Fathers meant it, containeth whatsoever a penitent should do in the humbling himself unto God, and testifying by deeds of contrition the same which confession in words pretendeth.'[26] Hooker goes on to say: 'Amongst the works of satisfaction, the most respected have been always these three, Prayers, Fasts, and Almsdeeds.'[27] But Hooker was explicitly critical of the Church's claim to impose temporal punishments and chastisements for sins as something 'strange and preposterous'. For Hooker confession of sin and the pronouncing of forgiveness by a priest was for the purpose of assuring the penitent of God's forgiveness, not for the purpose of imposing punishments so as to inculcate virtue.[28]

Though the medieval superstructure of the penitential system was dissipated through the course of the Reformation, Christ's 'satisfaction' for the sins of the world continued to mean not so much an adequate payment of compensation to God for all the offences committed by humanity, but rather a complete, perfect and appropriate or suitable acknowledgment of human sinfulness — something that imperfect human beings cannot perfectly perform. At the same time it was a complete, perfect and unwavering pledge of the human desire for amendment of life — something that fallen and backsliding humans of their own effort cannot achieve. Against the background of the Church's penitential system Christ's death on the Cross could be understood as a full or complete acknowledgment of human repentance and a perfect human turning in obedience to God. Given that the ecclesiastical practice of the undertaking of a penance or satisfaction was usually necessary before forgiveness was pronounced, the sacrifice of Christ may therefore be understood to have been a full and complete satisfaction which made good the defective repentance of sinners and thus supplanted the need for additional 'penitential works' to achieve reconciliation with God. As such it was viewed as a necessary prerequisite before God's forgiveness could be accessed and appropriated. The term does not necessarily carry the implication of placating an angry God,[29] or suggest any kind of behind-the-scenes transaction between the Father and the Son, but signalled a complete and perfect acknowledgment in history of human sinfulness and disobedience with which all humanity could thereafter associate itself through faith. 'Faith alone', says Hooker, 'maketh Christ's satisfaction ours; howbeit that faith alone which after sin maketh us by conversion his.'[30]

How reconciliation with God might be further understood without recourse to the idea of the Son's bearing a required punishment will be discussed below. For the moment it is sufficient simply to note that the patristic and more distinctively Anglican post-medieval and Reformed use of the concept of satisfaction or penance can clearly be separated from crude ideas of retributive justice. It may certainly be set at a distance from the view of much popular preaching — that the Cross was a penalty or punishment inflicted on the Son in order to satisfy the offended sensibilities of an angry God. Insofar as the death of Christ is referred to in the Consecration Prayer of the 1662 Prayer Book as a 'full, perfect and sufficient sacrifice, oblation, and satisfaction for the sins of the whole world', it may be understood as a full, perfect and sufficient acknowledgment of human rebelliousness and repentance, such as might 'draw the pity of God towards us'. The effect of the sacrifice of Christ is to nullify the need for further good works or further human striving to effect a complete reconciliation with God, in the sense that it makes good our imperfect and defective acts of repentance, confession and contrition.

† † †

But let us return to some of the other problems associated with the penal substitutionary theory. R. C. Moberly also argued that Anselm's theory failed because, while it dealt with sin in abstract quantitative terms and by appeal to the concept of retributive justice, it had no place for the transformation of personality. This problem was originally pointed out, almost as soon as Anselm articulated the theory, by Abelard, who conceived the classic exemplarist theory of the Atonement. For him the Cross of Christ was essentially a showing of the divine love that works because of its power to move the pious subject to penitence and obedience. The pitiful death of Christ on the Cross has its effect insofar as it inspires the most searching penitence and the most ardent love. In other words, we are drawn by the self-giving of Christ to self-giving in our own lives. Bernard of Clairvaux, somewhat unfairly, criticised Abelard by implying that he had explained the *whole* meaning of the Cross as only supplying humanity with a pattern to follow. As such it left the objective state of human sinfulness and the alienation from God which it causes unaddressed. He charged that the Cross of Christ was understood by Abelard as *only* a graphic instruction or exhibition or commendation of steadfast and unwavering love of the kind which refuses to save itself in the service of others. In fact, Abelard also spoke of the Cross with the help of such New Testament interpretative terms as 'ransom' and 'purchase' which Bernard chose to overlook. Nevertheless, Abelard's exemplarist view of the Cross as an incentive to love has often since been criticised for being purely subjective in its effect, leaving the objective state of the sinfulness of the world entirely as it is.

According to this kind of alternative to Anselm's view, instead of effecting a change in God by reconciling an alienated God to sinful humanity, the Cross of Christ is said to work because of its effect on humanity. In this way it serves to reconcile humanity to God, and it can be argued that this is more in line with the emphasis of the Bible. For it can be pointed out that scripture itself speaks not of the reconciliation of God to us but of the reconciliation of humanity to God. As Paul says in Romans 5:10: 'We were reconciled to God by the death of his Son.' Likewise in 2 Corinthians 5:18 he declared that God 'reconciled us to himself through Christ'. In other words, the Cross has its effect on sinful humanity rather than on God. In this way of thinking, the Cross is the consequence of God's love and forgiveness not its cause.

To some degree this is out of kilter with Article II of the Anglican Thirty-nine Articles, which speaks of Christ's work of 'reconciling his Father to us'. Calvin also speaks in this way, and the Article may reflect a Calvinist influence. Alternatively this may be little more than a slip of the pen, given the scriptural emphasis on humanity's being reconciled to God rather than the other way around. Where scripture and Church formularies are at variance scripture must prevail.

Nevertheless, while it is conceded that Abelard's exemplarist approach in this way takes account of these biblical emphases it is still open to the charge that it relies on a subjective response to the Cross on the part of humanity but leaves the objective state of the world's sin precisely where it was before.

This defect can, to some extent, be addressed by noting a deficit that is found in the thinking of both Anselm and Abelard. One fundamental flaw of their Atonement theologies is that both theories seek to explain the meaning of the Cross in complete independence of the Resurrection, thus oversimplifying and fracturing the Paschal mystery. Indeed, this is the first difficulty that may be directed at almost all theoretical explanations of the meaning of the Cross. It very notably applies to the penal substitutionary theory. For an exclusive focus on the Cross alone suggests that even had Christ not been raised from the dead, his sacrificial death upon the Cross, standing by itself, would have been sufficient to accomplish the salvation of the world.

We do well to note, however, that the death and Resurrection of Christ belong together as complementary parts of the one narrative story. The Cross and Resurrection constitute two identifiable poles, if you like, of the one indivisible divine-human act of God in Christ for our redemption. Indeed, in thinking about the saving work of Christ it is a serious mistake to separate Cross and Resurrection. Rather, the Resurrection should be understood, as an integral part of the reconciling work of God in Christ. As St Paul says, Christ 'was handed over to death for our trespasses and was raised for our justification' (Romans 4:25). Or again in I Corinthians 15:17 he declares: 'If Christ has not been raised ... your faith is futile and *you are still in your sins*' (my emphasis). We would therefore be unwise to wrench the Cross and Resurrection apart as if to imagine that the saving event of God can be adequately understood by concentrating on one element to the exclusion of the other. It is the total Christ event which initiates the new order in which we stand in reconciled confidence in the presence of God.

Though we naturally speak of the historical sequence, first the Cross and then the Resurrection, the first Christian community was essentially the Easter community of faith in the Raised Jesus Christ. Having encountered the presence of the Raised Christ amongst them in a concrete way, and having actually experienced within the life and worship of the Christian community something of the new life in Christ and of the fellowship of the Spirit, they then reflected on, and drew meaning from, the historically prior episode of the Cross. In a sense, their reflection on the meaning of the Cross explained their newfound experience of new life in Christ and of communion with God. But the Cross never stands alone, for it is always viewed in conjunction with the Resurrection and from the perspective of Resurrection faith. This is why for Christians the Cross is never to be understood as a wholly negative and humanly evil happening, though it certainly was partly that. It is rather the preliminary to something that produced an outcome that can be assessed as essentially good. That is why the Friday on which Christ died is spoken of to this day as 'Good Friday'. As part of a greater totality which included the Resurrection, the Cross can be seen to be not wholly bad. In the light of Easter faith it can be interpreted not just as a cruel death but as an event with a positive value and outcome. We thus separate Cross and Resurrection at our peril.

Indeed, it is by holding these two aspects of the Christ event together in some kind of synthetic tension that each is able to throw light upon the other. What happened at the foot of the Cross, for example, helps us to understand an important aspect of the Resurrection. The embryonic community was scattered by the traumatic arrest, passion, public execution and death of Christ on the Cross. When Christ died, therefore, he died isolated and alone, deserted by his friends. As the Gospel record has it, with the exception of some of the women, those who had been with him observed all that happened only from a distance. After all, Christ had died, but they had gone free. 'Take me, but let these go', Jesus had himself said at the time of his arrest. Some, like Peter, vehemently denied knowing him at all in order to save themselves. It does not take much by way of imagination to appreciate their very mixed and confused feelings as a consequence of what had happened to Jesus — feelings of anguish and grief, of anger, of outrage at the injustice of it, of disbelief that it could have happened at all. Naturally they were traumatised. But they probably also entertained feelings of guilt. So Jesus died, while they saved their own skins by denying and deserting him. And part of the miracle of Easter is the reconstitution of that scattered and traumatised community, as the community of forgiven people who self-consciously understood themselves to have been regathered around the presence of the Raised Christ, the Forgiver.

So it cuts both ways: we understand the Easter experience by first observing what happened on Golgotha. But equally what happened on Golgotha is interpreted in the light of the Resurrection. The Christ Event and the reconciliation with God which it effected cannot therefore be understood by concentrating on the saving significance of the Cross alone.

When viewed in this way as an essentially historical event, rather than some kind of behind-the-scenes transaction, the saving significance of the Cross of Christ can also readily be appreciated in terms of sacrifice. In a sense, from the point of view of those Apostles who at the last hour had deserted him, the kernel of the idea that Christ had died as a sacrifice for the sins of others is already present. Jesus had died on behalf of others in the straightforward historical sense that he died while they all denied him, scattered in all directions and escaped to freedom.

It is understandable that, as they processed the trauma of it and their own guilt in relation to it, they began to describe what had happened in metaphors: their freedom was won in just the way that the payment of a ransom by someone secures the freedom of others. Or else, using language from their religious tradition, they spoke of Christ's death as a kind of sacrifice of which they were the living beneficiaries. Thus, they naturally remembered his own saying about there being 'no greater love than this, that a man should lay down his life for his friends'. Once again, it is clear that the Cross is thus the consequence of the love of God not the cause of it. It is not that some kind of change of attitude is effected in God or a concession manipulated out of God the Father by the sacrifice of the Son on the Cross, for God is changeless.

The Easter release of new life put their guilty scattering from the Cross into reverse. In the light of their joyous regathering in community around his forgiving presence, his death can be seen to have secured their freedom, way back then; and somehow, it has significance by obtaining an eternal deliverance for all. Jesus' death began to take on a unique and cosmic significance as it came to be understood as a death that had meaning, not just for that small band of followers who had actually escaped the vindictive Jerusalem crowd and gone free, but for all humanity and for all time. Hence the claim that Christ died once and for all, and for the sins of the whole world.

Thus the reconciliation with God effected by the sacrifice of Christ, occurred in history, on Golgotha outside of Jerusalem, and it continues to be appropriated in history through its regular commemoration in the breaking of bread and the sharing of the cup. In this believers do not just *believe* in atonement and reconciliation with God as the outworking of some kind mythological or otherworldly behind-the-scenes heavenly transaction, but actually *experience* a life of victory over sin through reconciliation both with God and with one another in the communion of God. They understand themselves to be thus caught up in the mutual self-gift of Father and Son, standing as it were with Jesus where Jesus stands at the right hand of the Father as Jesus eternally pleads the sacrifice of the Cross.

This means that reconciliation with God is not just a subjective human response to the Cross of the kind that Abelard said moved the subjective believer to a life of repentance and obedience. Rather, it is an objective achievement of God's own initiative though the Resurrection, Ascension and, very importantly, the gift of the Spirit to his people. The reconciling of humanity to God and the restoration of human communion with God is not just due to the Cross of Christ alone, but to the total act of God in Christ. Indeed, as we shall see, perhaps we should speak of the total event of Cross, Resurrection, Ascension *and* the gift of the Spirit as all part of the reconciling work of God in Christ.[31] Clearly, this is not an exemplarist view of the kind that Abelard developed by unwittingly focusing exclusively on the Cross, because, as a consequence of the Resurrection and the gift of the Spirit to the community of faith, that community receives the love with which it is enabled to respond. This is a positive act of God. That is why in Romans 5 Paul can speak of the love of Christ not just as an exemplar — a pattern to follow — but as an objective reality that has been 'poured out in our hearts by the Holy Spirit who has been given to us'. All this brings about reconciliation with God.

Abelard came close to the truth that reconciliation or atonement cannot be handled as Anselm had done by dealing with sin in purely quantitative and abstract terms, by discerning that there must also be a place for the transformation of personality. Unfortunately, however, by focusing exclusively on the Cross and failing to take account of the Resurrection and the gift of the Spirit as also part of God's reconciling work in Christ, he failed to see that it was not just up to humans to respond to the exemplary sacrificial love or self-giving of Christ on the Cross. It was an actual and objective gift of God to humanity that made this response possible. Thus, in *Atonement and Personality*, R. C. Moberly observed that Abelard 'totally failed to interpret the production of Divine Love within us, not as a mere emotion of ours, elicited in us as our response to an external incentive, but as being the doctrine of the Holy Ghost: — that presence of Christ as constitutive Spirit within ...'[32] Instead, like Anselm, he tended to focus exclusively on the Cross.

However, the death of Christ upon the Cross can be understood to have become necessary in a causal sense, as preliminary to the Resurrection victory over death and the gift of the Spirit to his people. Calvary has a positive, restraining and transforming influence upon our characters; it achieves reconciliation with God by providing us with an incentive to love, but it also triggers the Resurrection, Ascension and the gift of the Spirit. This nexus of events results in the generation by God of love within us, actually transforming us in Christ and restoring us to communion with himself. This total Event of God in Christ is what overcomes the alienation of rebellious human sinfulness. This kind of understanding of things deals not just abstractly with a quantity of sin but with sinners, and meets Moberly's requirement that the Atonement can only achieve reconciliation with God if it also includes an account of the transformation of human personality.

† † †

Contrary to any suggestion that the Atonement was secured in some kind of mythic behind-the-scenes transaction between the Father and the Son, we must therefore insist that Christ died in history, in time, outside Jerusalem, and that it was precisely there that an understanding of the Atonement is to be focused. The sacrificial offering of his life on behalf of others happened in time at a specific place. The first Easter experiences likewise occurred in time at specific locations, on an axis between Jerusalem and Galilee, some time close to the end of the third decade of the first century. Ever since, people of faith have gathered to commemorate that once-and-for-all sacrificial death of Christ in the sacred meal of the breaking of the loaf and the sharing of the cup. This sacrificial meal in which Christ's death and resurrection is commemorated is the way in which the benefits of Christ's sacrifice are appropriated by God's faithful people. The gift of the Spirit also continues to be known in the continuing life of the Christian community in history. Reconciliation with God is therefore a concrete and objectively verifiable experience of grace which is known by acquaintance and not just by description. It is out of this experience of the new order in which they stand in reconciled confidence and in peace with God — enjoying their restoration and renewal in communion with him in Christ — that baptised Christians give thanksgiving and praise to God.

From this perspective the Atonement does not really need a theory; what it needs is a liturgy. Reconciliation with God is a fact of Christian experience achieved through the proclamation of the saving event of Christ in word and sacramental sign, through the response of repentance and renewal of faith, and communion with God. Once the penal substitutionary theory is simply believed as something that happened long ago, the theory itself becomes the object of belief. But Christian faith comes to centre on more than just a theory.

† † †

It is useful here to return to the point with which this chapter started, the concept of mystery. This is where the penal substitutionary theory begins to go wrong. In a nutshell, this theory of the Atonement presumes to know too much. This is not so much a charge that can be directed at Anselm as at his modern followers. For Anselm well knew that he was dealing with a surpassing mystery and that his attempted explanation of it was in a sense bound to be inadequate. He speaks a number of times of truths surpassing his powers of expression, which he cannot reach even with the developed logical skills for which he was acclaimed. As a thoroughly orthodox Christian skilled in logic he also appreciated the implications of the changelessness and impassability of God who is in all respects absolute and cannot therefore be manipulated into a change of heart in relation to humanity, or in any way acted upon in order to achieve some end. Anselm knew full well that he was grappling with a surpassing mystery.[33]

Interestingly enough, Calvin also seems to have recognised something of the inadequacies of human language. He says on a couple of occasions, at least at the beginning of his exposition of the saving effect of Christ's death upon the Cross, that the language describing human sinfulness and corruption and our consequent need of somebody to save us from the wrath and punishment of God is *accommodated* to our human capacity and is intended to produce an effect in us.[34] In other words, he recognises the rhetorical force of the language to bring us to an awareness of our human need of redemption. Unfortunately, however, he leaves these remarks behind in his subsequent effort to expound the Atonement and to commend its truth. Anselm, it seems, would not have himself been surprised at the long history of discussion of his work which has ensued through the centuries, including the many expressions of misgiving about it. He is already aware of the shortcomings of his humble attempts to probe both the necessity of Christ's incarnation and death and the way it has its effect. All this for Anselm falls within the overall project of Christian theology as *faith seeking understanding*. Would to God that Anselm's successors had been as alert to the concept of mystery!

It is interesting that this point surfaced in the nineteenth-century debate between John Henry Newman and Thomas Erskine to which reference has already been made. One of Newman's criticisms of the theology of those who were of a more rationalistic frame of mind, including Erskine, came to focus on this very doctrine. Indeed, given Newman's commitment to the basic importance for theology of the category of 'mystery', it is understandable that to Newman's mind the penal substitutionary theory provided a paradigm of the human desire to reduce the surpassing divine mystery of the Atonement down to the proportions of limited and finite categories of mind. In particular, the definition of the penal substitutionary theory illustrated Erskine's fundamental theological mistake of attempting to define everything as manifestly clear and distinct, and in so doing to make the object of faith into an assent to a rationalistic system of abstract propositions and formulas.

Newman noted, for example, that Mr Erskine 'exalts the doctrine of the Atonement into the substance of the Gospel', and that the first flaw to be discerned in his way of thinking of the good news of the Cross was Erskine's assumption that God's justice was fully and clearly *manifested* in it. By contrast, Newman highlighted the paradoxical tensions, or even plain contradictions, involved in affirming that God's justice demanded that somebody should suffer the death penalty for the sin of Adam's disobedience while at the same time believing that God's love means that he sends his own Son to die as a substitute for the rest of us — 'in the stead of the whole apostate, disobedient and sinful world'. For Newman the meaning of Christ's death is to be understood essentially as a mystery, a death on our behalf and a supreme sacrifice for the sins of the whole world, with a clear, practical effect in relation to the reconciliation of humans with God and with one another in him. But it is the surpassing experience of reconciliation with God that is actually known, and it passes our understanding in a way that allows us only to discern hints and glimpses of the transcendent meaning of it.

At Erskine's hands the mystery of the Cross is reduced to a mere formula insofar as Christ is said simply to have died in our stead bearing a penalty to satisfy the demands of God's justice. Newman insists, in response to this kind of thinking, that the Atonement should be understood essentially as a mystery, not as a simple manifestation of God's justice: 'Mr. Erskine is remarkable for several reasons', he says:

... first, for the determination ... not to leave us anything in the Gospel system unknown, unaccounted for. One might have thought that here at least somewhat of awful Mystery would have been allowed to hang over it; here at least some 'depth' of God's counsels would have been acknowledged and accepted on faith. *For though the death of Christ manifests God's* hatred of sin, *as well as his love for man, (inasmuch as it was sin that made His death necessary, and the greater the sacrifice the greater must have been the evil that caused it,)* yet how *His death expiated our sins, and what satisfaction it was to God's* justice, *are surely subjects quite above us. It is in no sense a great and glorious* Manifestation *of His* justice, *as men speak now-adays; it is an event ever* mysterious *on account of its necessity, while it is* fearful *from the hatred of sin implied in it, and most* transporting and elevating *from its display of God's love to man. But Rationalism would account for everything.*[35]

The gnostic tendency of much evangelical theory to know too much about ultimate things has frequently been matched by a nervous refusal of engagement, a sect-like tendency to isolate itself from commerce with any thinking that might be disturbing to its life. Inevitably this results in a hostile tendency to lash out at those who are willing to grapple openly with a deeper but more mysterious truth. Certainly, Mr Erskine is still around in Australia. Indeed, it will probably not be too hard to find him in many congregations, if not within mainstream Anglicanism, then certainly at its edges, and in the life of other Christian denominations as well. It was certainly clear from the volume of correspondence I received after the *Bulletin* article that many good Christian folk, like Mr Erskine, were labouring under the misconception that the penal substitutionary theory of the Atonement was not only somehow coherently clear and distinct, but the essence of the Christian Gospel! Christian faith, however, involves our having to do with something much more mysterious than assent to a mere theory.

✝ ✝ ✝

It remains that the final thing to emphasise about the penal substitution theory of the Atonement is its lack of dogmatic status.

As Jaroslav Pelikan has correctly pointed out,[36] while imagining they were defending Christian orthodoxy against the critique of contemporary Liberal Protestantism of the late nineteenth century, the original fundamentalists in fact unwittingly departed from orthodox Christianity themselves. For while the doctrine of the person of Christ was defined by the Church councils of the first five centuries, there has never been a similar attempt to formulate and define the doctrine of the salvific work of Christ. The first ecumenical council of the Church held at Nicaea in 325 AD sought to specify how Christ was related to the Father as a person of equal status within the mystery of the Holy Trinity. In the Creed of Nicaea the cataclysmic events of his Incarnation, Passion, Resurrection and Ascension were declared to have occurred 'for the sake of us human beings and for the purpose of our salvation', but the credal definition of Nicaea did not specify precisely how this salvation was won. We can say quite categorically that in her wisdom the Church of Christian orthodoxy has never dogmatically defined the saving work of Christ. This observation is by no means new. As long ago as 1926, when the fundamentalist movement was at its height, the Anglican scholar Kenneth Kirk was already pointing out that 'Conciliar definition has never asserted any one theory of the manner in which Christ's death avails for the salvation of man.'[37] If there is no legitimate warrant for elevating any particular theory of the Atonement to the status of a required belief, then *a fortiori* and quite clearly it is entirely illegitimate to allege that the penal substitutionary view of the Atonement is an essential element of orthodox Christian belief.

Indeed, the language used in the Creed does not really support, even by implication, the penal substitutionary view. The original Greek text of the words 'for us men and for our salvation' in the Creed reads *di' hemas tous anthropous kai dia ten hemeteran soterian*. The use of the Greek preposition *dia* with the accusative indicates the reason why something exists or happens or results. The assertion that Christ's Incarnation, Passion, Resurrection and Ascension were 'for us' may simply mean 'for our benefit' or 'on our behalf'. By contrast the idea of substitution would have been indicated by the use of the Greek preposition *anti* meaning 'instead of' us but not *dia*. It is entirely arbitrary to interpret *dia* in the sense of 'instead of'.[38] Thus Pelikan says:

> *Those closest to the Council of Nicaea, chronologically and theologically, did not in fact take its formulas to be speaking about 'vicarious atonement', but went on employing an abundance of metaphors for the involvement of God the Father, Christ the Son, the human race, and the devil in the redemptive transaction.* [39]

Of even more importance is the fact that the concept of satisfaction on which the penal substitutionary view relies so heavily is not even a scriptural term. Not only does it not feature as an article of the Creeds of orthodox Christianity; the term 'satisfaction' is not so much as found in the Bible. It is one of the unexplained puzzles of our time that folk who pride themselves in being 'Bible believing' are so wedded to an entirely unbiblical theological motif! So we find in some evangelical seminaries generations of theological students, for example, who appear to have been schooled in the unwitting mistake of thinking that the penal substitutionary theory of the Atonement is a doctrinal necessity. The imperative of truth demands that we call on all those who have been so indoctrinated to think again about this theory and its lack of dogmatic definition and biblical grounding. If the Bible is the ultimate court of appeal for judging the authenticity of doctrine, it fails exactly here.

However, as we have seen, contemporary scholars find much more that is unsatisfactory about this theory of the Atonement even as an item of theological reflection. In other words, its failure to attract a following in the contemporary world of serious theology is not just because it has never been formally defined or is focused on an unbiblical concept. Even if we place the doctrine in the outer circle of more speculative theological reflection, it remains more an item of interest in the history of the development of doctrine, rather than a live option for the preaching of the Gospel of reconciliation today.

CHAPTER 5

LAY AND ORDAINED MINISTRY

There is today a very lively debate in the Church at large about the meaning of ordination. In one sense, this is not new. There has been hardly a time when ministry was not, at least potentially, a Church-dividing issue. However, the most intense debates of the past have been about bishops and whether or not they are necessary in the Church. At the time of the Reformation those who had no truck with bishops opted for a less hierarchical model of Church order and became presbyterians, the work of oversight being put into the hands of groups of presbyters. While the necessity of bishops continues to feature in ecumenical debate, not least between the Anglican Church and the Uniting Church, the contemporary environment has tended to focus on the issue of whether even the ordained ministry of presbyters or priests has a future.

There are a number of contemporary factors and pressures that have raised questions about the nature of the ordained ministry. For example, the 'fit' of the seventeenth-century parson in the post-industrial urban conglomerates of the twenty-first century has become problematic, and the contemporary need for sacramental ministry in sub-centres of country parishes and remote rural areas is frankly not being met by the increasingly sparse dispersion of stipended clergy. The world has changed; we cannot imagine that the patterns of ministry in the Church can deal adequately with a new environment by staying fixed.

At the same time, increasing theological education amongst the laity and the development of various lay ministries along with the emergence of team ministries which include both lay and ordained people also have implications for the exact role of those admitted to full-time ordained ministry.

There are a number of other sociological factors behind the contemporary need to rethink the role of ordained ministry. The fall-off of vocations to priesthood in the Roman Catholic Church has meant that deacons, lay acolytes and religious sisters have been called on to fill the void. Often worshipping communities have had to come to terms with the lack of an ordained priest, or the occasional ministry of a visiting priest. By force of circumstance, the priest's role is reduced to that of an itinerant 'sacramentalist', who consecrates sufficient bread and wine to be distributed between his visits by others who are not ordained. These unordained people cannot but become *de facto* pastors and leaders of the local community in its day-to-day life.

Within Anglicanism, where by and large the pressure of lack of vocations has not been so keenly felt, the role of the laity has nevertheless become increasingly valued, in the first instance as an enrichment of priestly ministry. We talk a lot these days about 'total ministry', the ministry of the whole people of God, with every individual having a God-given gift which can be brought to the building-up of the community of faith and the Church's work of service in the world. The Church, as it is often said these days, 'is not a community gathered around a minister, but a ministering community'. Gone are the days when the ordained priest was a one-man band who led an otherwise passive community. The whole community is now clearly seen to have a role to play.

While this emphasis on the collaborative ministry of the whole people of God is undoubtedly a good thing, its downside is that we have tended, perhaps unintentionally, to devalue the importance of the ordained ministry, and even to blur the boundaries between the respective roles of ordained and lay people. It is easy to slip from talk of the 'complementary' ministry of lay people to so emphasise the role of the laity as to question the necessity of having an ordained minister at all. A serious focus on the specific contribution of those ordained to ministerial priesthood is thus something that runs contrary to the mood of the prevailing ecclesial culture. Without a doubt, we live in the age of the ministry of the laity. Indeed, I sometimes wonder if we are not beginning to experience a minor crisis of identity amongst those ordained to ministerial priesthood as a result.

This challenge to priestly identity has been magnified too because the traditional pastoral role of the parish priest has largely been usurped by a range of secular workers: the social worker, the child welfare officer, the local schoolteacher, psychologist, psychiatrist, and trained counsellor, the secular marriage celebrant and even by the talkback disc jockey. Somehow there are fewer and fewer functions that fall exclusively and uniquely within the job description of a priest. And I suppose this may be one reason why distinctive clerical dress is no longer as evident on our streets as it once was. These days ordained clergy tend to become anonymous as they blend more and more into the community. Indeed, there are some places where distinctive clerical dress has even disappeared from the sanctuary! While this may be motivated by a contemporary quest for 'relevance', I find myself asking whether all this is not ultimately a kind of liberal accommodation to the ways of the world. Or is it just symptomatic of a loss of nerve? Certainly, the distinctive place of clergy in society is no longer as clearly defined as it once was.

† † †

The debate over the role of the clergy has taken an idiosyncratic twist in Australia with recent proposals from the Diocese of Sydney to allow lay presidency of the Eucharist. According to these proposals, ordained clergy would continue to minister both in a pastoral and liturgical sense as shepherds and overseers of the flock. They would preside in a seamless way both over the general life of the community and over its worship, but at one remove, insofar as they would not actually be present at Eucharists which would be delegated by them to lay people. Though the Church has not yet chosen to adopt these proposals, the constitutional validity of such a development within the Anglican Church of Australia was upheld in a majority opinion of the Church's Appellate Tribunal, which was handed down on 24 December 1997. Despite this the discussion has so far been very localised; for most dioceses the debate arouses little interest. Indeed, for most Anglicans around the world it does not appear to be an issue worth expending time and energy on. Even within Australia it has not been easy even to facilitate a national conversation and debate on the matter. In 1998 a working group was appointed by the Standing Committee of the General Synod in response to a request of the General Synod itself.[1] The initial working group[2] was asked simply 'to identify critical issues'. Subsequently, the group was asked by the Standing Committee to take these 'critical issues' as a brief to prepare a report on 'the meaning and place of ordained ministry' in this Church so as to address General Synod's request.

An explicit reference in the relevant General Synod Resolution 42/98 to the Appellate Tribunal majority opinion indicated that the question of concern did not focus on the three-fold nature of ordained ministry, or on such questions as the necessity of the episcopate in an Anglican understanding of Church order, or on the renewal of the diaconate as a distinct order in the life of the Church. Rather, it more concerned the nature of ordained ministry as distinct from lay ministry, and the essential and unique functions of ministerial priesthood in particular.

As the original chair of the working group which was commissioned to pursue this conversation across diocesan boundaries, I therefore have first-hand experience of just how difficult it has been to find any common ground at all — whether about the precise meaning of ordination; the place of the sacraments in the life of the Church; the nature of the Eucharist, in particular; even the nature of the Church itself, let alone the question of why it might be appropriate only for ordained persons to preside at celebrations of the Eucharist. The General Synod of 2001 received the working group's initial report, which could do little more than signal something of the unresolved diversity of view between Sydney proponents of the idea of lay presidency and others who were resolutely opposed. This report was not so much a theological discussion as simply a first attempt to define issues and alternative or opposing viewpoints. Indeed, it read almost as a list of polar opposites.

Since becoming Primate of Australia and leaving the working group I have also been involved in discussions at the international Anglican Primates' Meeting at which I have tried to interpret the thinking of those from Sydney who have a particular interest in the idea of lay presidency of the Eucharist. To many in the Anglican Communion at large this idea appears to pull the rug from under the ordained ministry, in terms both of its meaning and purpose. The primates of the thirty-nine member Churches of the Anglican Communion are of a common mind in not supporting the idea, and have put in place a strategy for dealing with this question should it be pursued in Australia. It has been agreed that, should there be unilateral action of the kind that has at least been threatened in recent years to implement lay presidency, questions relating to internal discipline within the Anglican Church of Australia will be handled by the national Church's own legal instruments, while questions relating to intercommunion with other member Churches of the Anglican Communion would be be handled by the Archbishop of Canterbury. It is the Archbishop of Canterbury who has the prerogative of declaring who is in communion with him, the See of Canterbury and the Church of England in England, and who is not.

I think we should not be premature, however, in jumping into a discussion of the legal implications of lay presidency. Rather, I think we must be grateful for those in the Diocese of Sydney who have raised the question, and who have argued in favour of it with a great deal of energy and tenacity. At the very least this has forced us all to re-examine the inherited theological tradition with regard to the meaning of ordination and the specific role in the Church of those ordained to ministerial priesthood.[3] In particular it has obliged us to pursue the precise reasons why it might be appropriate only for those ordained to ministerial priesthood to preside at the gathering of the Christian community for the Eucharist. Certainly, there is some serious theological thinking to be done before we retreat into a consideration of international and ecumenical reverberations, and the dire practical implications and legal questions that would face us as a national Church.

To begin a discussion on the nature of ordained ministry, there are a number of items to note on which there is already widespread agreement. I do not think, for example, that there would be any contention about the overriding aim of the contemporary desire to free up formal Church structures so as to release latent vitality and spontaneous enthusiasm amongst lay people within the Church. It may well be that a rigidity of ordered structure has in the past suppressed much active lay involvement beyond a somewhat passive Sunday attendance at worship. It is acknowledged that in many minds the hierarchical structuring of the Church seems the exact opposite of the kind of church they want. Charisma, the life of the Spirit, rather than a preoccupation with Church order, is characteristic of our time.

The contemporary emphasis on the free movement of the Spirit rather than on Church order certainly reflects an important emphasis of the New Testament. In the New Testament comparatively little is explicitly said about order. The Church is not a community that lives primarily because people have decided upon some kind of ordered structure; it lives by the Spirit. It is clear from the writings of St Paul, for example, that the one thing to be earnestly desired by a Christian community is the life of the Spirit. Hence, the Pauline injunction 'Do not quench the Spirit' (I Thessalonians 5:19). And St Paul seems to have believed that each individual man or woman would bring his or her gift, or charism, to the service of the Christian community. Paul's understanding of the distribution of gifts of the Spirit is outlined in I Corinthians 12. Despite the diversity of gifts, Paul seems to have hoped that all baptised people would work together in a kind of free and spontaneous harmony. 'To each is given the manifestation of the Spirit', his or her own gift, but it is to be exercised 'for the common good' (I Corinthians 12:7). Paul may have had at the back of his mind the spiritual gifts of non-Christian mystery religions, which were often used to impress others or for a person's own self-aggrandisement. By contrast the genuine charism of each Christian is to be brought to the edification and building-up of the community.[4]

The actual concept of order is stressed on only one occasion in the entire New Testament. In I Corinthians 14:40 St Paul declares that 'all things should be done decently and in order'. However, while he mentions the concept only once, it is clear that Paul himself spent a good deal of time actually working to establish good order within the communities with which he was connected, particularly those which he founded. His declaration about the need for decency and order is in the context of trying to regulate disturbances in the assemblies of the Corinthian community, in which enthusiasts were not behaving in a manner that was edifying. Indeed, it is perfectly clear that already in Paul's own time his ideal of an unorchestrated, harmonious exercise of a diversity of individual gifts was not being achieved. Although he insisted that the life of the Spirit should not be quenched (I Thessalonians 5:19), he spent a great deal of his own time trying to curb excesses of enthusiasm. His concern was to introduce order, harmony and peace into the life of communities that were tending towards ungodly disharmony. As St Paul himself says a few verses before his classic call for decency and order: 'Our God is a God, not of disorder but of peace' (I Corinthians 14:33). Nevertheless, most discussions of St Paul's treatment of the gifts of the Spirit in I Corinthians 12 tend to overlook Paul's own apostolic and shepherding ministry, which was clearly designed to preserve harmony and order and to build the community into the Body of Christ.

One of our contemporary mistakes has been to place an emphasis on total ministry and collaborative ministry amongst all the people of God, based upon those passages of Paul that focus on the exercise of individual gifts, but to forget the important ministry of Paul himself, for Paul worked earnestly to shepherd and order the life of these very communities. Moreover, in the generation after Paul it became necessary for the early Christian community to devote time and attention to questions of good order. In the Pastoral Epistles (I and 2 Timothy and Titus) which, if they were not written by Paul himself (for Pauline authorship is disputed by New Testament scholars), certainly originated within communities that he founded, we readily detect a different emphasis. In these documents an appeal is made back to the apostolic authority of Paul to secure the authority of a more structured kind of ministry in which ordination clearly played a key part. Indeed, by this time the gift of the Spirit had become closely associated with the laying on of hands (2 Timothy 1:6). This indicates also that in the very communities that Paul founded an unorchestrated exercise of gifts by all the baptised appears not to have worked. Certainly, in the generation after the Apostles the shepherding ministry examplified in Paul appears to have passed without dispute or controversy to bishops and their councils of presbyters.

In the historical developments of the first few centuries of the Christian era, the ordering of commonsense, the ordering of reason and coherence within belief, the ordering of worship, the ordering of consistent moral standards, the ordering of definitions of faith all became necessary to maintain the unity of the Church, its boundaries and its purity of faith in what was a very fluid and pluralistic environment not at all unlike our own. We should therefore pause to reflect on the reasons why a structured ordained ministry arose in the life of the early Church. When we stress lay ministry at the expense of ordained ministry we put ourselves in peril of forgetting the lessons of the past and why it was that an authoritative ordained ministry was needed in the first place.

† † †

Fortunately, a residual sense of the importance of ordained ministry continues to inform the debate about lay presidency of the Eucharist even amongst the chief proponents of the idea. For, while lay ministry would certainly be enhanced were lay people to be authorised to preside at Eucharistic celebrations, it is not envisaged that ordained ministers would then have no further role. Rather, it is proposed by those in the Diocese of Sydney who are most wedded to the idea that those ordained and in full-time priestly ministry would continue to exercise a general oversight both of the pastoral and liturgical life of the parish community.

The unity of the pastoral and liturgical leadership of the ordained ministry is accepted by those who support lay presidency insofar as it is acknowledged that, were it to be introduced, lay people would be permitted to preside at Eucharists but *only under the general oversight and direction* of an authorised ordained person. This, as I understand it, is why the term 'lay administration' is sometimes preferred to 'lay presidency' amongst Sydney proponents of the idea. Even though in the 1662 Ordination service the newly ordained priest is given authority to 'preach the Word of God and *minister* the sacraments' (my emphasis), the proposal is that, while an ordained person would not necessarily be the minister of the communion, he would remain in a role of general supervision and control. A residual responsibility for the supervision of the liturgical and pastoral life of the congregation would remain in the hands of the ordained, and thus the priest would *preside* over its life and liturgy in this general sense, while arranging for and authorising lay *administration* of the Holy Communion.

At this point we may also note in passing that the discussion of lay presidency at the Eucharist within the Diocese of Sydney may also be driven by an additional complicating agenda, which some may find more sinister. This is the idea that lay women might be allowed to preside at Eucharists so as to satisfy the growing demand for the ministry of women to be recognised in dioceses which are reluctant to ordain women, while at the same time leaving the overall power of headship securely in the hands of ordained males. Lay women might be authorised to preside at services of Holy Communion, but only under the oversight of ordained men.

In the thinking of the Appellate Tribunal, which we shall look at more closely in the next chapter, the role of the leadership of the ordained person as shepherd of the flock is said to remain in place even in a situation where the role of presiding at Eucharists is delegated. The Tribunal acknowledged that this is an element of the leadership to be exercised by the ordained as enshrined in the ordinal of the 1662 Prayer Book. It is on the basis of this delegated authority — precisely because it is delegated — that it was held that the constitution does not legally rule out the possibility of lay presidency for, it is argued, the priest's pastoral and liturgical oversight remains intact.

It seems to be agreed amongst all Anglicans that we are constrained by the clear teaching of scripture and our reformed theological tradition to avoid some noxious views of priesthood of the pre-Reformation period, which tended to think of priestly power as something personally possessed by the ordained minister, almost as an isolated individual in separation from the Church as a whole. At times in the history of the pre-Reformation Church, this understanding of personal priestly powers tended to see the priest alone as able to administer the sacrament while the people passively attended and received grace dispensed by him. Sometimes these views of priestly power were understood to presuppose a particular understanding of the sacrifice of the Eucharist offered by the priest as a kind of addition to the sacrifice offered once and for all by Christ himself upon the Cross. At the time of the Reformation this was viewed as a kind of human work effected at the hands of the priest that is inimical to the doctrine of justification by grace through faith alone. Sometimes it seemed to the reformers that the priest produced upon the altar a kind of repetition of the sacrifice of Christ in which Christ was offered again in a way that is foreign to the 'once and for all' and sufficient nature of Christ's sacrificial death on the Cross.

Those who argue for lay presidency are clear in their rejection of such almost occult views of ordained ministry. But this view is shared also by those who continue to argue for the appropriateness of having Eucharists actually presided over and administered only by the Church's ordained leaders. And I think it is clear that arguments for reserving the presidential role at the Eucharist to those ordained to ministerial priesthood based on personally possessed priestly powers would not muster much, if any, support amongst Anglicans.

These points are common ground in this debate. Nevertheless, given the radical and far-reaching nature of the Sydney proposals about lay presidency in the context of a more wide ranging tendency to whittle away functions that were formerly unique to priesthood, one cannot help wondering what the future may hold for ministerial priesthood. Are there really any functions unique to priesthood? Or is the ordained priest to slip into a role by way of making his or her way to the top of the heap? Is it that the priest exercises leadership and control in the Christian community by virtue of his or her individual gifts, and in this way pursues a ministry that is essentially no different from that of any other of its baptised members who exercise other gifts in other ways? Such questions indicate that the relationship of ordained and lay ministry is in urgent need of more precise clarification and definition.

† † †

A further development which bears upon the relationship of ordained and lay ministry has surfaced in a report entitled 'For the Sake of the Gospel', written for the Anglican and Uniting Churches in Australia. This report is to be warmly welcomed as an important step forward on our ecumenical journey.[5] Given that the goal of the current dialogue between the Uniting Church and the Anglican Church is 'the mutual recognition of ministries' it has been usual to focus on differences between the two Churches in relation to the role of bishops. 'For the Sake of the Gospel' foreshadows this as an outstanding concern that has yet to be resolved. However, I think there is yet even more work to be done, particularly in the crucial area of the theology of ordination and the relation between ordained ministry and the priesthood of all the baptised people of God.

The report indicates, for example, that in the Uniting Church, when a lay person acts as moderator or as presbytery chairperson, he or she may on occasion preside at Eucharists and also participate in ordinations.[6] While the question of lay presidency at the Eucharist has been under discussion in the Anglican Church of Australia for some years, the participation of lay people in ordinations has not been on the Anglican agenda. It is not a practice that Australian Anglicans, not to mention members of other Churches of the Anglican Communion, would be likely to countenance.

The participation of lay people in the essential matter of the laying on of hands at ordinations has not been part of Anglican practice. The only Anglican theologian I have been able to locate who would think sympathetically of the participation of lay people in ordinations in this way is Robin Greenwood, who was formerly the Ministry Development Officer in the Diocese of Chelmsford in England and is now the Ministry Officer in the Church of Wales. In *Transforming Priesthood*,[7] he suggests not only that lay representatives might in the future present candidates to the bishop for ordination, but that a 'small group of laity and clergy' might be involved 'in the laying on of hands with the bishop'.[8] Certainly, Anglican formularies appear to be quite explicit in requiring ordination at the hands of a bishop. In view of the constitutional importance of the ruling principles of *The Book of Common Prayer*, the Ordinal, and the Articles of Religion in the Anglican Church of Australia, it may be noted, for example, that Article 23 clearly speaks of those lawfully called and sent as those who have been 'chosen and sent to this work by men who have publick authority given unto them in the Congregation, to call and send Ministers into the Lord's vineyard'. They are not sent and commissioned by the congregation as a whole but by a subset of authorised ministers. This echoes the requirement of the Preface to the Anglican Ordinal of 1662 that a person cannot be taken to be a lawful bishop, priest, or deacon 'except he be called, tried, examined, and admitted thereunto following, or hath had formerly Episcopal Consecration, or Ordination'.[9] Apart from the concentration on 'lawfulness of ministries' in these Anglican formularies, I believe there is an important theological principle to be noted concerning the authorising ministry of ordination. Clearly, this is an issue that should be clarified in Anglican consciousness and also addressed in Anglican–Uniting Church conversations.

However, rather than focus narrowly on the manner in which it is proper for lay people to be involved in Eucharistic celebrations and in ordinations, let us try to define the theological area of concern more broadly. There appear to be two different ways of understanding the relation between the ministerial priesthood of the ordained and the priestly ministry of the whole people of God in the world. Definitive expressions of these alternative ways may be found respectively in the World Council of Churches Faith and Order document, *Baptism, Eucharist, Ministry* (the Lima Document, known as *BEM*), and in the document on *Ministry and Ordination* published in the *Final Report* of the Anglican Roman Catholic International Commission (ARCIC I). Briefly put, *BEM* tends to see ordained ministry as an extension or a focusing in leadership of the priestly ministry of the whole Church, whereas the ARCIC I *Final Report* explicitly says of ministerial priesthood that it is 'not an extension of the common Christian priesthood but belongs to another realm of the gifts of the Spirit'.[10] There is thus a significant difference between these ecumenical consensus documents on this point.

Given that those ordained have a responsibility to coordinate lay ministries and to harmonise the life of the community in the interests of securing its unity, the question at issue is therefore whether the priestly ministry of the ordained is simply an intensification or concentration of the more general priesthood of all believers, different only in degree from the priesthood of the rest of the people of God, or whether it is a ministry that is different in kind.

These different viewpoints, in turn, condition attitudes with regard to the propriety of lay involvement both in Eucharistic presidency and in ordinations.

Unfortunately, however, in Australia we do not seem to have studied nearly carefully enough the relevant sections of these ecumenical documents, even though we already have at least some formal interest in them as stakeholders. For example, with reference to the Lima Document, *BEM*, which Anglican representatives played a part in producing, the Australian General Synod of 1985[11] provided a response of a generally positive kind and asked for further exploration of a number of items. But the relation between the priesthood of the whole people of God and the ministry of those ordained was not one of them. This does not seem to have registered at that time as even an issue. Whether there has been any really serious exploration of *BEM* at all across Australian Anglicanism is doubtful.

In relation to the *Final Report* of ARCIC I, on two occasions (in 1981 and 1985) General Synod approved Australian responses — once again of a generally positive kind — and on the basis of these and similar responses from other Churches of the Anglican Communion, the Lambeth Conference of 1988 endorsed the *Final Report* all but unanimously. When a resolution to the effect that the *Final Report* is 'consonant in substance with the faith of Anglicans' was put to the vote it passed overwhelmingly with only a couple of dissenting votes amongst over 500 bishops.[12] What may be called 'the ARCIC view' of the nature of ordained ministry and its relation to the priesthood of all the baptised therefore has a claim to authority within the Communion if anything greater than the view to be found in *BEM*.

However, the report 'For the Sake of the Gospel', while noting the agreed statement on ministry of the *Final Report* of ARCIC I, nevertheless relies more heavily on *BEM*. A good deal of inspiration appears to be drawn from it. Some individual Anglican thinkers certainly also incline towards its view that ordained ministry is a focusing of the ministry of the whole people of God. Once again, in the international literature this view is clearly represented in the writings of Robin Greenwood. Anglican members of the Anglican–Uniting Church Joint Working Group may also share these views; others may not be very conscious of them.

I cannot detect any evidence that Anglican contributors to the conversations have proffered the view of the ARCIC I *Final Report*, despite the fact that it has already been commended by two successive General Synods of the Anglican Church of Australia and by the Lambeth Conference of 1988, which declared the theology of the *Final Report* to be 'consonant in substance with the faith of Anglicans'.[13] The ARCIC view should, therefore, be taken into account in discussions between Anglicans and the Uniting Church, particularly given the importance of maintaining consistency in relation to our already agreed position with the Roman Catholic Church.

† † †

Rather than align conflicting viewpoints as those of particular Churches or as differences of emphasis between *BEM* and the *Final Report*, we can to try to clarify our Anglican mind by conducting the discussion as an intra-Anglican discussion. This can conveniently be done by focusing critically on the views of Robin Greenwood, which, as has already been mentioned, appear to be broadly similar to the position to be found in *BEM*. Within the international Anglican world this view has also been adopted as the starting point in considering the ordered nature of the Church and Anglican ordination rites by the International Anglican Liturgical Consultation.[14] Under the heading of 'Baptism and Ministry', the findings of the Sixth International Consultation declare:

> In order that the whole people of God may fulfil their calling to be a holy priesthood, serving the world by ministering Christ's reconciling love in the power of the Spirit, some are called to specific ministries of leadership by ordination.[15]

The adequacy of this position may be tested by looking at the historical continuity of the institution of the ordained ministry secured in our tradition by the outward and visible sign of episcopal ordination with the laying on of hands. This is what used to be called the apostolic succession of the ordained ministry. Generally speaking, Robin Greenwood's writing does not exhibit a sense of the Church's catholicity through time. He has little interest in pursuing a conversation about apostolic succession. Indeed, he denies the importance of 'institutional pedigree' in the interests of defining the catholicity of the Church by appeal to 'Christlike qualities and concerns'. These are said to be related to a commitment to God's 'universal, all embracing concern for all creation'.[16] Catholicity is clearly understood as a universal interest in all that is in the present at the expense of an interest in a connectedness with all that has been through time.

This is hardly unusual in our age. I think we must own that the idea of apostolic succession has not fared well in recent times. As has been noted, the Church has become much more pragmatic in its thinking, much more focused on the ministry needs of the present and on the involvement of lay people in the work of ministry than on the nature and role of ordained ministry. Talk of 'collaborative ministry' or 'total ministry', the ministry of the whole people of God in the present world, is more characteristic of our day.

If we think of apostolic succession at all, we tend these days to speak of a continuity through time of the whole Church, a continuity in faith and worship going back to the Church of the Apostles. And by contrast we tend to speak disparagingly of 'the old pipeline theory' of a tactile succession of semi-occult priestly powers transmitted at the hands of the bishop alone.

The New Testament idea of the priesthood of the whole people of God (I Peter 2:9) undoubtedly informs much of the contemporary egalitarian push to stress the total ministry of all the baptised, and following, St Paul in Romans 12:4–8 and I Corinthians 12:4–12, we thus talk much about every baptised person having a God-given gift, which is to be brought to the building-up of the community of faith and the Church's work of service in the world.

This contemporary emphasis on the collaborative ministry of the whole people of God seems to lead to an understanding of ordained ministry in terms of the concept of enablement — the role of the ordained priest is to enable lay ministry to function as a priestly people in the world. For example, the starting point of the International Anglican Liturgical Consultation, significantly entitled 'To Equip the Saints', is that 'God bestows upon the church a variety of gifts to build up the body of Christ and to participate in God's mission in the world. Within the Spirit filled body, different charisms are given by God to every member, including prophecy, evangelism, teaching, healing, discernment, wisdom, administration and leadership.'[17] Robin Greenwood, as one of the Anglican world's leading exponents of collaborative ministry, both in his *Transforming Priesthood*[18] and in his very recent book entitled *Transforming Church, Liberating Structures for Ministry*,[19] also endorses an idea of ordained ministry understood in terms of the exercise of just another of the diverse gifts of the Spirit which are shared equally amongst all the baptised. He says 'there is nothing that could be said of bishop, priest or deacon that is not in some way true of the Church as a whole'.[20] Because all the baptised have individual gifts and distinctive roles to play, a priest, as also 'a baptised disciple',[21] can be understood to have a specific vocation and ministry.[22] This allows Greenwood to say that 'a blurring of identity and function between clergy and laity is ... to be resisted' but he is unable to explain how or why.

Greenwood, in fact, has enormous difficulty in identifying and defining the uniquely distinguishing role of the priest. The best he can do is to speak of the priest as a kind of ministry development officer, discerning the gifts of the Spirit amongst lay people and equipping them for ministry. The priest, he says, is to preside both liturgically and pastorally in such a way as to 'enable the priesthood of the baptised'.[23] He or she is, in other words, a kind of training officer, not unlike a personal trainer in a gym — an encourager of others.[24] Whether Greenwood conceives of all priesthood in his own image as a ministry development officer is a moot point, but what is clear is that ministerial priesthood is assimilated to the ministry of all the baptised. The priest exercises leadership amongst them almost as a chairman of a group to facilitate its effective functioning.

Greenwood therefore argues that the ordained, whether bishops or priests, are to be understood as representatives of the Church as a whole; because of their training they are acknowledged to have the gifts and the 'ministerial competence' to 'speak and act on behalf of the Church'.[25] This inevitably begs the question whether lay people might be 'equally competent'[26] to exercise some of the priest's functions. After all, lay people today are certainly able to access theological education and may excel in competence. We are therefore left with the impression that the real difference between ordained and lay ministry is basically a matter of degree — with an alleged higher degree of competence involved. Greenwood is, generally speaking, against hierarchy and in favour of equality, but he cannot avoid speaking in terms of a hierarchy of competence.

Now, I really do not think this will do. While there is, of course, something important to be said about the priest as teacher and encourager of the ministry of others, I want to suggest that these views are problematic because of what is left unsaid about the nature of ministerial priesthood. So, what more can we say?

First, while all the baptised obviously have a ministry in the world as part of the priesthood of the whole people of God, it is just as certain that there never was a time when the Church did not have specifically authorised ministers. We rightly encourage and promote lay ministry with gusto, but the Church was never an undifferentiated community of believers without a clearly called and authorised ministry. At the very beginning, the Church's ministry was in a sense co-terminous with the Church's founding, for the very Apostles who were called apart and who shared the Last Supper with the Lord on Maundy Thursday and who were mandated to continue to make remembrance of him with loaf and cup were the very ones who, three days later, were commissioned to minister as witnesses to the Resurrection. They received a mandate to go into all the world proclaiming the good news of the Kingdom. From the start, the Church had a mandated ministry of sacrament and word. Talk only of baptism and the gifts of the Spirit will be insufficient to furnish the Church with a theology of ordained ministry without reference to the mandating of the apostolic ministry of sacrament and word by Jesus.

Secondly, there is a sense in which this apostolic ministry is logically prior to the Church itself, insofar as the Church comes to be around the ministry of word and sacrament. The starting point for our understanding of ministry is the mission and ministry of God who calls the Church into being; the ministry of word and sacrament is a share in, and an instrument of, this ministry, which is constitutive of the Church. It is not, as Greenwood imagines, that authorised ministry is thrown up by the Church, but the other way around. This means that it is wrong to say that 'the Church is not a community gathered around a minister but a ministering community'; in fact it is both. It is a community gathered around a minister, insofar as it is gathered by the ministry of word and sacrament and by the continuing shepherding ministry of pastoral care and oversight of the ordained. We do not have to deny this in insisting that the Church as a whole is also a ministering community in the world. In advocating 'total ministry' or 'collaborative ministry' we do ourselves no service by overlooking or devaluing the distinct and unique gathering role of the priest as shepherd of the flock.

This means that those set apart by prayer with the laying on of hands have a ministry that is not just different from that of lay people in degree of competence, but different in kind. This is the insight that is correctly preserved in the *Final Report* of ARCIC I when it says, quite explicitly in reference to the ordained ministry that it is 'not an extension of the common Christian priesthood but belongs to another realm of the gifts of the Spirit'. I do not think either the International Anglican Liturgical Consultation or Robin Greenwood have really understood this at all. The priesthood of all God's people is a ministry exercised by the whole Church in the world — the transforming ministry of representing God in and to the world and praying to God for the world. The unique ministry of those admitted by ordination to ministerial priesthood is primarily a ministry in and to the community of faith. The role of the ordained priest, as defined in the Ordinal in the 1662 Prayer Book by appeal to the controlling image of the shepherd, is not just an enabler of the ministry of others — a personal trainer. A priest is commissioned for a unique pastoral and liturgical ministry of leadership, involving responsibility for the gathering and oversight of the community as shepherd of the community. Lay people will in varying degree be collaboratively involved in the liturgical and pastoral ministry of helping to build up the body of Christ, but the primary focus of the priestly ministry of the whole people of God, priest and lay people together, will be in the world. Otherwise, we stand in danger of clericalising lay people by drawing their ministerial focus away from the world and into the internal life of the Church itself.

Those today who, like Greenwood, emphasise the total ministry of all the baptised on the basis of Paul's words in I Corinthians 12 and Romans 12 about the exercise of individual gifts of the Spirit and the building up of the Body of Christ tend to delete Paul himself from the equation. We need to note Paul's own shepherding ministry, his earnest striving to form a dysfunctional community at Corinth *as* the Body of Christ.

The third point I want to make is that ordination to this shepherding ministry is always effected by predecessors in the same office. As far as we can see, this always has been so. Within the lifetime of the Apostles, presbyters were appointed by the Apostles and hands were laid on them; in I Timothy 4:14 presbyters lay hands on presbyters. While we have no definite evidence of Apostles explicitly handing this role on to bishops, the same pattern is at least preserved insofar as after the death of the last Apostle this authorising process signalled by the laying on of hands seems to have passed without controversy to the presiding chief shepherd or bishop who, from that time onwards, came to exercise the apostolic responsibility. To this day bishops consecrate bishops, and the college of priests joins the bishop in ordaining priests.

Though the Church as a whole assents to ordinations, and though ordinations take place within the context of the whole community of the baptised gathered for worship, ordination is thus effected at the hands of predecessors in the same office. The matter of the sacrament, the laying on of hands, is not performed by the whole Church but by those who already minister in the same office. The Anglican scholar R. C. Moberly defined the principle expressed in this standing practice in his magisterial work of 1897, *Ministerial Priesthood*, in these words: 'Those only are duly commissioned who have received commission from such, before them, as were themselves commissioned to commission others.'[27]

There are a number of things at stake in relation to this standing practice. The first is that the setting apart effected by the outward sign of the laying on of hands with prayer by predecessors in the same office is not just a setting apart of a person from the world, but a pastoral distancing of an individual *from the rest of the Church.* The outward and visible reality of the institution of ordained ministry signals that this shepherding ministry comes not from the community but from Christ, the great high priest and shepherd of our souls. In this sense ordained ministry is not to be assimilated to, and defined by, the ministry of all the baptised. Nor is it a focusing of the ministry of the whole Church in its leadership, but is a gift *to* the Church. Those who are ordained are separated by the outward ordering of the laying on of hands from the Church *for* the Church, so to speak. This clinches the truth that priesthood is not just a kind of intensification, a focusing of the priesthood of the whole people of God. Nor is it a ministry that is derived from the community by a kind of social contract: 'do this for us' or 'enable us to minister by equipping us'. Rather, the priest's ministry is different in kind from the priesthood of all believers, or as the ARCIC I *Final Report* said: it 'belongs to a different order of gifts of the Spirit'.

The importance of this is that it makes for an utterly crucial dynamic within the life of the Church. For those ordained to the ministry of word and sacrament are not just expected to speak what the Church wishes them to speak; and priests do not just speak on behalf of the Church to the world, as Greenwood actually says at one point.[28] Rather, the Word of God must be on their lips. They must speak not just *for* the Church or on behalf of the Church but rather, in the name of Christ *to* the Church reminding it of its origin in Christ, calling it to fidelity to Christ, and, very importantly, taking responsibility for its formation *as* the Body of Christ. This point is amplified in the ARCIC *Elucidation* of *Ministry and Ordination* published in 1979. This document speaks of the distinctiveness of ministerial priesthood and of the particular sacramental relationship of ordained ministry with Christ as High Priest.

Moreover, the historical continuity of ordained ministry, which is outwardly signalled by the ordination of the priest by predecessors in the same office, also means that the priest in his or her very person is a living sign to the community of its apostolic origin in Christ. It therefore also signals the unity of the Church in the present with the great company of believers through time in the communion of saints. For the Church's communion is not just a reality of the present that stretches geographically across space; it also stretches across time. In the technical language of contemporary theology, the Church's communion is both synchronic (of the present) and diachronic (through time). It is the communion of saints of every time and place. Catholicity is not just about a universal or inclusive interest in the things of the present devoid of a sense of the continuity of the Church through time. Thus in the Great Prayer of Thanksgiving at every Eucharist the presiding priest actually reminds the community that it is one 'with angels and archangels' *and* with 'all the company of heaven', or one with 'apostles and prophets, and holy men and women of every age'.

Apostolic succession is not about the transmission of some kind of semi-occult priestly power, as in the old pipeline theory; rather, the significance of the laying on of hands by predecessors in the same office lies in its signage: what you see is what you get: the priest is a living and visible sign to the community of its apostolic continuity in space and time.

One other point I want to make is this: the role of the ordained priest is to interpret the Church to itself, reminding it of its historical continuity through time and of its intimate relation to Christ, recalling it to its origin in Christ, and calling it to sustain and renew its identity as the Body of Christ. In all this the Church is built up *as* the Body of Christ. This happens *both* in pastoral ministry in the general day-to-day life of the Church *and* in its gatherings for worship, especially its Eucharistic worship.

It is normal, of course, for the presiding priest to bless and absolve at the Eucharist. But neither the blessing of the people nor the forgiveness of sins is essential to a Eucharist. However, the recital of the Great Prayer of Thanksgiving over loaf and cup, the *anaphora*, is quite different.[29] This prayer of blessing is the second element of the four-fold action of taking, blessing, breaking and sharing, which Our Lord himself commanded to be done in remembrance of him. It is an essential part of the Eucharist, the 'verbal centre' of the Eucharistic event. Indeed, the *anaphora* is the quintessential prayer in which the Church prays what it believes. It is no coincidence that it has the same Trinitarian structure as the Creed: thanksgiving is made for Creation by God the Father, thanksgiving for redemption through Christ the Son, and thanksgiving for our continuing human transformation and renewal through the gift of the Spirit. It is a prayer that moves from *berekah* (blessing) to *haggadah* (narrative) to *shikhinah* (presence).

In this very central prayer of our worshipping tradition, the Church itself is able to grasp its Trinitarian identity. Worshippers come to know themselves as the children of God the Father, as the Body of Christ, in the communion of the Holy Spirit. It is in the course of the prayer of thanksgiving over loaf and cup, and culminating in communion, which is received 'by faith with thanksgiving', that the community is not just reminded of something but actually formed and renewed *as* the Body of Christ. Indeed, as the bread is broken in preparation for its being shared, this fact is declared, using the words of St Paul: 'the bread which we break, is it not a communion of the Body of Christ; the cup which we share is it not a communion of the Blood of Christ? We who are many are one body, for we all partake of the one bread.'

This means that it is in this prayer *par excellence* in which we see the ordained person actually doing exactly what he or she is authorised and commissioned by ordination to do as shepherd of the community — interpreting the Church to itself and forming it as the Body of Christ. Peter Waddell, whose thesis has informed this discussion, has helped me to appreciate that this is perhaps the single most important and compelling reason why it is appropriate that those ordained to this distinctive ministry in the life of the Church do actually lead the Great Thanksgiving. It is the central prayer in which, culminating in communion, the community *is* formed as the Body of Christ. And, given the seamlessness or unitary nature of the ministry of liturgical oversight and pastoral oversight, this is why it is appropriate for those authorised by ordination for this distinct ministry to lead the reciting of it. To do otherwise would be to perpetrate the symbolic confusion of saying one thing and doing another. At this point the pastoral and the liturgical oversight of those ordained priest coincide: their pastoral work becomes a liturgical work and the liturgical becomes the pastoral. This is why it is appropriate that those ordained to ministerial priesthood should preside immediately and directly at the Eucharist, and why it is inappropriate for lay people to do so. To fracture this seamless pastoral and liturgical ministry at this point would result in a symbolic nonsense.

Moreover, the suspect notion of personally possessed priestly powers to which I referred earlier, which in the pre-Reformation era tended to separate the ordained in an unhealthy way from the laity, are, in fact, overcome in this prayer. For this is a prayer which establishes the intimate relationship between priest and people. In the dialogue of the *Sursum Corda* of the Eucharistic president with the gathered congregation ('Lift up your hearts/We lift them to the Lord'), an interdependent relationship between priest and people is established. It is appropriate that the person ordained to ministerial priesthood and commissioned to pastoral and liturgical oversight of the community should lead this prayer in the presence of the community, just as he leads and cares pastorally for the community in his day-to-day ministry. What happens in the great Eucharistic prayer, culminating in the communion, is what the ordained person is explicitly given responsibility for doing in his or her leadership role, not only pastorally but liturgically.

The priest is thus not just an enabler of lay ministry or just a personal trainer; nor is priestly ministry some kind of a focusing or intensification of the ministry of the whole Church. Rather, a role is assigned by ordination to those within the people of God who are separated and consecrated for this specific ministry. If ordained ministry is agreed to be a share in the shepherding ministry of Christ which comes from Christ to the Church, and if this is what is signalled by the received practice of the outward and visible laying on of hands by predecessors in the same office going back to the time of the Apostles, then it would be very difficult for Anglicans to come to terms with the inclusion of lay people as representatives of the whole Church in the laying on of hands at ordinations. Indeed, this too would constitute an entirely unhelpful symbolic confusion. This is why it is necessary, before the Anglican and the Uniting Churches engage in discussions about *episcope* and the episcopate, that they address the more fundamental question of the relation of the shepherding ministry of those who are ordained to the ministry of the whole people of God.

The same reasoning explains why it is so appropriate for the ordained to preside and lead the community not just in some general sense, or some minimal and detached sense by a kind of remote control, as would be the case if they delegated and authorised lay people to preside at Eucharists. The priest actively presides, not by just giving the blessing and pronouncing the absolution, but also and quite specifically in the rehearsal of the *anaphora* in the presence of, and in dialogue with, the people of God. In this prayer is expressed the essence of ministerial priesthood as distinct from the priesthood of all believers which the whole people of God, priest and people together, are to exercise to the glory of God in the world. It is not appropriate that all or just any believers might perform this task. Indeed, this would cause role confusion of the first magnitude. It would ultimately be inimical to the identity and integrity of the role of the shepherd-leader.

We may therefore affirm with confidence that there *is* indeed a unique leadership role for those admitted by ordination to ministerial priesthood which is both pastoral and liturgical. This is exactly what those ordained to ministerial priesthood are set apart by prayer with the laying on of hands to do in authorised ministry to and for the community. In relation to the ministry of all the baptised in the world this simply belongs to 'a different realm of the gifts of the Spirit'.

CHAPTER 6

LEADERSHIP AND PRIESTHOOD

We have already noted that on 24 December 1997 the Appellate Tribunal of the Anglican Church of Australia delivered an Opinion, which indicated that, in constitutional and legal terms, it would be possible for the General Synod of the Church to enact legislation which would allow both deacons and lay people to preside at celebrations of Holy Communion. This is despite the fact that, since the Council of Nicaea in 325 AD, deacons, who are assistant ministers to bishops and priests, have been explicitly inhibited from presiding at celebrations of the Holy Communion.

This is not to say that the Church is minded to take this action. Rather, the effect of the Appellate Tribunal Opinion is simply to declare that such action is a theoretical option: it is a legal and constitutional possibility for the Church to follow, should it so wish. Clearly, the Appellate Tribunal Opinion demands very careful scrutiny and attention. It must be received with respect. But that does not make the Tribunal infallible. Because the Opinion involves legal argument, this chapter will necessarily involve a rather more legalistic and philosophical than theological treatment, with close attention being paid to the interpretation of legal formularies and the exact meanings of words.

The first critical issue that arises explicitly out of the Appellate Tribunal Opinion has to do with what is understood by leadership and with the precise nature of the priestly leadership of the Christian community. Generally speaking, in the reasoning of the Tribunal, the distinctive role of the priest in the Christian community is understood by appeal to the concept of leadership. Leadership, it is said, is implicit in the imagery of the shepherd with respect to the flock over which he or she is given pastoral responsibility at ordination. This is a form of leadership that involves the pastoral oversight of the congregation.[1]

As we noted in the previous chapter, traditionally this broad ministry of the pastoral oversight of the community has also been liturgically focused — in the leadership of the congregation gathered for worship. Amongst other things, the 1662 Ordinal assigns to the priest ultimate responsibility for preaching and for 'the administration of the Sacraments', as well as the pastoral care of the community. In the reasoning of the Appellate Tribunal Opinion, however, while upholding this seamless connection of duties as essential to the office of priesthood, it is argued that their expression in immediate presidency over word and sacrament may be detached from it. There would be sufficient pastoral oversight for the integrity of the office to be maintained, it is argued, even if a less immediate kind of oversight were to be exercised. This would be the case, for example, if presidential functions at the Eucharist were on occasion to be delegated to lay people. Indeed, it is contended that the concept of 'delegation' itself implies sufficient ultimate oversight to sustain the integrity of the priestly office.[2] The priest is thus understood to be able to exercise the pastoral leadership essential to the office, even at one stage removed from the actual celebration of a Eucharist which may occur by virtue of a delegated authority either to a deacon or to a lay person.

Only one of the Appellate Tribunal members (Ian George, Archbishop of Adelaide) recognised the iconic and definitive value of immediate, specific and visual oversight of word and sacrament, with respect to the more general and in many ways hidden expression of day-to-day pastoral oversight. The majority of Tribunal members accorded no particular value to this. On the other hand, the Tribunal did not envisage that lay presidents of the Eucharist would also assume responsibility for the more general oversight or pastoral care of the community. The responsibility for this kind of oversight is acknowledged to have been conferred by prayer with the laying on of hands on the community's ordained leaders. This reverses and negates the usual nexus between a specific responsibility of oversight of the gathered community for the Eucharist and the more general oversight of the scattered community which is assigned to ordained leaders, and which I sought to defend in the previous chapter. Whether, in the longer term, the authority necessary for the general oversight of the community by ordained ministers would be sustained in public consciousness without reserving to them the visual and iconic oversight of the community gathered for liturgical worship may, of course, be very problematic in practical terms.

† † †

It has already been noted that one element of the biblical tradition that is relevant to this matter is Paul's teaching that everything should be done 'decently and in order' (I Corinthians 14:40). This demand for good order does not just arise out of an aesthetic sense of social neatness, but is theologically grounded. As Paul says a few verses earlier, God is a God not of disorderly confusion but of peace (I Corinthians 14:33). The Church is an ordered community and in the 1662 Ordinal it is made clear that the bishop is the authoritative minister of order, the Ordinary. Indeed, the bishop is the one who not only governs and moderates, but who ordains as part of the specific function of oversight appropriate to his or her *episcope*. By definition, the bishop is the one who orders in this ministerial sense. Amongst other things the bishop promises to ordain ministers when he or she is consecrated.

These ordering functions may be said to be essential and necessary among the various functions assigned to those who occupy the office of bishop, and not transferable to anybody else in the Church without compromising the integrity of the office itself. The bishop may share a general pastoral and liturgical oversight with the college of presbyters associated with him or her, but not the role of being the *source* of order and unity in this immediate and very practical sense. The presiding minister of ordination is thus uniquely the bishop with his or her presbyters and not presbyters in independence of the bishop by virtue of some delegated authority. Indeed, this defining function of the bishop in and with his or her college of presbyters is a matter of episcopal identity which in an important sense distances the bishop from the college of presbyters. Most other functions of a priestly kind may be shared with presbyters, but not the ultimate responsibility for ordering the community by ordaining. This may not be delegated away any more than the defining leadership functions that are essential and necessary to the office of priesthood may be delegated.

The character of the Church as an ordered community, governed by and in communion with the bishop, has at some times in Christian history been regarded as the mark of orthodoxy. This contrasted with heretical and deviant Gnostic groups, which separated themselves from the bishop. Early in the second century, Ignatius of Antioch taught that without the bishop 'the name Church is not given', for this reason. Since the discovery and identification of the letters of Ignatius in the seventeenth century, this key role of the bishop as the minister of order and unity in his or her diocese has become very important in Anglican ecclesiology. It even conditions the language of the Constitution of the Anglican Church of Australia which states that 'the diocese is the fundamental unit of organisation and shall be the see of a bishop.'[3]

The biblical doctrine of the unchangeable steadfastness and love of God, whose 'faithfulness extends to the clouds' (Psalm 36.5), may also condition the Church to speak in terms of the steadfastness and faithfulness of an indelible or 'for life' commitment to ordained ministry. Once again this is an expression of good order. If the Church not only reflects but 'participates in' the divine nature of the God who is a God 'not of disorder but of peace', then it follows that the allocation of specific responsibilities and functions to the ordained is intended to be permanent, involving a covenant commitment of faithfulness for life. For the same reason, the covenant relationships established by baptism and marriage are also intended to be for life. Indeed, ministerial priesthood is a particular individuation of discipleship amongst some of the baptised, who are ordered for a specific function and purpose. It seems to follow that the Church has been consistent in the view that those ordained are ordered unchangeably and for life, just as all those ordered to take their place in the life of the Church by baptism are called to faithfulness for life.

To allocate the specific functions belonging to this covenant relationship to those who are not wedded to them for life may be inimical to the thrust of this biblical norm. This may be one reason why some functions have been reserved only to those who are ordained, for they are prepared to make a solemn lifetime vow and promise.

Up until now the functions that have been assigned uniquely and permanently to priests for life have been liturgically focused in the priest's role of presiding over word and sacrament at the Eucharist. However, as we have noted, in the thinking of the Appellate Tribunal Opinion the permanent defining characteristics of ministerial priesthood are of a more general kind of leadership involving the power to delegate responsibilities.

However, the principle that the Church is an ordered community and that everything should be done 'decently and in order' because 'our God is a God not of disorder but of peace' at least provides one good reason why the casual and occasional performance of uniquely priestly tasks by lay people may be held to be inimical to the life of the Church. An echo of the Pauline appeal to good order may be heard in Tertullian's criticism of Gnostic groups, for example:

> First, it is unclear who is a catechumen and who one of the faithful; they all come, listen, and pray on the same footing. Even if pagans should come they throw what is holy to the dogs and pearls (fake ones, however!) before swine. They want 'simplicity' to overturn discipline, our care for which they term pedantry ... They are all puffed up; they all promise knowledge. The catechumens are 'perfect' before they are instructed ... Their ordinations are reckless, trivialised, and inconsistent: one time they install neophytes, another time those enmeshed in the world, then even our apostates, so that they may

bind them with honours since they could not be bound by the truth. Never is it easier to get ahead than in the camp of rebels, where just to be there is to merit honours! So one is bishop today, another tomorrow; he who is deacon today will be reader tomorrow; today's presbyter will be tomorrow's layman (for they entrust priestly functions even to the laity).[4]

Insofar as priests are exhorted by the bishop in the 1662 Ordinal to be 'messengers, watchmen and stewards' of the Lord, they are commissioned also to exercise a ministry of oversight and to share in the ministry of good order. The good ordering of the celebration of the Eucharist is an essential ingredient of this. Normally this is conferred by ordination for life. The dangers of disorder implicit in allowing just anybody to preside over gatherings of the people of God for the Eucharistic offering may be held to be entirely foreign to Anglicanism for this pragmatic reason, given the fundamental theological imperative of achieving the good order, peace and harmony, and steadfast stability of the divine life.

† † †

This theologically grounded but essentially pragmatic consideration is not the only difficulty to be found in Appellate Tribunal reasoning. We have noted that the understanding of the role of those admitted to the office of priest is handled in Appellate Tribunal reasoning as a form of leadership in which the power of the delegation of functions is the defining characteristic. The power to delegate, in other words, is understood to be an essential aspect of the leadership of those admitted to the priestly office. Insofar as this is so, the delegation of functions is understood to be a sufficient ingredient to sustain the essential character of the office.

The difficulty with this element in the reasoning of the Appellate Tribunal Opinion is that priestly leadership is handled as though it were little different from managerial oversight in the commercial world where functions and responsibilities may be delegated to others. While appeal is made to the biblical imagery of the shepherd of the flock in establishing this essential function of leadership and oversight, the Appellate Tribunal Majority Opinion takes no cognizance of the fact that in the same biblical tradition of the shepherd and the flock the delegation of functions actually appears to be frowned upon. In this tradition absolute dedication to the duty of care characterises the shepherd. The shepherd is in a close personal relationship with the flock; he knows each of them by name and is prepared to give up his life for them. This does not necessarily characterise the hireling. Indeed, because he is a hireling and not a shepherd, the hireling is not expected to exercise the same degree of steadfast commitment. Certainly, an understanding of leadership which comes to expression in the delegation of responsibilities to others does not appear to flow from the biblical imagery of the shepherd and the flock. Can it be that the Tribunal has assimilated the leadership exercised by a priest to an entirely secular form?

Of course, the biblical suspicion of hirelings does not feature in modern commercial management theory, where delegation to hirelings is normally regarded as a good thing. But this very fact immediately signals that the Appellate Tribunal Opinion's understanding of leadership and oversight, may not be entirely adequate to an understanding of priesthood. Indeed, this lapse into liberalism, involving the accommodation of essential priestly functions to the world of contemporary commerce and business management, may be the single most critical issue arising out of the Appellate Tribunal Opinion.

Moreover, the idea of 'delegation' can hardly be said to be *essential* to the concept of leadership, since in the commercial world there are leaders who delegate and others who do not. The philosophical categories of Immanuel Kant may help us achieve clarity of thought at this point. In the language of Kant, the judgment 'that leaders delegate tasks' is not an analytic judgment, but a synthetic judgment. An analytic judgment is one which derives from the meaning of the term itself and which is known by reflection on the meaning of the term. As Kant said, it is 'cogitated through identity', rather than by empirical observation. An example of an analytic judgment is the judgment that 'all bachelors are unmarried'. The analytic judgment that 'all bachelors are unmarried' does not add to our knowledge of bachelors, but simply clarifies the meaning of the concept of a bachelor; a synthetic judgment, by contrast, does add to our knowledge. Such a judgment would be the judgment that 'all bachelors are lonely'. This judgment, like all synthetic judgments, has the potential to increase our knowledge and can be verified by observation. By contrast the judgment that 'all bachelors are unmarried' is true by definition.

Now, the idea that leaders delegate tasks to others cannot be derived from the concept of leadership simply by reflecting on the term itself. It is not an analytic truth. Rather, the judgment that leaders delegate tasks to others is clearly verified by observation. Such a judgment is undoubtedly a synthetic one. It may or may not be true. If it is true, it adds to our knowledge of leaders, whereas what is necessary and analytically true of leaders would not add to our knowledge of leaders. In other words, while it does not add to our knowledge of leaders that they lead and direct others, the judgment that leaders delegate tasks does add to our knowledge of leaders.

It is thus logically flawed to argue that the power of delegation of tasks is essential and necessary and thus analytically true of all leaders, including Church leaders. Rather, we must conclude that in the Appellate Tribunal Opinion the power of delegation is arbitrarily and synthetically associated with the concept of leadership.

This is not to deny that it may nevertheless make sense to speak of the priest sharing or delegating some tasks in the exercise of the office of ministerial oversight. Even if the delegation of responsibilities does not appear to be an element in the biblical imagery of the shepherd and the flock and is not analytically true of leaders, he or she may ask a lay person to read lessons and assist at the administration of the Holy Communion, for example. This seems unexceptionable and canonical provision is made for it in the Authorised Lay Ministry Canon (No. 17, 1992) of the General Synod of the Anglican Church of Australia.

This canon also allows a lay person from time to time to preach, but in *The Book of Common Prayer* of 1662 it is clear that preaching takes place in the context of the proclamation of the Word in the ministry of Word and Sacrament at the Eucharist. There is no Prayer Book provision for preaching at Matins and Evensong. And, should preaching be delegated to a lay person on occasion at the Eucharist, this would, according to current norms, be done while the priest remains clearly in his or her presidential role of immediate liturgical oversight. In this circumstance it is possible for the priest to maintain good order by exercising some quality control even in relation to the ministry or preaching as 'watchman and steward' of the mysteries of God. This is achieved not just through the choice by the priest of the readers and people to assist in the administration of Holy Communion, and occasionally of a lay preacher at the Eucharist, but also by monitoring the quality of performance and the content of what is said. The priest thus fulfils his or her ordination promise to 'drive away all false doctrine'. In this sense the role of the priest at the Eucharist involves an element of presidential responsibility and leadership in the actual context of the liturgy itself, even to the point of raising an eyebrow from the presidential chair so as to assure a hesitant reader that it is time to move to the lectern.

The saying of the greeting at the beginning and the collect at the end of the rite of gathering, the pronouncing of the absolution and the giving of the greeting of peace at the end of the penitential rite, the recitation of the Great Thanksgiving over the gifts of bread and wine, and the blessing at the end of the whole rite, might all be said to be most appropriate to the leader of the community, given that he or she is the one who has a been commissioned to exercise pastoral oversight of the flock. As we saw in the previous chapter, of these functions that are appropriate for the priest to perform, the recitation of the Great Thanksgiving over the gifts of bread and wine is an essential element of priestly responsibility at the Eucharist, for this is where we see the priest forming the community as the Body of Christ both liturgically and pastorally.

In the first English Prayer Book of 1549, the priest is explicitly singled out, not just to lead the saying of certain parts of the service, but also to perform some quite specific manual acts in the course of his recitation of this prayer: He '*must* take the bread into his hands' at the words 'this is my body which is given for you' and '*shall* take the cup into his hands' at the words 'this is my blood of the New

Testament which is shed for you' (my emphasis). This rubric seems to have been intended to avoid any possibility of priestly detachment from the Eucharistic action, as was at the time the case in some Reformed services of Holy Communion which made do with the reading of scriptural accounts of the Last Supper in the general proximity of bread and wine. Essentially the same rubric was deliberately revived in *The Book of Common Prayer* of 1662, though it had dropped out of the intervening 1552 rite.[5] At the end of the Holy Communion service the priest is also explicitly charged with the responsibility of ensuring that unused sacramental elements are consumed by himself with the help of lay people so as to ensure that they are not put to a profane purpose. These specified functions provide detailed practical examples of what is meant in the ordination service when those to be ordained priest are exhorted to be 'stewards' of the mysteries of God as well as 'messengers and watchmen' of the Lord.

From a purely practical point of view, we must conclude that, while some functions in the liturgical life of the Church may be shared or delegated to lay people, it is doubtful if the integrity of the office could be maintained if this focal liturgical role were to be itself delegated. This is why preaching might be delegated, but the role of presiding over the gathering of the people or God which provides the context for preaching, may not. The chief difficulty of the Appellate Tribunal reasoning, however, lies in its tendency to reduce the presidency of a Christian community to a model of leadership more at home in the profane world of modern commercial activity than the sacred context of the gathering of the people of God for divine worship.

† † †

Something of the deficit of the Tribunal's thinking at this point may be discerned by attending to the meaning of the term 'priest' and what it entails by way of specific functions. These tend to be overlooked when ministerial leadership is understood predominantly in terms only of the business of management and the delegation of tasks.

The Preface to the Ordinal speaks of the 'office of priesthood' as something that is to be 'executed'. This entails that those admitted to the office of priesthood are intended to function in some specific way. However, in his Appellate Tribunal reasoning the Right Reverend Bruce Wilson, the then Bishop of Bathurst, noted that the ordination service for priests provides no concise statement of the office and its functions. This contrasts with the kind of statement of functions that *is* provided in the case of the service for the ordination of deacons. Bishop Wilson then argued that the office of priesthood may therefore be understood without reference to *any* defining or essential functions,[6] and then, by a strange logic, went on to fill the alleged deficit with a description of a specific form of leadership involving the delegation of tasks! This is particularly strange when this form of leadership through delegation is then said to be of the essence of the office, for this is so clearly a synthetic judgment that is only arbitrarily associated with the term priesthood.

In any event, the logic of dispositions and episodes may be brought to bear on this subject, particularly with regard to the relationship between the order and office of priesthood and the specific functions that may be essential in the execution of it. A baker, for example, must necessarily be involved in baking in order to be referred to as a baker. In Kant's terminology this is also an analytical judgment that is necessarily and universally true of all bakers. By definition bakers are people who bake. This does not mean, however, that at every minute of every day he or she will be found baking; it does mean that he or she will be disposed to bake from time to time. The dispositional nature of the term allows for a baker to be referred to as a baker, even when he or she is asleep. When we describe a person as a baker we will expect to find him or her baking from time to time. The term 'baker' is thus a dispositional rather than an episodic concept in the sense that a baker may not be found to be involved in episodes of baking at precisely the minute he is referred to as a baker, but he or she will normally have been or be involved in episodes of baking at least on occasion.

In the case of a baker, the disposition and the appropriate episodes that on occasion actualise it are logically related in an analytic rather than a synthetic sense. In other words, the defining function appropriate to a baker may be discerned by reflection on the meaning of the term 'baker' rather than by observation. Just as all bachelors are necessarily unmarried, so it is in the nature of all bakers to bake.

Another way of saying this is to say that the disposition of being a baker is a 'single track' disposition concept. This allows the function which actualises the disposition to be unpacked simply from a consideration of the meaning of the dispositional description of the occupant of the role. Bakers bake; they may also do other things like washing up and sweeping the floor, but what is essential to being a baker is the ability to bake. Whether bakers wash up or sweep is established by observation rather than by reflection on the meaning of the term. The capacity to bake is contained in the concept of a baker.

In the case of solicitors, on the other hand, there is no single activity that may be said to be essential to the role of 'solicitoring'; rather, solicitors draw up wills, represent people in court, give legal advice to clients, etc. This, rather than being a 'single track' disposition concept, is a generic disposition concept, which may be actualised in a wide variety of different episodes. These are synthetically associated with the dispositional concept, not analytically derived from it. This synthetic association may be established by conventionally agreed upon arrangement, through tradition and custom, or by constitutional and legal definition.

Now, elders or presbyters are, strictly speaking, the older people in the community, the natural leaders. In the Roman World in which the average life expectancy was less than thirty years, the older members of the community would have been much younger than older people as we think of them today. In the course of time, younger people were admitted to the role of presbyter or elder. At this point the elder or presbyter came to be admitted to an office rather than qualifying simply by being an older member of the community. While the minimum age of ordination to the priesthood has remained static, average life expectancy has increased to the point where presbyters or elders have become, comparatively speaking, very young in terms of years, despite being called 'elders' or 'presbyters'. As a result, though young in terms of actual years of age, through admission to the office by ordination they receive the status of an 'elder'.

In any event, the most pressing question for our present purposes is: do those referred to as presbyters or elders, regardless of their actual years of age, necessarily *do* anything specific that is logically entailed simply by the dispositional description of them as elders? Is there a single function which must be regarded as essential to the actualisation of the office of presbyter because it is analytically true, and thus contained in, or logically entailed by, the meaning of the term itself?

In strict logical terms the dispositional description of a person as an 'elder' appears to be functionally neutral; there are no specific episodes in which an elder person might be necessarily involved. Indeed, the concept of an 'elder' appears to be a generic disposition concept, which may be actualised in a wide range of different functions of an episodic kind: an elder might be imagined to be a person sitting on a veranda in a rocking chair as much as a person exercising leadership in a community. Because these are synthetic not analytic judgments they are verified by observation of what happens amongst older people in the world, rather than by reflection on the meaning of the term.

It is perhaps conventional in most traditional societies for roles of leadership to be associated with older members of the community because of their long experience of life and acquired wisdom. This is changing in modern societies where community leaders may retire much earlier than hitherto, and where managerial roles are tending to go to younger men and women. Either way, the specific tasks to be assigned to the elders and natural leaders of the community seem to be entirely open; there is no single function or task that is necessarily entailed by the dispositional description of a person as being older than others.

This raises an important question: if Paul, for example, appointed elders, by contrast with the 'younger men' to exercise a leadership role and to perform a set of specific functions, can the Church of today simply decide what specific function to give to them? Can this vary from age to age? If bishops shared their presidential role with their presbyters/elders in the post-Constantinian period when there was a demand for more Eucharistic presidents because of the exponential growth of worshipping communities across the Empire, and if the Church at around the same time by conciliar decision explicitly denied deacons the right to preside at Eucharists, can the Church of today itself simply determine what functions to assign to those who hold the office from time to time according to need?

The answer to these questions, logically and theoretically may be 'yes', but in actual practical terms 'no', because of considerations of tradition and convention. These considerations may include a reverence for the actual historical trajectory of development of priestly functions from New Testament origins. The belief that these developments are God-guided in accordance with his promise to lead his people into all truth may also inhibit random change. Alternatively, the same decision may be determined by considering the importance of maintaining visible communion as a divine imperative with respect to matters of church order. Ecumenical prudence, or a lack of really pressing need, given that there are alternative ways of providing ministry, including sacramental ministry in remote rural areas, may also discourage the Church from making radical changes to the nature of priestly ministry.

There may be a natural inclination to expect that the older members of a community assume a natural authority to preside over community gatherings. Indeed, it is suggested that this is an operative principle in the Pastoral Epistles where younger men are exhorted to respect their elders. However, in terms of the strict logic of the concept 'elder', the disposition is functionally neutral. A very wide range of functions might be assigned to elders.

I think we have to conclude, therefore, that the term 'presbyter' or 'elder' does not entail that those who occupy the office simply by virtue of considerations of age must be involved in any specific function. Nothing is logically entailed by the term itself that might be said to be essential and necessary to the office. Apart from being old in terms of years and enjoying the natural authority of seniority in a community, there is no judgment about what is necessary and essential to the role of an elder or presbyter that may be said to be analytically true. Rather, whatever the specific functions are that are to be assigned to 'elders' or 'presbyters' in the Church, they must be synthetically added to the concept. This is particularly so once the term is used to refer not just to older people in terms of years of age, but to the holder of the office of elder at whatever age.

† † †

However, when the logic of dispositional and episodic concepts is applied to the term 'priest', it yields a somewhat different result from the logical analysis of the term 'elder' or 'presbyter'. There is no instance in the New Testament of the Christian minister being called a 'priest', just as there is no reference, for that matter, in the major Pauline Epistles to the term 'presbyter' or 'elder'. The earliest stratum of New Testament evidence speaks of Christian ministers as deacons (servants) and bishops (overseers) (e.g. Philippians 1:1). This is also the case in the Didache. Both the term 'elder' and the term 'priest' appear to be later arrivals in Christian parlance. The term 'elder' appeared only in the second generation of Christian writings, in Luke, Acts and the Pastoral Epistles, and the term 'priest' perhaps waited another 100 years, for there is no concrete evidence of this occurring before Polycrates of Ephesus (c. 190 AD). From then on the notion of priesthood gradually became the most influential notion for filling out and interpreting the function filled by elders/presbyters in the early Church.

The term 'priest' is favoured above 'presbyter' in *The Book of Common Prayer* of 1662 and securely rooted in the Ordinal and in the Anglican tradition. This is despite, as R. C. Moberly observed, the Reformer's 'close fidelity to the language of Scripture' and the fact that the term priest was 'thought to have been most deeply misused' in the Middle Ages and was 'so savagely attacked'.[7] Indeed, no less influential a person than Richard Hooker preferred the term 'presbyter' to that of 'priest', 'because in a matter of so small moment I would not willingly offend their ears to whom the name of Priesthood is odious'.[8] Despite Hooker's support for the substitution of 'presbyter' for 'priest', the terms 'priest' and 'priesthood' have remained in continuous Anglican usage. For a while, the term 'presbyter' entered the textual tradition of Anglican liturgy in the Scotch Liturgy authorised by Charles I,[9] which by and large otherwise followed the 1604 Prayer Book of James I after the Hampton Court Conference. However, following the Savoy Conference, the Restoration liturgy of 1662 consciously and intentionally retained the use of the term 'priest', which has thus been consistently used in all English Prayer Books from 1549 onwards, even despite Reformation pressures to change it. Because this is the term used in the Ordinal and in *The Book of Common Prayer* of 1662, the term 'priest' must be accorded an importance in the Anglican tradition over and above the term 'presbyter'. This is particularly the case in the Anglican Church of Australia where the principles of doctrine and worship embodied in the 1662 *Book of Common Prayer* have constitutional force.[10] In this sense the term 'priest' occupies a definitive position in determining the understanding of the office and function of those who exercise leadership roles as ministers of Word and Sacrament in this Church.

Now, while 'presbyter' is a dispositional concept which entails no particular episodes that might be said to be essential to the actualising of the disposition, the term 'priest' as a dispositional concept is necessarily associated with a set of quite specific functions. Generally speaking these focus in the first instance on cultic activities relating to services of worship. These functions derive through association of the Prayer Book term 'priest' with the scriptural use of the same term, in the original context of the rites and ceremonies of the Old Testament. Further to that, the meaning of the term has been developed through its metaphorical use by Christians, first with respect to the priesthood of Christ, who is actually called *hiereus* in the New Testament — the eternal high priest and representative not only of God but of all humanity (Hebrews); and secondly from its use as it is applied to the whole people of God (1 Peter 2:5). In other words, the meaning of the term 'priest' in *The Book of Common Prayer* to denote the ordained minister of Word and Sacrament in the Church cannot be divorced from its family resemblance to the scriptural use in the Old and New Testament. Insofar as it is argued in the Appellate Tribunal reasoning that the priest might delegate lay people to preside at the Eucharist and, further, that this would not be inimical or vicious with respect to his or her own role, for he or she would be still be exercising a form of managerial oversight, the Appellate Tribunal ruling is very seriously flawed. For the real problem with understanding the essential functions of the priest in the form of managerial oversight is that it detaches an understanding of priestly ministry from its biblical roots in the cult of the offering of sacrificial worship, and this is necessarily associated with it in an analytic rather than a merely synthetic sense.

The failure of the Appellate Tribunal majority opinion to associate an understanding of what is essential to the office of ministerial priesthood with a discussion of Christ the eternal high priest of the Epistle to the Hebrews, who ever lives to make intercession for us, (Hebrews 7:25) and eternally pleads the sacrifice once and for all offered in time on the Cross, may be the most crucial omission of its Opinion and reasons. The liturgical role of the priest when he or she leads worshippers, as together at the Eucharist they associate themselves with the eternal prayerful pleading of the 'once and for all' sacrifice of Christ is suggested by the term itself. The commemoration of the sacrifice offered in history by Christ as high priest and eternally pleaded at the right hand of the Father is normative in any Christian understanding of the meaning of the term. Likewise, the necessary connection between 'the priestly people of God' and the offering of 'spiritual sacrifices' acceptable to God (I Peter 2:5) also affects the use of the term priest in reference to the individual who leads 'the offering of spiritual sacrifices acceptable to God' in the ministry of Word and Sacrament. The Christian use of the term 'priest' cannot be separated from this nexus of ideas. For the meanings of words are established by their use in particular linguistic communities. The Church operates as a linguistic community which is rooted in the tradition of the Old and New Testament, and this provides the context for establishing the meaning of the term 'priest' as the Church uses the term.

Moreover, in order to understand the sacrificial aspect of the function of those who occupy the office of priesthood, it is necessary to place priestly ministry not just in the context of the offering of sacrificial worship, but in the more general ecclesiological context in which the Church is understood as 'the Temple of God'. Indeed, ecclesiological considerations become very important at this point.

In the Church of the New Testament the natural household seems to have provided an initial model which conditioned thinking about the nature of the Church. Moreover, the household was not just a theoretical model, but an actual model, since the Church originally met for worship and fellowship in an actual house. But there was another model which also conditioned ecclesiological thinking, as New Testament Christians pursued the early quest of self-understanding. This is the model of the Temple. Once again this was not just a theoretical model. For at least up until 70 AD, and for the entire first generation of Christian faith and practice, early believers had at hand the actual model of the Temple as the dwelling place of God. The Temple had been the chief place of worship in ancient Israel. After the destruction of the Temple in Jerusalem in 70 AD, Christians could claim to have replaced the old with the new in a particularly clear and graphic way. The New Israel could now claim to have replaced the Temple as the chief place of worship, for the Church saw itself as the dwelling place of the Spirit of God. This is what marked the Church as holy, just as the Temple had been a holy place. It followed that the chief place of worship was anywhere the new Temple of the Holy Spirit — the Church — was. Initially, of course, the reference was not to a building at all, but to a people — a people called to be holy. The destruction of the Temple in Jerusalem made it all the more easy to speak of the Church as the new Temple, though the shift from appeal to the household model to speak specifically of the 'household of God' and the Temple is already clear in Ephesians 2:19–22:

> Now therefore you are no more strangers and foreigners, but fellow-citizens with the saints, and of the household of God. And are built upon the foundation of the apostles and prophets, Jesus Christ being the chief corner stone; in whom all the building fitly framed together grows into an holy temple in the Lord. In whom you also are built together for an habitation of God through the Spirit.

This kind of ecclesiological appeal to the Temple model could hardly fail to have an influence on Christian language about ministry and worship. Indeed, it is highly probable that the very title 'elder', for example, which originally belonged in the context of the household, eventually gave way to the term 'priest' under the influence of the ecclesiological presupposition of the Temple model. In this case, the linguistic move from the functionally neutral term 'presbyter' to the theologically loaded and functionally much more specific term 'priest' was made as the Church also made the move from understanding itself as a 'household' to think of itself in terms of the 'Temple of God'. This development may be illustrated in I Clement, where a comparison is made between the worship of the first Christians and the ordered Temple worship: Clament says Jesus 'commanded us to celebrate sacrifices and services' (60:2), and Clement goes on to speak of ministers as those who 'offer their oblations'. He goes on: 'For to the High Priest his proper ministrations are allotted … and to the priests the proper place has been appointed' (60:I). There are similar sacrificial allusions also in the Didache 14:1–3.

From the first allusions to the Temple as a model for understanding aspects of Christian worship and ministry in the New Testament and in the Didache and I Clement, it is an easy step in the third century to call first bishops or overseers also 'priests'. Then presbyters were called 'priests', as the bishops more and more shared their priestly ministry with them. Inevitably this led to an understanding of their essential function in quasi-sacrificial terms.

The Old Testament connection of priests with sanctuaries and with the cultic acts performed in them is very ancient.[11] When the cultus became fully centralised in Jerusalem the offering of sacrifices became the exclusive privilege of the priests.[12] The classic definition of the priest in the Old Testament is found in Deuteronomy 33:8–10:

> Give to Levi your Thummim,
> and your Urim to your loyal one …
> they observed your word,
> and kept your covenant.
> They teach Jacob your ordinances,
> and Israel your law;
> they place incense before you,
> and whole burnt offerings on your altar.

For all the obvious differences between the priesthood of the Old Covenant and that of the New, it may be argued that both an essential association of the term priesthood with the concept of sacrifice and the exclusive nature of the functions uniquely associated with the inherited term 'priesthood' continue on in Anglican Prayer Book use in relation to the leaders of congregations. For the role of leading and presiding over the offering of the 'sacrifice of praise and thanksgiving' and leading the commemoration of the once-and-for all sacrifice of Christ upon the Cross cannot be disassociated from the term. Indeed, there is a necessary association of the term 'priest' with the leadership of the sacrificial offering of worship. This is an analytic judgment, for a role in the offering of sacrifice (in some sense of the term) is contained in the very concept of a priest as Christians have received it. This is not an ampliative synthetic or contingent judgment whose truth or otherwise might be established by observation. In other words, it belongs to our *conception* of a priest, not our *experience* of priests, that priests play a key role in the offering of sacrifice, in some sense of the word 'sacrifice'.

The idea of sacrifice is clearly capable of nuanced explication and argumentation. As Archbishop Cranmer, author of the First English Prayer Book, said, 'it is necessary to know the distinction and diversity of sacrifices' in order to understand the sacrifice of Christ and the manner of the appropriation of its benefits amongst believers. 'One kind of sacrifice was offered by Christ once and for all', he said, but 'Another kind of sacrifice there is, which ... is made of them that be reconciled to Christ, to testify our duties unto God, and to shew ourselves thankful to Him; and therefore they be called sacrifices of laud, praise and thanksgiving'.[13] This is a point he had probably learned from Calvin, who argued that there are different kinds of sacrifices and that the Eucharistic sacrifice and the offering of prayer and worship to God generally were perfectly acceptable forms of sacrificial worship.[14] We may firmly reject any suggestion that priests offer propitiatory sacrifices for the manipulation of God, or that they offer Christ anew in the Eucharist in a way that might repeat or add to the once-and-for-all sacrifice of Christ on the Cross. However, Anglicans would at least contend today that priests lead the people of

God 'in the offering of the spiritual sacrifice of praise and thanksgiving' for all the benefits won by Christ upon the Cross. This is the sacrifice that is vitally commemorated in each Eucharistic celebration.

Something of the necessary rather than contingent connection between the ideas of priesthood and sacrifice may also be illustrated by Richard Hooker. As we have already noted, Hooker thought that the 'word *Presbyter* doth seem more fit and in propriety of speech more agreeable than *Priest* with the drift of the whole Gospel of Jesus Christ'[15] precisely because he feared that the term 'priest' could not be disassociated from the noxious medieval ideas of sacrifice to which I have already referred. Thus, it was because of the association of the idea of priesthood with the sacrifices of the Old Covenant and the misuse of the idea of sacrifice as a propitiatory sacrifice by Roman authorities at the Council of Trent, that Hooker favoured the use of 'presbyter' amongst Anglicans so as to avoid misunderstanding. However, Hooker was well aware that this was not the only sense in which the associated words 'priesthood' and 'sacrifice' could be used. He noted, for example, that 'the Fathers of the Church of Christ ... call usually the ministry of the Gospel *Priesthood* in regard of that which the Gospel hath *proportionable* to ancient sacrifices, namely the Communion of the Blessed Body and Blood of Christ'. In other words, Hooker appreciated that a certain proportionality, or analogy, holds between the literal sense of references to the sacrifices of the Old Covenant and the extended use of the term 'sacrifice' by Christians. By an analogous application of the terms, even though the Church 'have properly now no sacrifice' in the strictly literal sense of the 'sacrifice of the law' of the Old Covenant, Hooker recognised that there was a use of the term that the early Church Fathers found amenable.

In the nineteenth century R. C. Moberly observed that there are significant differences of meaning between the Old Testament use of the term which was superseded by the Gospel of Christ, and the real and right sacrifices of the new dispensation, and that it was the former to which Hooker was reacting when he stated that 'sacrifice is now no part of the Church ministry' and so affirmed his preference for the term 'presbyter'.[16] Certainly, Hooker's apparent discomfort with the terms 'priest' and 'priesthood' indicate that he was well aware of their necessary association with the concept of sacrifice and of the difficulty of shaking an understanding of sacrifice from its original Old Testament context. The same dynamic seems to inform the reasoning of the Bishop of Bathurst in support of the Appellate Tribunal Majority Opinion when he says that 'The priest is a presbyter or elder not a priest *in the Old Testament sense*' (my emphasis).[17] Unfortunately, this statement entirely fails to take account of the necessary function signalled by the use of the word 'priest' in relation to the real and right offering of the spiritual sacrifices of the new dispensation. Instead, the meaning of the term 'priest' is dissolved at the hands of Bishop Wilson into the functionally neutral term 'elder'.

Nobody imagines that the references to the order of priests in *The Book of Common Prayer* intended to import the specific literal meaning associated with the priestly sacrifices of the Old Testament. On the other hand, while the terms 'presbyter' and 'priest' denote the same person, they clearly do not connote the same meaning. These are both terms whose meaning, like all terms of our language, is established by conventional use; in this case the Christian meaning of the term 'priest' has been established in nearly two thousand years of use after a pre-history in the Old Testament. One cannot, outside of the world of Alice in Wonderland, simply determine that the words 'presbyter' and 'priest' from now on are to mean the same thing. They may denote the same subject; in the English language they do not connote the same meaning.

† † †

That it is analytically true that a priest is a religious functionary who leads the offering of sacrifice in some sense of the meaning of the term 'sacrifice', whether in the literal sense of the Old Testament law or some analogous Reformed Christian sense, means that this function is covertly 'contained in', as Kant would say, the conception itself *a priori*, or prior to our experience of priests. That is, by virtue of reflection upon, and analysis of, the term and its explication we come to a clearer understanding of it. It follows that it belongs to the unique identity of a priest that a priest takes a leadership role specifically in the offering of sacrifice. That the holders of the office of priest have in certain periods of history found themselves involved in a range of additional functions that might be expressed in judgments of a synthetic kind and verified by observation is entirely irrelevant with respect to the necessary and analytic meaning of the term which establishes the essentials of priestly identity.[18] That priests 'have moved from being Mass priests to ministers of the Word, from the English role of being officials of the State to the Australian role of being paid leaders of the local branch of a voluntary association'[19] has nothing whatever to do with the essential functions that are assigned uniquely and universally to those to whom reference is made in the Church by use of the term 'priest'.

As Anglicans we naturally wish to keep a clear distinction between the Atonement won once and for all by Christ's sacrifice and the extended meaning of the same term when it is used in relation to Christian life and worship as 'the sacrifice of praise and thanksgiving'. As the Dublin Report of the Fifth International Liturgical Consultation (1995) put it: 'The sacrificial character of all Christian life and worship must be articulated in such a way that does not blur the unique atoning work of Christ.'[20] However, given its refurbishment by the sixteenth-century Reformers and the Church's subsequent rethinking of the relation of the sacrifice of Christ and its memorial (or anamnesis) in the Eucharist, the association of the term 'priest' with the commemoration of the sacrifice of Christ once offered on the Cross appears to be unavoidable. The term 'priest' remains from its point of origin an essentially cultic term. By contrast, the judgment about whether a priest might delegate functions to others is clearly a synthetic judgment which might or might not be true, and which would be verified by observation rather than reflection on the meaning of the term.

† † †

Moreover, it is the inherited cultic use of the term 'priest' that explains why the Preface to the Ordinal makes it patently clear not only that no one should be admitted to the office 'unless he be called, tried, examined, and admitted thereto' according to the appropriate form specified in the Ordinal, but also that no one should be 'suffered to execute' any of the defining functions of priesthood without being ordained.

It may not be widely understood that there are clear scriptural grounds underpinning the Ordinal's injunction against presuming to execute the office without authorisation and, in particular, apart from the due manner of authorising such ministry by prayer with the laying on of hands.

Generally speaking, in the Old Testament the role of priesthood was confined to a particular subset of authorised people within the Jewish community, the house of Aaron. Because the offering of sacrifice in ancient Israel was the prerogative of the House of Aaron, it was not a role to be distributed in an undifferentiated way amongst the Jewish congregation. In addition, and very importantly, there is a biblical tradition of condemnation of those who, without authorisation, presume to take holy things by force. The unauthorised taking of sacred things, wrenching them from the hands of their authorised stewards, unworthily and by force, by Korah and his cohort in Numbers 16 and the divine punishment of this by the instantaneous imposition of the death penalty, is a good example. In this story Korah and his cohort assemble 'against Moses and against Aaron' and, on the basis of the egalitarian claim that 'all the congregation are holy, everyone of them' (verse 3), ignore any need for the differentiation of roles within the congregation. Instead they presume to 'seek the priesthood' for themselves in addition to their own assigned role as Levites (verse 10). This passage may be read with the story of Uzziah in 2 Chronicles 26:18, where Uzziah is similarly punished for making an unauthorised offering of incense at the altar. In this case he was punished, not by instantaneous death, but by being afflicted with illness. The teaching of this ancient scriptural tradition is that one should not presume to take holy things by force and without due authorisation. If one does, one must heed the consequences of sickness and death rather than wholeness of life.

The stories of these incidents help us to understand why St Paul can say in I Corinthians 11:30 that the misuse of sacred things by

Corinthian Christians at celebrations of the Eucharist may lead to weakness, sickness and even death. The fact that we no longer teach confirmation candidates that if they take the Holy Communion unworthily they will get sick and die is simply an indicator of the fact that we have, in the modern world, tended to detach our understanding of the Eucharist and priestly ministry at the Eucharist from its original context in the sacrificial theory of the biblical world. Instead today we tend to overconcentrate on the meaning of the Eucharist merely as a fellowship meal.

The Appellate Tribunal Majority Opinion has certainly, though perhaps unwittingly, detached both the understanding of the Eucharist and the function of those admitted to the office of priesthood from this aspect of the original biblical context. Once we acknowledge that the Eucharist is more than a fellowship meal, insofar as it involves a commemoration of the sacrifice Christ offered once and for all, we can begin to understand the sacrificial nuances in Paul's talk in I Corinthians relating to the dire consequences of failure to discern/divide the Lord's Body by reducing the Eucharist to a kind of mundane party.

In other words, this biblical evidence suggests to us that the unauthorised taking of the holy things of sacrificial worship and handling them with mundane familiarity, involves a failure to discern their true significance. This, indeed, is what is said by Paul to lead to sickness and death. For us the point is that the sacred significance of the Eucharist may only be properly understood by placing it in the context of a world in which the concept of the offering of sacrifice was presupposed and clearly understood. In that world of meaning, sacrificial theory held a normative place that it does not retain in the thinking of many today; it is certainly entirely missing from the Appellate Tribunal ruling with regard to the constitutional possibility of lay presidency. As a result, the Appellate Tribunal's reasoning fails to place an understanding of the role of the priest at the Eucharist in the context of the sacrificial theory of the biblical world. Instead its reasoning reflects the world of contemporary commercial activity and business management insofar as it is prepared to whittle priestly oversight down to the form of leadership expressed in the delegation of duties. This simply will not do.

The authorised role of the priest is essentially a role of leadership associated with the sealing and strengthening of covenant relationships within the worshipping community and between the worshipping community and God by the sacred commemoration of the sacrificial death of Christ. In the offering of the Eucharistic sacrifice of praise and thanksgiving, Christians appropriate the benefits of Christ's sacrificial death to themselves by faith. The role of the priest as leader of the community at Eucharistic worship is necessarily, essentially and as a matter of unique identity focused in this activity.

The authorisation of ordination for the task of priestly leadership establishes the essential and unique preserve of the stewards of holy things in accordance with these biblical traditions. This is not just a function that may be arbitrarily and synthetically associated with priesthood at the whim of the Church, but something intrinsic that inheres in the meaning of the term 'priest' as Christians have inherited it. For Anglican Christians, in particular, the term 'priest' has been deliberately and consistently retained to refer to one who necessarily leads and presides over the offering of the commemoration of the sacrificial death of Christ, even though the theology relating to this has varied from time to time. Just as all bachelors are unmarried, and all bakers bake, so all priests lead and preside over the offering of the sacrifice of praise and thanksgiving. This is a sacred and nontransferable prerogative of those who are explicitly authorised by prayer with the laying on of hands to do so, and who are thus separated out for life to exercise this particular onerous responsibility as a service to God's people. To argue that the function of actually leading and presiding over the Eucharist can be detached from priesthood and replaced by a general form of pastoral oversight and leadership with a power of delegation fails to appreciate these analytic implications of the term.

Finally, one simple practical test of the correct use of the term 'priest' and what it essentially and necessarily involves arises out of a consideration of the question of vocation and priestly self-identity: it has already been observed that, in the Appellate Tribunal Majority Opinion's reasoning, the distinguishing marks of priesthood can be reduced to the concept of leadership of a community of Christians where 'leadership' is understood in a managerial sense. However, a generalised sense of call to 'leadership' or 'presidency' in the Church of an essentially managerial kind would not be sufficiently adequate to allow the Church to affirm a vocation and admit a person to an ordination training program and eventually to Holy Orders. If one were to ask a candidate for Holy Orders why he or she pursued a calling to priesthood, a response in the form 'I think I am good at management and the delegation of tasks' simply would not do. On the contrary, it would reveal that such a person has no clear understanding of the office of priesthood and the functions that are necessarily involved in the execution of it.

CHAPTER 7

WOMEN IN THE EPISCOPATE?

As the Anglican Church of Australia begins to tackle the question of the possible admission of women to the episcopate, I think it may be helpful for everyone to be aware of the journey over which we as a Church have come since 1968. The Lambeth Conference of that year invited the member Churches of the Anglican Communion to commence a study of the possibility of ordaining women. This put the question of women in ministry very firmly on the international Anglican agenda. The subject has dominated Anglican Church life and absorbed an enormous amount of energy over the last generation. The discussion of the issue has also spilled over into the life of other Churches.

In the Anglican Church of Australia the initial work of theological exploration was assigned to its General Synod Doctrine Commission, which, after some years of study, produced a report entitled 'The Ministry of Women' for the General Synod of 1977. Noting the report, the General Synod of 1977 resolved:

> that this General Synod endorses the conclusion of the Commission that the
> theological objections which have been raised do not constitute a barrier to

(a) *the ordination of women to the priesthood, and*
(b) *the consecration of women to the episcopate, in this Church.*[1]

This resolution was carried by majorities in all houses: forty-four votes to thirty-three in the House of Laity; fifty votes to thirty-three in the House of Clergy; thirteen votes to six in the House of Bishops. This thus became the authoritative theological position of the Anglican Church of Australia, but it needs to be noted that there remained a significant minority who were of a dissenting viewpoint.

Following this determination of the General Synod on the theological issue, the Church's highest court of appeal in legal and constitutional matters, the Appellate Tribunal, was asked for its advice as to the constitutional validity of these possible developments. Just prior to the General Synod of 1985, the Tribunal advised in the affirmative with respect to the question of constitutional validity, but went on to say that it had not been asked a question about whether a canonical provision of General Synod was required in relation to adapting male personal pronouns so as to include the female in ordination services. The Tribunal therefore gave no answer to that question. However, the Opinion then went on to say that '*if* this was required' (my emphasis), a canon to amend the text of ordination services should take a particular recommended form. The use of the conditional 'if' immediately raised a question about whether a General Synod canon was really necessary at all, or whether the matter could perhaps be handled in a more piecemeal fashion, diocese by diocese.

Many of us argued that whether a General Synod canon was a legal requirement or not, it would nevertheless be a good thing for the issue to be handled nationally by the Church's General Synod as a matter affecting the national unity of our communion as Australian Anglicans. Though no bill for a canon was on the business paper in 1985, I myself argued that we should as a General Synod, consider one. Because the Appellate Tribunal's ruling was delivered only within a few days of the commencement of the Synod, this matter had first to be argued onto the business paper, in view of the impossibility of giving the usual required notice. The General Synod voted affirmatively to consider the matter, but on that occasion a bill for a canon to provide for the admission of women to ministerial priesthood failed by the narrow margin of two votes in the House of Clergy (that is to say, one clergy person voting one way rather than another). It was certainly a near run thing. Nevertheless, while no mandate was given for the admission of women to ministerial priesthood, the same General Synod passed a canon allowing for women to be admitted to the diaconate.[2]

Bills for a canon to provide for the admission of women to ministerial priesthood then came before General Synods on two subsequent occasions during the 1980s, now in the more complicated context of a Church with a growing number of women deacons who aspired to priestly ordination. Some of these women became members of the House of Clergy of the General Synod itself. At the same time, in the life of the Church outside and between General Synods, the issue became both increasingly polarised and, I think it is fair to say, increasingly politicised on both sides of the debate, and therefore increasingly difficult to resolve. Both those rigidly opposed to the ordination of women and members of the Movement for the Ordination of Women were very active and vocal during this period. It became an issue in which the media and the wider Australian community also began to take a very keen interest. Legal and constitutional problems abounded, including the residual issue of whether a canon of General Synod was really required at all. At one point, a lawyer from Sydney observed that just to address the legal problems that the Church faced at that time was 'like swimming in shark infested custard'.

In this atmosphere of contentious theological and legal debate, a substantial body of opinion, notably in the Diocese of Melbourne, came to the view that the process had become unhelpfully divisive at national level, and so determined on pursuing a more piecemeal approach. The Diocese of Melbourne therefore began to develop diocesan legislation to authorise the admission of women to ministerial priesthood independent of General Synod. At the last General Synod at which a bill for a General Synod canon was promoted (1989) the clear message was received, particularly from supporters of the ordination of women from the Diocese of

Melbourne, that they no longer intended to support a General Synod canon, and really preferred that the matter should not again come before General Synod.

The matter was nevertheless debated in principle at the General Synod of 1989 in order to once again canvass the theological issues at this level, but with the clear indication that the General Synod would be asked for leave to withdraw the proposed legislation before any vote was taken. Interestingly, given that there was no explicit canon warranting the ordination of men (for it was simply assumed that ordination candidates would be men), it was argued that if a General Synod canon was needed to authorise the ordination of women, then there should also be one authorising the ordination of men. After a debate on matters of principle, which obliged opponents of the measure to rehearse what arguments they could muster, leave of Synod was sought to withdraw the bill. It was therefore, out of deference to the Melbourne viewpoint that a General Synod canon was not desirable, never put to the vote. Indeed, with respect to the ordination of women, one resolution was passed that actually affirmed the belief that diocesan synods might have the power to enact local canons to admit women to ministerial priesthood.[3] Another even affirmed an alleged 'ancient authority of a diocesan bishop, subject only to such qualifications and conditions as are imposed by lawful authority, to ordain by virtue of his office canonically fit deacons to the order of priesthood in his diocese'.[4] In other words, the dominant thinking seemed to be that, unless restrained by his diocesan synod, a bishop had an inherent power to ordain whom he willed. It was argued that, as the minister of order in the Church, the choice of candidates was simply his decision. Whether he chose to take matters relating to the chromosomes of candidates into consideration was also purely his decision.

I myself voted against this resolution in the belief that such an important development in the life of the Church should be taken by the Bishop-in-Synod — the bishop not acting alone, but along with clergy and laity in Synod. I was still of the view that this should preferably happen at a national level by a decision of General Synod. Whatever we might make of the suggestion of Resolution 25/89, about a bishop's absolute autonomy in this matter of ordination, it was clearly the case that a majority of supporters of the ordination of women had determined that a General Synod canon was not the way to go. Certainly, those of us who were supporters of General Synod as the appropriate decision-making forum found ourselves in the minority and had to accept that this view was no longer shared even by a substantial number of those who supported the ordination of women.

Ironically, when the Appellate Tribunal considered the validity of the local diocesan canon of the Diocese of Melbourne, it came to the view that the *Melbourne Diocesan Constitution Act* of 1854 did not actually confer the constitutional power to enact such a canon. This effectively prevented the Diocese of Melbourne from proceeding independently of General Synod. But the Tribunal went on to say, very significantly, that this ruling might not necessarily apply in the case of other dioceses of the national Church. What was apparently being indicated was the fact that there were other dioceses which had been differently constituted in the colonial era and whose constitutions might allow for such action. This gave the signal to those dioceses which were constituted by consensual compact rather than by an Act of Parliament to entertain the possibility that, even if their constitutions did not clearly provide for such a power, it might be possible for them to amend their constitutions and so to pass diocesan-enabling legislation. Any amendment to a diocesan constitution would have to be in accordance with the provisions allowed in the national Constitution of the Anglican Church of Australia (1962) for the amendment of diocesan constitutions.

Meanwhile, the Appellate Tribunal had also been asked for an opinion to clarify the question of whether a General Synod canon was in fact required or whether diocesan legislation was all that was needed. In 1989 this resulted in an unfortunate legal impasse, when the Tribunal found itself in the embarrassing position of not being able to furnish the Church with an answer either way. In order to give an opinion at all on matters of ritual, ceremony or discipline, a majority of at least four of the seven Tribunal members was required; but in addition, the majority of four had to be comprised of two bishops and two lay judges. Failure to meet this requirement meant that the Appellate Tribunal could give no answer to this crucial question. The question of whether a General Synod canon was required or not had thus gone to the highest court of appeal within the Church's own legal structure and no answer could be given! The Church has since acted to rectify this constitutional defect, but at the time it found itself in a legal limbo.

There thus seemed no alternative for interested dioceses other than enacting local diocesan legislation, first to alter their constitutions and then to pass a canon. As a consequence, since October 1991 the Constitution of the Diocese of Perth has provided, for example, that the words 'bishop', 'priest' and 'deacon' all include the feminine; they are no longer to be interpreted as exclusively masculine terms.

The taking of the local diocesan route did mean, however, that in the absence of an Appellate Tribunal ruling about whether a General Synod canon was necessary, those dioceses enacting local legislation might have to face the possibility of legal challenge elsewhere. This led to the series of very strained, unedifying and divisive civil legal actions, unbecoming of the people of God, which ended in hearings before State Supreme Courts on both sides of the nation in 1991 and 1992.

While an injunction was obtained to prevent an ordination of women candidates from occurring in the Diocese of Canberra and Goulburn, in the Supreme Court of Western Australia on 6 March 1992 Mr Justice Kerry White refused to issue a similar injunction to prevent an ordination from occurring. This ordination had been planned in Perth for 7 March, the Feast of St Perpetua and her Companions,[5] in accordance with the amended Perth Diocesan Constitution of 1991 and subsequent diocesan legislation to permit the ordination of women. The first women were thus ordained to the priesthood in Australia in St George's Cathedral in Perth on 7 March 1992. The judgment of the West Australian Supreme Court raised the prospect of a series of similar outcomes in secular courts elsewhere across the country. Indeed, it was followed a short time later by a similar ruling in the Supreme Court of New South Wales in relation to the delayed ordination of women in the Dioceses of Canberra and Goulburn.

It was in this context that General Synod had little alternative other than to pass a clarification canon in July 1992 so as to eliminate any continuing doubt about whether diocesan synods had power to proceed. This avoided the prospect of further action in civil courts. The inability of the Appellate Tribunal to produce an answer in 1989 to this question was in this way finally resolved.

I think Anglicans all learned a good deal from this strained and difficult train of events. To my mind far too much energy was sapped away during this process, energy which might well have been put into other pressing and more productively evangelical matters. It was also naturally very costly in financial terms. It is not a process to be repeated.

† † †

Almost certainly, the determination not to repeat this kind of exercise brought the Church to the point at its 1998 General Synod sitting in Adelaide to set up a Working Group on Women in the Episcopate. The aim was to chart a way forward on the question of the consecration of women as bishops which would avoid the difficulties that had been encountered during the saga leading to the ordination of women as priests. The Report of this Working Group came before the most recent General Synod in Brisbane in July 2001. This Group had worked very earnestly and hard, and exceedingly harmoniously, over the years between Adelaide and Brisbane. It was a very representative group which included opponents as well as proponents of the admission of women to the episcopate, and there was a huge amount of consultation in the Church at large in order to find a way forward. Dr Muriel Porter of Melbourne and Dr Anne Young of Sydney and their colleagues on that Working Party provided a paradigm for working consensually to resolve the conflict of ideas. Their work together on this process was universally applauded.

The result of their work was to produce as the preferred option General Synod draft legislation in the form once again of a clarification canon which would have made it clear that those dioceses which wished to elect a woman bishop certainly had power to do so, while not requiring those of a contrary mind to vote for such a measure at General Synod level. As I understand it, the proposed legislation was designed to end any possibility of continuing legal argument, which might end up in the civil courts, as to the question of whether a General Synod canon was necessary or whether a diocesan canon alone would be sufficient to warrant the election and consecration of a woman to the episcopate. Also, if passed, the legislation would have ensured that all dioceses, and not just a subset with congenial constitutional provisions, would have been given a green light to pass diocesan legislation to allow for the appointment and consecration of a woman bishop should they wish to do so. At the same time, and to my mind very importantly, the desire was to develop creative ways of providing pastoral care for those unable to accept the ministry of a woman diocesan bishop in a particular diocese.

When the matter came before the General Synod it soon became clear, however, that the protocols for providing pastoral care to those unable to accept the ministry of a woman bishop were the sticking point. The measure to approve the admission of women to the episcopate was approved in principle by the General Synod by one hundred and thirty-five votes to ninety-five. However, the Synod was clearly divided over protocols which would have given metropolitan dioceses the responsibility of providing alternative pastoral care within the diocese of a woman bishop should a particular parish seek to avail itself of that alternative. For one thing, many were concerned that a woman bishop's authority would be compromised and the integrity of the diocese she administered would be fractured at least in some degree. Others were clearly unimpressed by the idea that metropolitans would be given a power to interfere directly in a diocese other than their own.

The utter impossibility of redrafting the protocols on the floor of the Synod resulted in a decision to refer the matter back to the Standing Committee of the General Synod for further work before bringing the matter back to the next General Synod. A Working Group has therefore been established to bring draft proposals to the General Synod in 2004.

† † †

Now, it seems to me there are a number of things to be said about the present situation of the Anglican Church of Australia on this issue. First, insofar as no concrete action was taken with regard to the proposed clarification canon that came before the General Synod of 2001, the Church is in a difficult predicament. For this bill for a canon sought to find a way of dealing with this matter from within the Church so as to head off any possibility of future recourse to civil courts. There are still those who are of the view that a General Synod canon is not really necessary at all. It seems likely that if dioceses were to enact local legislation today and that legislation were to be challenged in civil courts, the outcome would be the same as in the case of the ordination of women to ministerial priesthood. In other words, it is unlikely that civil courts would act to prevent a diocese from proceeding to appoint and consecrate a woman bishop. The failure of the General Synod to act in 2001, thus leaves a gaping legal void. This was in fact pointed out from the floor of the General Synod in Brisbane by Mr Justice David Bleby of Adelaide.

It is also surely unfortunate and undesirable for the Church to find itself facing a future situation in which some dioceses, differently constituted from others in the colonial period, might today be legally able to proceed, should they wish to do so, while others almost certainly do not have the same constitutional powers. There is an added complication, because the Appellate Tribunal has already ruled that women ordained to the diaconate, priesthood or episcopate overseas in a Church in communion with this Church may be invited to minister in this Church. But, even worse, the General Synod's failure to act in 2001 has left the Church in a situation in which there is no agreed provision for the pastoral care of those unable to accept the ministry of a woman bishop. The Church must therefore exist for the present in a legal void in which all these matters are entirely unresolved. In this situation the responsibility has fallen on the bishops to act collegially in a way that will serve the best interests of the unity of the Church. Their best counsel has been to encourage patience. As Isaiah says: 'One who trusts will not panic' (Isaiah 28:16). But protracted indecision will be equally undesirable. It is therefore very important that this matter be resolved in 2004.

Then there is the question of the protocols and whether or not at the end of the day a decision will be taken to require dioceses to make adequate provisions for those who cannot accept the ministry of a woman bishop. This might be provided, for example, by a male bishop from a neighbouring diocese who could be invited by a female diocesan bishop to minister to dissenting parishes within her own diocese. This would be an issue in a diocese that elected a woman to the episcopate as diocesan, though it does not appear to be such a problem in the case where a woman is appointed to be an assistant bishop. Where there are two bishops in a diocese, one male and one female, it is pastorally uncomplicated to ensure that a male bishop makes visitations to parishes preferring maleness.

It now appears very likely that when General Synod next considers a bill for a canon to allow for dioceses to elect a woman bishop, protocols will be proposed which, if adopted, would require her to make arrangements within her diocese for the pastoral care of dissenting minorities. It has to be admitted that this would still raise an anomaly, insofar as a woman bishop would be subject to restraints to which male bishops are not subject. There are probably people in the Church who would be uncomfortable with the protocols on these grounds. Nevertheless, the Church inevitably faces a new and pastorally demanding set of circumstances, and it may have to accept a degree of anomaly, at least as a temporary measure in a period of reception while the Church as a whole comes to a common mind. A compromise may be unavoidable. The reality is that there may be no way to resolve the question of women in the episcopate other than with alternative or extended episcopal oversight of some kind. Here I have frankly to declare my own hand. It may be a matter of having women bishops who minister under the restraint of some kind of protocol or of not having women bishops at all. Given that it will take time for some people to come to terms with, and be able to accept, the ministry of a woman bishop, some way has to be found to meet their needs. In some situations anomalies have to be tolerated while new developments are processed and managed.

There are already many examples of arrangements which are designed to provide episcopal ministry to meet specific needs that the current diocesan bishop may not be able to meet. For example, the bishops of the Anglican Church of Australia already work quite effectively with agreed protocols that govern the ministry of visiting Indigenous bishops. Both the Aboriginal and the Torres Strait Islander bishops minister under agreed protocols to Indigenous communities within dioceses other than their home diocese of North Queensland.

The last Lambeth Conference may provide us with a paradigm for our handling of this. In relation to ecumenical dialogue, the Lambeth Conference of 1998 in the report of Section IV: Called to be One, Chapter 4 on Consistency and Coherence, began to speak of the need to live with anomalies of some kind in periods of transition following ecumenical agreements. For example, the Church of South India lived with an anomalous situation over an interim period of thirty years. It was accepted that, while all new ordinations were to be episcopal from 1948 onwards, there would be some ordained clergy who had come from non-episcopal traditions and who would continue to minister in that Church without episcopal ordination. The same Lambeth Report of 1998 notes that similarly anomalous situations are countenanced by both the *Porvoo Declaration* and the *Concordat* for intercommunion between the Lutheran Church and the Episcopal Church in the United States of America. Similarly, in the Roman Catholic Church, following Vatican II, and the switch to vernacular liturgies, some congregations have been permitted to continue to use the Tridentine Latin Mass. Overlapping Latin Rite and Eastern Rite administrative structures and parallel liturgical traditions within a single geographical diocese are also not unknown in the Roman Catholic Church. A principle of economy dictates that uncompromising purist positions sometimes have to be accommodated to what will be of most pastoral benefit to people, particularly as they process and come to terms with new developments in relation to matters of Church discipline.

This suggests to me that those who support the possibility of the consecration of woman bishops, particularly a diocesan bishop in a diocese where there are no assistant bishops who are male, may have to consider living with a form of extended episcopal oversight, even if this, to a purist's way of thinking about a bishop's jurisdiction, contains an element of anomaly. Such situations should, of course, be kept to a bare minimum to serve practical pastoral necessity. But in a diocese where there is a difference of opinion, careful attention, as a matter of pastoral principle, should be paid to the needs of minorities. The Church should do all in its power to ensure that those in this situation will be appropriately ministered to in the most satisfactory way that can command agreement. In the interests of responding to the overarching need to provide adequate and acceptable pastoral care, a jurisdictional anomaly may therefore have to be countenanced.

Whether the Church at large is currently ready for the ministry of a woman bishop, and whether the protocols need to be enshrined in a schedule to legislation or simply in conventionally agreed upon guidelines of the House of Bishops, are things which will have to be addressed at the General Synod in 2004. But it seems that some form of arrangement by protocol may certainly be needed if a provision to allow for the possible consecration of women to the episcopate is to succeed at all.

† † †

Meanwhile, Anglicans must also continue to address the theological questions relating to the ordination of women, both internally within their own Communion and at the ecumenical level, for there is no doubt that the ordination of women to ministerial priesthood in many Churches of the Anglican Communion during the 1980s initially strained relations, particularly with the Roman Catholic Church and the Churches of Eastern Orthodoxy. Despite the fact that the admission of women to ministerial priesthood has been spoken of since the time of Pope Paul VI as a 'new and grave obstacle' to unity, it is gratifying that the theological dialogue on this question has continued. Anglicans cannot claim a monopoly on truth and must listen carefully to arguments brought forward by other Christian traditions. On the other hand, Anglicans will naturally expect theologians of other denominational traditions to assess their own thinking in an open and respectful way. All the while, continuing dialogue is informed by the shared belief that if something is theologically right, it will eventually be found to be ecumenically right.

It is certainly encouraging to Anglicans that the question of the place of women in ordained ministry is currently being addressed with seriousness in the Churches of Eastern Orthodoxy and in the Anglican–Orthodox international dialogue. In *The Ordination of Women in the Orthodox Church*, Elisabeth Behr-Sigel and Kallistos Ware, Bishop of Diokleia,[6] urge that the matter must be revisited within Eastern Orthodoxy 'with an open mind and an open heart'.[7] This book calls for a theological reassessment of the question of the place of women in ordained ministry in the Orthodox Churches. Given the reverence for the ancient tradition of the early Fathers, the question of the nature and authority of tradition, and particularly of the *silence* of Church tradition with regard to the explicit question of the ordination of women, will be crucial for Eastern Orthodoxy. In relation to this, Kallistos Ware quotes Professor J. Erickson with approval: 'We must admit quite simply: while the Fathers have blessed us with a multifaceted yet coherent teaching on the priesthood, they have not given us a complete and altogether satisfactory answer to the question of the ordination of women.'[8]

The significance of this observation about the position of the early Fathers is that it invites closer examination of the most clearly articulated Roman Catholic argument against the admission of women to ministerial priesthood. For the argument 'from the weight of tradition' was originally of quite decisive importance in the Roman Catholic Church's negative assessment of the question. After the initial examination of the relevant biblical material by the Pontifical Biblical Commission in the 1970s failed to produce conclusive results in relation to the ordination of women, the argument in the Roman Catholic Church has tended to revert to an appeal to tradition. The Vatican Declaration on the Admission of Women to Ministerial Priesthood, *Inter Insignores*, contended that, despite the inconclusiveness of the New Testament material, the weight of tradition is against women's ordination. This Declaration remains the most authoritative statement of the Roman Catholic Church on the question of the ordination of women.

Unfortunately *Inter Insignores* was issued by the Sacred Congregation for the Doctrine of the Faith on 15 October 1976, but it was not officially published until early in 1977, after the first ordinations of Anglican women in the United States of America had occurred, and thus could not be assessed prior to this decisive Anglican action. There had, however, been extensive Anglican–Roman Catholic dialogue within the United States of America which left Anglicans thinking that the Roman Catholic view was that they would be 'esteemed the more' if they did what they, in the end, themselves thought to be right. It may well have been that Roman Catholics in the United States were more open to the possible admission of women to ministerial priesthood than Vatican authority turned out to be.

Since its publication, the argument of the Vatican Declaration has been submitted to careful scrutiny. When it speaks of the 'weight of tradition' it does not just mean that nothing can happen in the life of the Church for the first time, or that the Pope is a prisoner of the past to the point where it is impossible for him to sanction anything new. Though it may be difficult for a Pope to reverse the decision of a predecessor, given that the aura of infallibility attaching to papal teaching would be seriously weakened, there is more hanging on the appeal to the weight of tradition than a simple surrender to inertia because something has not happened before. When it is said that the weight of tradition is against the admission of women to ministerial priesthood what is meant is that there is an ancient theological tradition clearly articulated by the early Fathers which positively speaks against the possibility of such a development. Given the acknowledgment of the ambiguity and inconclusiveness of the arguments based on the New Testament material that has been noted above, it therefore becomes important to examine this alleged theological tradition.

When *Inter Insignores* is actually consulted, the evidence of the existence of such a considered theological tradition amongst the early Fathers is confined to a footnote. Footnote 7 of the

Declaration says that 'A few heretical sects in the first centuries, especially Gnostic ones, entrusted the exercise of the priestly ministry to women: this innovation was immediately noted and condemned by the Fathers, who considered it unacceptable in the Church.' Then references are provided to a number of texts of the early Fathers. Michael Slusser, in an article entitled 'Fathers and Priestesses: Footnotes to the Roman Declaration',[9] has examined them in detail, though little international or interdenominational attention has been paid to Slusser's work. We may profitably look at them in turn.

First, Irenaeus of Lyons, writing around 180 AD, refers to a Gnostic magician named Mark who is said to have pretended to consecrate cups of wine 'and drawing out the prayer to great length' he was able to make them appear purple and red. But then he apparently gave the cups to women and ordered them to consecrate them. Then he is said to have poured wine from a smaller cup into the larger ones held by the women until they overflowed, thus driving the miserable women mad.[10] Clearly, this case has nothing to do with ordained women in ministry in the Church. It is a reference to some alleged miracle-working of a confidence trickster at the expense of gullible women. There is no suggestion that these women were ordained or purported to have been ordained to the priesthood of the Church.

The second reference is to the condemnation by Tertullian, not of women in ministry, but of a total lack discipline amongst Gnostics, to which reference was made in Chapter 6. This passage is not about the ordination of women so much as about the lack of good order in the assemblies of these Gnostic sects; it bears repeating:

> First, it is unclear who is a catechumen and who one of the faithful; they all come, listen, and pray on the same footing. Even if pagans should come they throw what is holy to the dogs and pearls (fake ones, however!) before swine. They want 'simplicity' to overturn discipline, our care for which they term pedantry. They exchange the peace with everyone ... for it does not bother them that they all disagree with each other, so long as they are conspiring to fight the one truth. They are all puffed up; they all promise knowledge. The

catechumens are 'perfect' before they are instructed. The heretical women themselves, how shameless! They dare to teach, argue, exorcise, promise healings, perhaps even baptize. Their ordinations are reckless, trivialised, and inconsistent: one time they install neophytes, another time those enmeshed in the world, then even our apostates, so that they may bind them with honours since they could not be bound by the truth. Never is it easier to get ahead than in the camp of the rebels, where just to be there is to merit honours! So one is bishop today, another tomorrow; he who is deacon today will be reader tomorrow; today's presbyter will be tomorrow's layman (for they entrust priestly functions even to the laity).[11]

Clearly, as Michael Slusser points out, there is no accusation concerning the ordination of women in this passage; nor is there any suggestion that women celebrate the Eucharist, or that they exercise priestly ministry. Rather, it is precisely the lack of ordination and good discipline amongst the Gnostics that is complained about by Tertullian.

Firmilian of Caesarea, in the third reference cited by the Declaration,[12] speaks in a letter to Cyprian of a possessed woman who claimed the power to cause earthquakes. But she also pretended to exercise priestly functions using authorised Church texts. She is not ordained, and when Firmilian rejects her baptism as invalid he does not give her sex as the reason, but the fact that those whom she baptised had already been baptised by a demon who was said to have possessed her. This is hardly a considered expression of viewpoint about the possibility of ordained women ministering in the Catholic Church, but a passing reference to a demon-possessed unordained woman taking priestly functions to herself.

The fourth reference is to a comment from Origen on Paul's prohibition against women speaking in Church.[13] However, Origen refers not to ordained women and the exercise of priestly functions, but to women prophetesses in Phrygia in the late second century. Irenaeus also referred to these two prophetesses closer to their time but did not condemn them. Instead, he noted that Paul knew both men and women prophetesses. The primary point is, however, that Origen's reference is not to ordained women in priestly ministry.

Then there are three passages from Epiphanius (c. 315–403 AD).[14] The first reference is to a group which followed a woman named Quintilla who had close ties with the Phrygian prophetesses mentioned by Origen. In the gatherings of this group seven virgins dressed in white enter with lamps and 'prophesy' to the people. 'Working up a species of enthusiasm, they dupe the people present and reduce them all to tears, as if bringing about a catharsis of repentance, gushing tears, and lamenting after a fashion over the life of human beings.' Among them are women bishops and women priests, and Epiphanius mentions that they used bread and cheese in their liturgy! This is hardly a reference of the ordination of women in the Church Catholic.

The next group mentioned by Epiphanius are the Collyridians who sacrifice a little cake in the name of the ever-Virgin Mary and celebrate to her name. Once again this is clearly a reference to a deviant practice, rather than a considered reference to the possibility of the regular ordination of women in the Church.

Of all the references cited by the Declaration only these of Epiphanius really refer to ordained women, but his complaint is more about the worship of Mary and about strange and irregular practices than about the gender of women in the regular ministry of the Church.

On the basis of these references it would be very difficult to sustain an argument to the effect that the early Fathers of the Church seriously considered the possibility of the ordination of women to ministerial priesthood in the Church and decided against it. The references cited in the Vatican Declaration actually refer to bizarre and deviant practices in irregular and identifiable Gnostic sects. Certainly, it would be very difficult to sustain the contention that the 'unanimous consent' of the Fathers was that the possibility of ordination of women to the priesthood, having been seriously considered, was rejected. It seems more likely that the non-involvement of women in ordained ministry was more a matter of unquestioned presumption in patriarchal society. Given that men would almost automatically occupy places of leadership, the possibility of the ordination of women to ministerial priesthood was a matter that was not really seriously considered.

† † †

The same presupposed patriarchalism is almost certainly reflected in the most popular conservative evangelical argument against the ordination of women. This is the so called headship argument, which contends that, as a matter of the divine will, males are always to be accorded a status over women. Proponents of this argument, such as Canon Broughton Knox, have claimed that this is not 'culturally originated'; rather, 'headship and its concomitant of subordination is a principle on which creation has been brought into being'.[15] Thus, in I Corinthians 11:3 Paul is said to establish a principle of subordination when he says that 'The head of every man is Christ, the head of a woman is her husband/man, and the head of Christ is God'. It is said that Paul supports this contention by reference to some features of the Creation narrative in Genesis 2. In other words, because this principle is said to be grounded in the Creation narrative of Genesis it is not culturally conditioned! Rather, these are 'divinely inspired expressions in the culture of the time of the unchanging relationship between man and woman'.[16] An alleged unchanging principle of the man–woman relationship is thus said not to be a reflection of the patriarchal social arrangement of the age which produced the Creation stories of Genesis, but a matter of the unchanging divine moral will for men and women of every time and place. This is said to be something that 'God's word makes clear'.

Canon Broughton Knox's argument rests upon some presupposed assumptions about the nature of the Genesis texts and the way they should be read. These are little more than arbitrary assertions. One only has to sample some of the plethora of commentaries on I Corinthians to know that it is really a bit of wishful thinking on the part of Broughton Knox to think that there is a clear meaning to be read from Paul's appeal to Genesis in I Corinthians 11:2–16. Indeed, there must be few biblical concepts that are less multivalent than 'headship'. Anthony Thiselton's recent work, for example, contains an exhaustive discussion of the possible meanings of Paul's use of the metaphor of the head.[17] Indeed, it is precisely because it is a metaphor that a rich diversity of interpretation results in the unpacking of its more literal and prosaic specification. Does 'head' mean 'ruler', 'source', or 'pre-eminence' and 'the foremost'? Some Anglicans may claim a privileged knowledge of the exact meaning of the metaphor of the head, as a kind of a gnostic knowledge of secrets, but the exact meaning of 'headship' is in fact a polymorphous and hence a much discussed matter.

One might also have thought that, apart from the possibility of the cultural conditioning of traditional patriarchalism, the subordinationist perceptions of the divine moral will that are said to be embedded in the statements of the Genesis Creation stories might just be subject to reinterpretation in the light of the Christian hope of the eschatological transformation of the natural created order by grace, and by a consideration of the values of the future dawning Kingdom of Heaven in which 'they do not so much as marry or are given in marriage'. The values of the dawning Kingdom may call for the transformation rather than the sustaining of subordinationist relationships amongst men and women. After all, in the vision of the eschatological future of humanity, all divisions based upon the superiority of one race over another, or one gender over another, or one social class over another, have to be rethought, for, as St Paul himself says, all such human arrangements of the created order are transcended in the eschatological community of the baptised where all are one in Christ (Galatians 3:28). In this sense the Church is the anticipation of the Kingdom, and should already reflect its values.

But even if we set aside such considerations as these, the headship argument fails as a formal argument even on its own terms. In other words, even if the exegetical question of whether there really is an unequivocal indication in the New Testament scriptures that men must in all circumstances and places exercise 'headship' over women is owned, the formal structure of the so-called headship argument fails in internal logical validity and force. In particular, we may ask: is it really valid to argue from a perception of God's alleged eternal moral will and intention for males and females, and how they should relate to one another, to the conclusion that God cannot today be calling women to his service in ministerial priesthood?

First, we have to note a flaw in the pattern of argument which crops up with persistent regularity in expositions of the alleged 'headship' of men over women. This takes the form of an implicit fundamental confusion between the categories of morality and providence, and between the human responses of moral duty and vocation. Let me explain this confusion by clarifying these terms.

Those who find the headship argument attractive contend that there is revealed in certain passages of scripture a 'natural order' which governs male-female behaviour and relationships. I Corinthians 11:3 is one of them. This is said to express the original will and intention of God at Creation and to require, as a matter of unalterable divine will, that only men should exercise a role of leadership both in the natural family and in the Christian community. When it is said that males are meant to be head of their wives, it means that ultimate authority in decision making in the natural family is theirs and that male priests are to exercise some kind of authority, even if it is responsible and loving, over women disciples of Christ in the family of the Church. Because our understanding of both priesthood and the oversight of *episcope* implicitly draws upon these capacities of leadership of the natural male leaders of society, it is argued that priesthood should likewise always remain an all-male affair.

Now, it may certainly be argued that God had a specific intention when he created the universe. In particular, God may legitimately be said to have had a specific will and intention for men and women and how they would relate. This divine will or intention may be said to be reflected in a revealed moral order. For example, in our understanding of the moral order of creation we may say that God intended that men and women would behave or relate to one another in specific ways and that the idea of 'headship' expresses one understanding of the intended relationship. But so does the biblical idea of 'mutual submissiveness' of those whose lives are transformed by saving grace, which seems to be in logical tension with the idea of the headship of one over the other, or the one-way subordination of one to the other. There can therefore be a debate about what God wills or intends for his creation — a debate about the moral norms governing the behaviour of men and women and their relationships. One form of this debate is the discussion of the precise meaning of the concept of the 'head'. Whatever the outcome of this debate, we are obliged to affirm that the moral order which we are seeking to define relates to generic groups and that it is unchanging, for what we are seeking to define is understood to be the original intention of God as it applies to all men and women at all times and places.

However, it is important to note that God's will is not limited to our understanding of his unchanging moral will (whatever its precise terms) for generic groups. In the Christian understanding of things, God also acts in history. He is creator; but he also acts within his creation. Apart from his original intention for generic groups, Christians believe he has a specific will for particular individuals at particular times and places. In an individual's awareness this finds expression in his or her sense of vocation. It may be God's general intention that men and women should settle down and live together as families and raise children. But this does not prevent God, in a specific set of circumstances, to call somebody to forsake family life and to go alone as a missionary to Africa. This specific will of God for individuals is distinguishable from the fixed nature of God's will for generic groups such as he may be said to have had in mind when he first created them. This is not a general moral will but a providential will, for it relates to history and what God intends for individuals in specific historical circumstances.

It may also be argued, for example, that God wills all people to be saved, and to live happily and peaceably together. That is a statement of God's general will. But, providentially speaking, we have to contend with evil and sometimes the evil happenings of history appear to be at variance with our perception of God's general will and intention. This is why Christians have to wrestle with 'the problem of evil'. The occurrences of this world which God in his providence *permits* may seem to be at odds with our understanding of God's original will for humankind as we discern it in the moral order of creation.

This should alert us to the truth that what God intends for humankind generally and what he intends for you and me right now under the circumstances of the present are two quite different things. One has to do with the moral order; the other with vocation. It is the moral duty of all to live peaceably; but it may be my specific vocation in a specific set of historical circumstances to go to war, while that may not be another person's vocation elsewhere in the world. Morality and providence, moral duty and vocation delineate two quite different areas of discourse. We should beware not to confuse them and take care not to slip promiscuously from one to the other.

Now, having made these distinctions, the next question is: is God inhibited in the exercise of his providential will by his general moral will? This seems to be the basic thrust of the headship argument. It is alleged that God cannot call a woman to the specific vocation of priesthood or episcopate because of a dominically (divinely) expressed or endorsed intention about the moral relation between men and women generally (e.g. in I Corinthians 11:3 or in I Timothy 2). Is God inhibited from calling a woman to a ministry of service and leadership in the Church because of a specific view about God's alleged original moral will for all men and women?

The answer to this question must be 'no'. For an affirmative answer to this question would suggest that God is somehow bound to act according to some fixed and uniform pattern *at all times and in all ages*. Such a contention would deny God's freedom to act providentially in history. For in the Christian view, God does not act out of necessity, but out of a free decision of will. He is, by definition, not limited. Not even the moral necessity implicit in a specific perception of his general will and intention in creation can inhibit or eliminate the exercise of his providential will. Indeed, whatever God wills is good, not vice versa. He is not obliged to will whatever is already understood by us humans to be good.

The evangelical Anglican moral theologian Oliver O'Donovan, in his excellent study of the basis of moral norms, *Resurrection and Moral Order*,[18] looks at the example of Abraham taking Hagar and producing a child. Here it could be argued God acted permissively, in accordance with his providential will, as a concession to Abraham the individual, in his particular historical and cultural circumstances. The episode involving Hagar was part of the working out of Abraham's individual vocation. But it would be a grave mistake to argue that the taking of concubines is good for all men at all times. We must not slide unwittingly from vocational discourse to moral discourse. God's specific providential will is not to be confused with his general moral will for humankind as a whole. Or to say that God's moral will is that men and women should marry and live together and then have children does not mean that it was not open to God to call Mary to conceive a child and bear the incarnate Son prior to her marriage. This is why it would not be true to the Christian's view of God to say that because God has a moral will or general intention for all men and women, he cannot freely choose to call particular individuals to a specific vocation in history.

In other words, what applies to humankind generally (morality and the obligations of duty) and what applies to individuals (providence and vocation) cannot be mixed up. We cannot slide from one to the other without being aware that we are moving between different areas of discourse.

Even if God has a moral intention for men and women in general, or as a whole, that does not inhibit or deny God's freedom to choose to call individual women to ministry should that be his providential will at a particular moment of history and in a particular set of circumstances. This could be argued to be providentially the case, for example, in the post-patriarchal age when women are educated and also able to control their fertility. To argue that God's moral will is fixed, so as to deny the divine capacity to act providentially with respect to individuals and their vocations in changing historical circumstances, is to deny the sovereign freedom of God to act other than the same way all the time.[19] Those who appeal to the 'headship' argument are in the unfortunate position of implying that God is not free to do a new thing. This is quite simply not the Christian view of God (cf. Isaiah 43:19).

Our God is a God of surprises. He does not simply repeat himself. It lies within his providential will to act contrary to moral expectation. That is part of his sovereign freedom precisely as God. To deny this is to deny the Christian view of God, though it should be said that God is also consistent, faithful and reliable, and that any new thing will probably be an expansion of our former perception of his will and intention rather than a complete reversal or denial of it.

On the other hand, our expanded perception of God as we experience his providential activity amongst us may lead us to a new and clearer understanding of his general moral will and intention in creating us all. Provided that we do not confuse these two areas of discourse, the one can be brought to bear upon the other.

Once again, Oliver O'Donovan provides us with an example. Once it was thought that it was God's general will and intention that a human individual would have two parents, one male and the other female. However, new advances in bioengineering have made it possible for an individual to have three parents — a mother, a genetic father and a social or adoptive father. What has occurred in the providence of God has allowed us to expand hitherto accepted views of what is involved in parenthood and the different ways in which a child may relate to parents.

It therefore cannot be validly argued that God is somehow inhibited from calling women to ministerial priesthood on the basis of our human perception of his moral will for men and women at Creation. This itself is an ever-expanding area of knowledge rather than some inhibiting and restricting gag on God, for God must ever retain his freedom to act providentially as he wills.

To return to the stories of Genesis, this means that, even if we for the sake of the argument concede that a perception of God's general moral will about how men and women should relate is expressed in the Creation stories of Genesis, in terms of formal argument this cannot ground a conclusion about God's providential will for specific people in particular historical times and circumstances. Though we cannot assume that Paul is consciously aware of this, it explains why he is able dialectically to hold together a gender-distinctive creation order along with the Gospel's call to reciprocity and mutuality. As the New Testament scholar Judith Gundry-Volf says in relation to the interpretation of I Corinthians 11:2–16, Paul appeals 'to creation to support instructions which presume a hierarchical relationship of man and woman as well as undergird their new social equality in Christ without denying their difference.'[20] What Gundry-Volf may not have noticed is that there is a fundamental difference between God's general moral will/duty and God's providential will/vocation. We must conclude, therefore, that in terms of formal argument the so-called headship argument fails to make it to weigh-in.

† † †

Finally, the view that women cannot be ordained to positions of leadership of the kind attaching to ministerial priesthood or the episcopate because God's alleged moral will is said to be against it, has been defended by appeal to the doctrine of the Trinity. The chain of superior to inferior beings, which is suggested by Paul's words in I Corinthians 11:3, when he is understood to speak of the subordination of men to Christ and of women to men, is said to be of a piece with the subordinate nature of Christ's relation to God the Father, and to reflect an eternal state of divine affairs. In other words, the claim that there is a relationship of superiority and inferiority between human persons on earth is said to be reinforced by an understanding of the internal relatedness of the three persons of the Trinity. Astonishingly, Dr Broughton Knox argued in 1977 that Jesus *is* subordinate to the Father. He quotes as a kind of proof text John 14:28: 'The Father is greater than I.' The apparent and undisputed functional subordination of the incarnate Jesus to God the Father in the course of his historical life on earth is then projected back into the eternal relation of the Father to the Son within the internal life of the Trinity. The alleged eternal subordination of the Son to the Father is, in turn, said to establish a normative pattern of interpersonal relationships. It is then held that this justifies the maintenance of an analogical relationship of superiority and inferiority of a permanent and unalterable kind between men and women. This is said to debar women from occupying places of leadership both in families and in Christian communities.

This pattern of argument has been endorsed by the Doctrine Commission of the Diocese of Sydney in a report[21] prepared in 1999 in response to a question about whether the traditional and orthodox Trinitarian belief in the *equality* of the persons of the Trinity entails a principle of equality amongst people of different gender in the Church. The conclusion of the Commission was that, even in post-patriarchal situations in which women are educated and appear to be equally as gifted and capable as men, and can control their fertility and are thus less constrained from entering the workforce, the role of the leadership of the Christian community is not open to them because of the alleged essential inferiority of women to men which is rooted in the doctrine of the Trinity.

There are a number of points one might take issue with in this report. First, the idea of reading back the functional subordination of the Son in his historical life as servant of others to the pre-existing life of the second person of the Trinity leads the Sydney theologians into pushing what is true of created time back into the timeless eternity of God. What is said to be true of the incarnate Son within the finite time of the created order is said therefore to be true 'as far as revelation permits us to see in any temporal direction' including 'from before creation'. Even if we pass over this suggestion of an alleged time before the creation of time, the report goes on to argue that the Son is 'incapable of doing other than his Father's will'. Subordination is not a matter of the freedom of the will. It is not that the Son freely and willingly offers perfect obedience to the Father. Rather, the response of loving obedience of the Son to the Father is portrayed as a mechanical and enforced, even automatic or programmed response. This is somehow said to be 'true freedom'! For example, the report argues that 'true freedom is enjoyed when a perfectly good person delights in doing good'. So it seems the eternal subordination of the Son means that the response of loving obedience to the Father is 'imposed by the inner reality of personhood'. One might have thought that love is, by definition, a genuinely free offering of oneself to another, and that the unity of the Trinity had to do, not with a set of enforced or coerced responses between persons, which would assimilate love to duty, but with free responses of mutual self-gift. One would also have thought that by the observation of a person's good deeds we might come to the judgment that the person concerned was, dispositionally speaking, a good person. But the Sydney theologians start with the static ontological idea of a good person who can do no other than goodness. This compulsive behaviour is then called freedom! It is as though the incarnate Jesus of historical time could not have sinned and that temptation was not real for him at all. How truly human such a Jesus would have been is open to question. Indeed, it is hard to see that this is not a form of the ancient heresy of Docetism.[22] For while Jesus *appears* to be a man he is said to be unable to sin because he cannot freely chose to do so. And how could such a Jesus really be tempted as we are?

In any event, in quoting the text 'The Father is greater than I' to ground and warrant a form of subordinationism, Canon Broughton Knox failed to note and draw out some of the implications of some other equally relevant scriptural texts. Indeed, his use of scripture is an all too atomistic one, which handles the interpretation of individual texts in an isolated way which fails to take account of the fact that a whole narrative and not just a single text may be the unit of meaning. Thus he does not hold texts that are in tension together, which involve some kind of paradox or dialectical reciprosity between apparently conflicting statements. Of these, the statements 'The Father is greater than I' and 'The Father and I are one' constitute a good example. It is not appropriate to interpret either one of these in a way that conflicts with the other; rather they must be held together so as to communicate a meaning to which both equally contribute. Certainly, the classical doctrine of the Trinity is the outcome of what John and Paul, particularly amongst the New Testament writers, begin to unfold in the rich texture of a number of interrelated scriptural texts, which speak of a balance between the distinctiveness of the divine persons, and reciprocity and one-ness between them.

Amongst a number of important texts which should be taken into account to inform the doctrine of the Trinity, we shall look at just three. The first of these is 'The Father and I are one' (John 10:30). The second is 'Whoever has seen me has seen the Father' (John 14:9). And the third, the Christological hymn quoted by Paul in Philippians 2:5–11.

Firstly, it is on the basis of the affirmation of the unity of Father and the Son in such texts as John 10:30 that the orthodox Christian doctrine of God holds that the Son and Holy Spirit are in fact not subordinates to the Father but equals. They do not relate as inferiors to a superior. Rather, they relate together as identifiable persons of equal divinity and status. All are equally to be worshipped as Lord. Indeed, to subordinate the Son to the Father from all eternity, and to fail to recognise their essential equality as persons of the same status and dignity in one unity of being, is to fall into the ancient heresy of

Arianism. Arius (d. 336) championed subordinationist teaching about the person of Christ, by holding that the Son was inferior to the Father. The members of the Doctrine Commission of the Diocese of Sydney seem prepared openly to embrace this heretical position. Indeed, they quote with approval a former Principal of Moore Theological College, T. C. Hammond, who, while trying to hold onto the equal divinity of the Son and the Father, was prepared to abandon their equality of status! He once openly affirmed 'the subordination of the Son and of the Spirit to the Father'.[23]

In the orthodox doctrine of the Trinity, however, the Father may be said to be the *first* person of the Trinity, but not in the sense of a superior to inferiors; rather, the Father is first amongst equals. The Father is the first person of the Trinity in the sense that the Father is the eternal source in different ways of the divinity both of the Son (who is begotten of the Father) and of the Spirit (who proceeds from the Father), and thus is the person from whom the unity of divinity derives. While in the Western Church the idea of the unity of the divine persons was said to reside in their sharing of a common divine substance, which logically if not temporally pre-exists them, in classical Eastern expressions of the social Trinity the unifying element is the person of the Father. Thus, in *Of the Holy Spirit* in 374 AD, Basil of Caesarea spoke not so much of three persons and one substance, but of three persons and one communion. The three are one insofar as they share a common will and a common purpose; what makes them one is a common exchange of love by mutual self-gift.

In the mystery of the Trinity, the coinherence of persons (*perichoresis*) in the Holy Communion of God means that the Father is everything the Son is, except he is not the Son, and the Son is everything the Father is, except he is not the Father, and the Father is everything the Spirit is, except he is not the Spirit, and the Spirit is everything the Father is, except he is not the Father, and so on. The three persons of the Trinity are so intimately related and interdependent as to be and act together in a perfect unity of will and operation. Basil of Caesarea says that the Father finds his own will freely reflected back to himself by the Son, like a reflection in a mirror, and thus speaks of a perfect 'coincidence of willing' within the divine life. When one person acts, the others also act. Like partners in a dance, they move and act together in perfect harmony as one unit. In the mystery of the Trinity the persons are therefore said freely to give themselves to one another so as to be one by mutual self-gift. In this way the persons of the Trinity preserve their individual personal identity, but within a strict equality of personhood in one unity of being. They are thus equal in divinity and equal in status. This is why we cannot speak of equality and subordination in the same breath. As soon as there is talk of the subordination of the Son to the Father the unity of the Godhead is fractured and the first step is taken towards an unacceptable tri-theism — three gods, rather than one.

Secondly, while the incarnate Jesus was in his historical life the humbly obedient and dutiful servant of God, he also claimed to 'show us the Father' (John 14:9). It is the unity and equality of the divine persons that makes this possible. The incarnate Jesus does not reveal a God who is other than he himself is. He certainly does not reveal a God who is the polar opposite to himself, insofar as the Father is said to be superior while he is inferior. Rather, Jesus declares: 'he who has seen me has seen the Father'. In other words, the humble obedience revealed in the historical life and death of the Son *reveals* something of the essential character of God. It is too much to claim, as Kevin Giles does, that the scriptural revelation can be trusted to 'accurately reveal the full truth about the whole triune God'.[24] God remains a mystery, beyond our understanding. But the revelation of God in Christ points us to something quite fundamental about the character of God in Christian understanding.

Thirdly, the way in which the Son reveals the Father can be very clearly seen in Philippians 2:5–11:

> *Let the same mind be in you that was in Christ Jesus, who, though he was in the form of God, did not regard equality with God as something to be exploited, but emptied himself, taking the form of a slave, being born in human likeness. And being found in human form, he humbled himself and became obedient to the point of death—even death on a cross. Therefore God also highly exalted him and gave him the name that is above every name, so that at the name of Jesus every knee should bend, in heaven and on earth*

and under the earth, and every tongue should confess that Jesus Christ is
Lord, to the glory of God the Father.

By way of preface to understanding this text we have to set aside nineteenth-century kenotic[25] views of Christology, which suggest that the pre-existing Son somehow emptied himself of some of the trappings of divinity when he became man, for this unacceptably introduces some kind of change into the Godhead at the Incarnation. It violates the ancient Christological principle in reference to the Incarnation of the Son that 'what he was he remained, what he was not he assumed'. Likewise, we have to set to one side an alternative kenotic view that the humanity assumed by the Son at the Incarnation clothed or concealed a true underlying divinity, as a way of explaining why Jesus came amongst us as a person of apparently limited knowledge, understanding and even power.[26] Once the lens of nineteenth-century kenoticism is removed, we can see that the self-emptying of the Son actually *reveals* the nature of divinity. For the self-emptying or humility of the Son was not just a decision of the pre-existing Son prior to the Incarnation, but a sustained and constant decision of the Son in the entire course of his incarnate human life. The condescension or self-emptying of the Incarnation is not the abandonment of some of the attributes of divinity in heaven in order to become man, but a free determination by the Son *as man* to abandon any tendency to grasp at divinity as humans usually think of divinity — in terms of coercive power and self-glorification. For the message of Paul in Philippians 2 is that, though in the form of God, having become man and 'being found in human form', he did not reckon God-likeness in terms of snatching at equality with God, but humbled himself, taking the form of a servant. Paul is communicating the early Christian contention, in other words, that the incarnate Jesus reckoned God-likeness, not in terms of grasping at power, but in terms of self-emptying, even to the point of being prepared to be elbowed out of this world and to die a humiliating death as a common criminal on the Cross. He lived life in the lowly form of a servant, of which, in the Gospel tradition, the *ikon* of the foot-washing is the most potent sign. We are not talking here of an involuntary or imposed subordination, but of a generous and freely offered or self-sacrificial love.

In this way Jesus' humanity does not conceal but reveals the true nature of divinity, for 'Jesus shows us the Father'. This means that a self-effacing humility is not only true of the incarnate life of the Son, but is true of God*self*. In other words, the *diminuendo* of the humanity of Jesus Christ is the *crescendo* of God, for the lowly humanity of Jesus speaks loudly and clearly of God. It follows that what is revealed in and through the lowly submissive humanity of the incarnate Son is true not just of the Son from all eternity in relation to the Father, but true of all three persons of the Trinity from all eternity. All the persons of the Godhead fully share the same character. Their self-giving is eternally the same, unchanging and steadfast in all respects. And if 'this mind is in us that is in Christ Jesus', it follows that it is Godlike for all, men and women alike, to subordinate themselves in self-effacing and lowly service of one another.

This means, as revealed in Christ, that God-likeness is freely and gladly to subordinate oneself for the good of the other. Just as the servanthood of Christ is towards both men and women, so both men and women must be as servants to one another. The washing of the feet is not just an *ikon* for women to follow in relation to men, but reciprocal.

The significance of the Incarnation was not just that Jesus assumed humanity and came amongst us as a human being, but that he assumed a distinctive kind of human being. For it is not just some general morally inert and neutral humanity that reveals divinity, but the unique and highly particular quality of the human life that Jesus lived, not to mention the death he died, that reveals divinity. The divinity is thus not changed at the Incarnation, but the humanity is assumed as the vehicle of its full revelation. In this way, the ancient Christological principle that at the Incarnation 'what the Second Person was he remained, and what he was not he assumed' is safeguarded.

It has to be admitted that the mystery of the humility of God as revealed in Christ has often been set aside in the Church, particularly as the Church became politically embroiled in the quest for assertiveness and power. A. N. Whitehead once said that 'the brief Galilean vision of humility flickered through the ages, uncertainly ... But the deeper idolatry, of the fashioning of God in the image of the Egyptian, Persian, and Roman imperial rulers, was retained. The Church gave unto God the attributes which belonged exclusively to Caesar'.[27]

The life of lowly service of the incarnate Son does not reveal God the Father as his superior, or as head of Christ in the narrow autocratic sense of 'ruler' or 'authority' over the Son; rather, it reveals the true nature of divinity itself. The life of the lowly service of others is not just something to be isolated and contained within the life and being of the Son alone in his alleged eternal subordination to the Father. Rather, within the unity and equality of persons of the Trinity there will be an equal and mutual submissiveness. This unity and equality of the divine persons in nature and status is therefore both what makes God one and what makes it possible for the Son to 'show us the Father'. The Father no less than the Son also is a self-effacing God, whose presence in the world is mysterious and ambiguous or hidden. Though this is what is regarded as weakness in the world's terms, God is not by nature one who comes down from the Cross in the manner of a Being of coercive force and power, but one who in self-effacing lowliness and meekness operates by love. Likewise, God does not compel our assent, but invites the free giving of ourselves in faith and love.

Now, the alleged chain of superiors to inferiors in I Corinthians 11:3 may reinterpreted from this kind of perspective. The unpacking of the metaphor of the 'head' involves us in a discussion of elements of rule and authority, source, and pre-eminence. As understood by Anthony Thiselton the section of I Corinthians of which Chapter 11 verse 3 is part warrants an emphasis on gender distinctiveness: men are to be men and women are to be women, but all are to be freed from any kind of competitiveness; 'rather the entailments of protection of, and respect for, "the other" hold greater prominence than issues of "authority" within the wholeness of Paul's dialectic'.[28] The rich complexity of Paul's theology does not therefore warrant the view that women should be excluded from ordained ministry because of some kind of alleged innate inferiority, but the view that when in ordained ministry they should relate to others as in Paul's day wives related in humility to husbands, and men were understood to relate to Christ and Christ to God. The primary quality of Christian ministry, in other words, is that of a servant. Not just women, but all Christians should have the same 'mind that was in Christ Jesus' in this sense. We are to humble ourselves and live as servants of others. Christ as the 'head' of every man, is also the servant *par excellence* of every man. God is the 'head' (source, pre-eminent) of Christ, but Christ reveals God's own essential humility, insofar as he did not think of divine status in terms of graspong at power, but, being in human form, he humbled himself and took the role of a servant. This is what the human Jesus actually revealed in history about divinity, not some privileged and highly speculative information about subordination in the inner relations of the divine persons. Christ revealed a quality of divinity that was visibly disclosed in his life and death and that can be put to practical purpose by men and women of faith who, having the mind of Christ, are committed to living by similar values.

It is thus entailed by the revelation of God in Christ that ordained women should act in humility as servants of the community, just as ordained males should also act in the service of the community. All ministry is grounded in the model of Christ the servant. This does not mean that one person cannot be called to lead others; it does mean that when a person leads others he or she must not lord it over others, but act in a spirit of service to those who are led as 'first amongst equals'. There is a kind of hierarchy or 'holy rule' that is expressed both in the Church's thinking about the monarchy of the Father as the source of the divinity and unity of the Son and the Spirit, and in the ministry structures of the Church. This contrasts with an undifferentiated kind of liberal democratic group lacking real leadership and direction. But in both cases the point is that leadership, whether exercised by men or women, should exhibit the moral character of Christ the servant-leader. The fact that the Father is 'first amongst equals' might ground a principle in the life of the Church, by which one person is the identifiable designated leader of others in a functional sense, as also a first amongst equals. How this can be made into a principle that rules out the possibility that a woman priest might minister in a parish community as first amongst equals, or that a woman bishop might minister in a group of priests and lay people in a diocese as first amongst equals is beyond comprehension.

Finally, the contention of the Sydney Doctrine Commission Report that the Son is eternally subordinate to the Father unfortunately calls in question his equal status with the Father as Lord. The Sydney view is, therefore, inimical to the fact that he is worshipped as God. One of the arguments that the early Church used to answer the Arians, who could summon a number of proof texts to support their belief that the Son was inferior to the Father and created by him (notably Proverbs 8.22), was that in the living experience of the life of the Church, Christ was worshipped as Lord and God. The Lordship of the Son is not less than that of the Father. This is the authentic monarchy of the Son. Unfortunately, the subordinationism of the Sydney Doctrine Commission raises a question as to why Christ the Son should be worshipped *as God* at all. We must conclude that the appeal to an alleged eternal subordination of Son to the Father, so as to warrant unalterable forms of subordinationism in human social arrangements, is a piece of special pleading. It is anathema to the doctrine of the essential equality of status of the persons of the Trinity.

The members of the Doctrine Commission of the Diocese of Sydney rightly appeal to the model of interpersonal relationality of God the Holy Trinity to envisage the correct way in which different and distinct persons should relate to one another in the communion of the Church, where all the baptised are 'partakers of the divine nature' (2 Peter 1:4). But this means precisely that to import notions of superiority and inferiority into a set of relationships which should exhibit a fundamental equality of dignity and status within a diversity of function is quite beyond the parameters of Christian orthodoxy. In resolving questions relating to the status of women it is right to appeal to the model of the Trinity of diverse but equal persons, but far from inhibiting women, this really opens the way for them to be admitted to positions of leadership in the Christian fellowship as equals of men. The Christian Church should embrace the possibility of the ordination of women both to ministerial priesthood and to the episcopate without further ado.

CHAPTER 8

DOING THE TRUTH

As we make our way in the world we are currently having to face a range of quite new moral issues which have been thrown up by the advances of modern science. Given that the world, no less than the Church, has not faced them before, and that there are no detailed biblical teachings that provide us with neatly packaged predetermined answers to the questions they raise, we must anticipate some conflict of ideas. The Anglican Church is not immune from the ethical difficulties that the modern scientific world poses to all humanity.

It is not possible within the compass of a single chapter to canvass the full range of issues that is currently exercising our minds. Rather than try to cover a number of moral issues in what would necessarily be a fairly superficial way, it seems better to focus on one interrelated set of issues that has already divided both Christians of different denominations and Christians within a single denomination, and which promise to occupy a good deal of our attention for some time to come. I have therefore chosen to focus on some fundamental issues pertaining to the modern development of high-technology medicine. Over the coming decade, the subject of reproductive technology and the burgeoning field of 'the new genetics' and, in particular, stem cell research, are bound to bulk large in public discussion.

Hopefully, along the way, as we grapple with these issues, it will be possible to provide some glimpses into the way a theologically committed person might operate methodologically. The discussion of a specific set of issues may illustrate a way of handling difficult moral questions more generally, and provide an indication of the way in which Anglicans, in particular, might come to terms with them.

† † †

In the course of a protracted public debate in 2002 about stem cell research, the Australian Federal Government Minister Tony Abbott made a welcome call for more analytical rigour in relation to current moral and ethical debate in this country. As it transpired, the Federal parliamentary debate on stem cell research in August 2002 was reported to be remarkable for the high standard of MPs' contributions. Generally speaking, in the press, and not least in the ecclesiastical press, however, the standard of public debate about stem cell research was disappointing. Christians at least, by and large, stood apart from a tendency of secular press reporting to degenerate into name-calling, but a good deal of what was said, both about the ultimate prospects and hopes of researchers, and about the relative merits of embryonic and adult stem cell research, actually deflected the debate from a careful discussion of the central issue concerning the moral status of the human embryo.

Anglican Media Sydney, for example, projected a negative stance with respect to embryonic stem cell research, by promoting the view that adult stem cell research was to be preferred. It was argued that it would bring benefits at least as great, if not greater than, embryonic stem cell research. Indeed, readers were encouraged by Dr Megan Best, who was identified as a Sydney bioethicist, to beware of practices which were motivated by 'financial motives' rather than genuine medical concern. Financial gain was somewhat gratuitously said 'to be the only way that priority being given to embryonic stem cell research can be explained'. Indeed, Megan Best was reported to have said that the argument that embryonic stem cell research 'could be used for vital research' is flawed because 'advocates are not explaining the step between the research and therapies'.[1] In particular, she thought it important to go beyond the hype to explain 'how long it would take' to make the step between research and therapies, and that human cloning would be required in the process. In a mood of apparent pessimism, she then concluded that the 'huge problems to overcome' raised the question of 'why are we pursuing it at all'. In other words, because hopes for stem cell research may not be realised, scientists should not try to achieve anything at all! Failing to note the basic utilitarianism of her own argument, Dr Best then contrasted 'a utilitarian and scientific perspective' with a clear portrayal of ethical issues!

Surely the Church can do better than just engage in a utilitarian discussion about the relative success rates and benefits of embryonic and adult stem cell research. An almost total concentration on utilitarian issues of this kind, however, meant that the debate in Australia in 2002 became unnecessarily polarised and difficult to resolve. With a little more analytical rigour of the kind Minister Abbott called for, and a little openness to rethink the issues, it might have been possible to cut a more direct path through the bracken.

† † †

All Christians come to this area of discussion with a shared theistic commitment to belief in the existence of God as creator, as against some alternative such as the atheistic belief that nothing made something, or that matter made itself, or that the universe is just a chance conglomeration of random happenings. Christians also come to the debate with a set of first-order moral commitments. Not least amongst these is the fundamental belief that, because God created us as unique human individuals, all human life is sacred, and that the killing of another human being is wrong. This, at least, is common ground amongst us. In relation to this first-order moral principle Dr Best this time rightly observed that even many non-religious people would agree that 'a human being is valuable and should be treated as such'.[2]

But just to cite this widely shared moral principle unfortunately does not immediately solve all our moral problems. For once we move from this shared first-order moral commitment to make judgments of a second-order kind relating to the application of the principle to particular situations, a wide variety of different opinion opens up amongst us. When opinions are in competition with one another, we naturally have to grapple with the question of moral truth, for not every position will be equally justified by appeal to evidence or supported by adequately cogent argument.

Given that we may all agree that human life is sacred, it is understandable that, since the widespread application of human reproductive technologies in the early 1980s, moral debate has been dominated by some interrelated questions relating to the origin of life — such as: when exactly does life begin? or at what point is an embryo to be accorded the status of an individual human being, with rights to care, protection and, indeed, life? These questions arose at the outset because of the destruction of some fertilised ova in the process of medically assisted reproduction procedures. In IVF procedures only some fertilised ova are transferred to the uterus in the hope of achieving a conception while others are discarded. This, rather than a utilitarian argument about success or otherwise of outcomes, raised a fundamental question: to what extent are IVF procedures acceptable at all?

Modern reproductive technologies raised some more detailed moral questions. For example, in the treating of infertile couples by assisted reproduction procedures, the process of fertilisation may be aided so as to allow a sperm and an ovum to 'dock' more easily, as it were. The outer skin, or zona pellucida, of the ovum is sometimes weakened so as to allow a sperm in. In this way fertilisation is helped to occur *in vitro* prior to implantation as the first step in the process of the conception of a human individual. The moral question that arises from this particular procedure is this: in allowing or assisting the sperm to penetrate the zona and to overcome some natural inability to do so (an inability that may not yet be fully understood), are we artificially, by human contrivance, overcoming a barrier that is operating in nature to prevent fertilisation from occurring — and perhaps for some good reason? Perhaps the sperm is not making it, as it were, because it carries some genetic defect that would issue in an inherited disease in the resulting child. In other words, perhaps there is a natural or God-given reason for screening out or not letting in some sperm. Are we running the risk of engineering deformities and inherited diseases by helping overcome a naturally erected barrier? In theological terms, are we unwittingly thwarting the good purpose of God? This concern is not just an idle speculation. While 90 per cent of IVF babies are born without deformities, a recent report of the Children's Medical Research Institute in Perth indicates that deformities are twice as likely in IVF babies than in those resulting from natural reproductive processes (9% as against 4.5%). This, at least, indicates that a degree of added risk attaches to IVF procedures.

This problem is exacerbated by the more recently developed procedure known as ICSI — intracytoplasmic sperm injection. In this procedure, a sperm is first intentionally selected then actually injected right into the ovum. And the moral question attending this procedure is: are we heightening the risk of genetically inherited diseases by providing this ultimate degree of assistance? This procedure has been in use in various parts of the world now for more than a decade, notably in Belgium, and while the figures at first seemed promising, there are now some first studies that suggest a possible increase in birth defects. But, of course, some genetic diseases are late-onset diseases. We will not really know for some years if anything is wrong. So there is an element of risk, and we must try to assess that risk and at the very least monitor experimentation very carefully.

Now, I think these concrete examples illustrate that in this area there is often a certain sense of fear: we *think* of possible negative outcomes, which tend to haunt us. How do we handle such fears? Well, I think it may help first to make a simple logical point. We must recognise that what is logically possible may not be actually possible. In other words, a thinkable risk may not be an actual risk. It is useful here to invoke a basic point of logic. Some things are just not possible as a matter of logic; it is just not possible even to think them without self-contradiction. It is not thinkable, for example, that there could be a bachelor who is also married. But it *is* possible without falling into a self-contradiction to think of a possible risk attaching to medically assisted reproduction. Even so, whether it is an actual risk is an open question, and the degree of risk therefore has to be assessed. Often the assessment of degrees of risk can only be settled by proceeding with caution and by trial and error.

It is very easy to slip, however, from what is thinkable to what is real, so that just by thinking that there may be a risk the conclusion is drawn that the risk is real. The same problem of slipping from logical possibilities to actual possibilities could be observed in the course of the debate that was triggered by the Australian High Court ruling in the Mabo case relating to Native Title. Because it was thinkable that 90 per cent of the backyards of Western Australia might be subject to a claim by virtue of Native Title, some notable politicians jumped to the conclusion that this was an actual possibility. This generated sufficient fear not only to create a climate of hostility towards the High Court itself and towards the whole idea of Native Title, but to trigger a general resentment in the community with regard to Australia's Aboriginal people who were cast in a threatening light. In fact, the extinguishment of Native Title in relation to people's domestic properties by freehold meant that these fears were unjustified. However, despite the fact that most people, by inspecting their title deeds and looking out of their back windows, could easily have allayed their fears experientially, by determining by observation whether or not there was continuous occupation of their backyards by Aboriginal inhabitants of this country, what was thinkable took on a life of its own as though it were actual. Just to have the idea was sufficient to allow some people to jump to a conclusion about reality.

So the logical point is: because something is logically possible, or thinkable, without self-contradiction, it does not mean that it is actually possible. Whether thinkable risks associated with IVF procedures are actual risks or not can only be determined by scientifically assessing the degree of risk that may be involved, and then by proceeding with caution, careful observation, investigation and research. This, after all, is why new drugs are usually first tried on animals, and then subject to human trials, before they are authorised for wider use in the community.

But, given the theoretical or thinkable risks that we imagine might be involved in reproductive technology, and a natural reticence about tampering with nature, as well as the need to weigh the risks, the abiding moral question inevitably arises: do we have a human right of entry to such a field at all? After all, the very first use of the atomic bomb raised the question: should we ever have made it? And the disaster at Chernobyl raised the questions: 'Should we ever have got into the business of trying to generate electricity with nuclear reactors? and will we live to regret it?'

Likewise, some may urge that we should adopt an attitude of conservatism and reverence, like Moses at the burning bush, in relation to our entry into the new world of stem cell research or genetic engineering. Should we not take off our shoes and tread wearily rather than be tempted to rush in where even angels may fear to tread ... into a very sensitive arena, the very beginning of life, with all its unknowable mystery? Are we intruding into an arena which is properly the province of God, the ultimate author of all life? Are we, indeed, usurping the role of God, even playing at being God by creating life ... but also by destroying some life in the process?

Moreover, is modern reproductive technology and genetic engineering not only an intrusion into a sensitive area, but a kind of uncontrollable and stampeding force, driven by an irresistible urge to break new barriers no matter what the cost, and which is out of control and threatening the quality of our humanity? Should not science be controlled? And is it not tending to be confusing to family relationships to have to speak these days of 'social fathers' and 'genetic fathers', and of 'natural mothers' and 'surrogate mothers'? Is all this a kind of dehumanising process, even an ultimately inhuman process?

And is this kind of problem not heightened in the case of tampering with genes? If a gene is the basic unit of inheritance, a particular sequence of DNA coding for the production of specific proteins that are the basis of life, and the index to the highly particular identity of each one of us as a unique individual human being, are we not tampering with the way we have each been 'designed by God', as it were? Or, to use more religiously neutral language, are we inappropriately tampering with the given laws or regularities of nature? And the moral question is: how far should we go in altering or tampering with the biological order of things? Are we on a downward slope towards some technologised but dehumanised form of life?

† † †

In response to this kind of talk, some moral philosophers and theologians argue that, far from being essentially inhuman, the intentional human intervention in reproduction, and even genetic interventions, should be seen fundamentally as a step more towards the physical perfecting of the human, rather than the destruction of the human. Such procedures are therefore to be regarded as pro-human rather than anti-human.

One moral thinker, the American Anglican Joseph Fletcher, argues (if you can forgive the sexist language) that 'man is a maker, and a selector, and a designer, and the more rationally contrived and deliberate anything is, the more human it is'. The Roman Catholic Jesuit theologian Karl Rahner also argued that 'the seemingly limitless capacity of man to experiment on himself is a sign of the creaturely freedom given to him by God'. In other words, God has made us with a capacity to reason that elevates us above all other animals, and this distinctively human endowment is intended to be used. What is willed, chosen, planned for, and rationally controlled is what distinguishes *homo sapiens* from other animals. This seems to suggest that the less random, less open to chance and the more planned and manipulated an activity, the more human, not the less human, does it become.

Though I suspect that most people out in the world tend to think the contrary, Fletcher says that we should be thankful, not fearful, when we reach a point of knowledge that puts us more in control of our destiny. Something of the difference of opinion over this kind of issue can be illustrated in a famous exchange between George Bernard Shaw and G. K. Chesterton. Shaw once commented that, despite the received inclination to place humans at the top of the order of creation by virtue of their superior intelligence, there are good reasons in the modern world for not doing so. For, said Shaw, in the age of automation and all kinds of labour-saving devices, it is now possible to milk a cow without the presence of a human being but never without the presence of a cow! But G. K. Chesterton, who never failed to miss the opportunity to have a go at George Bernard Shaw, said that Shaw had it wrong. Humans are still to be placed above all the other animals in the order of creation, said Chesterton, because it is possible to go up to a man at a bar who has been drinking too many whiskeys and put your hand on his shoulder and say 'Come on, be a man'. In other words, it is possible to appeal to what we call a person's commonsense, the basic sense of reason shared by all humans. But, said Chesterton, you cannot similarly go up to a crocodile who has been eating too many missionaries and put your hand on his shoulder and say 'Come on, be a crocodile'.

Of course, Chesterton was right. Humans are distinguished from all other animals by virtue of their unique ability to reason, to assess evidence and come to a considered conclusion and to act upon it. One of the fundamental religious truths of the Creation myth of Genesis is that humans have been placed at the top of the order of creation with responsibility to tend and perfect the rest of it — to be careful stewards of it. And, while the whole natural creation 'groans in travail', as St Paul says in Romans 8:22, it must be understood to be in the process of being brought to a more perfect state, moving, admittedly in fits and starts, towards the ideal of a more harmonious and peaceful end-time when by the grace of God 'the lamb will lie down with the lion, and the child will play in the adder's den', and there will be no more crying and tears, and all disease and humanly limiting physical imperfection will be done away with. This is the ideal end pictured in the images of the hoped-for perfect reign of harmony and peace of the Kingdom of God.

Indeed, since the Jesuit palaeontologist Teilhard de Chardin brought an evolutionary perspective to the Christian perception of where humans are to be placed in the order of things, we have tended to see the emergence not only of human reason and the human ability to make informed decisions and judgments, but the development of a moral consciousness, as the leading edge of the whole evolutionary process. This means that instead of resisting interventions using human reason in the evolutionary development of humankind, we should welcome them as a part of the process leading to an even higher stage in the order of creation. And instead of usurping the role of God we can understand ourselves to be involved in a cooperative exercise aimed at the elimination of physical defects and diseases and the perfection of all things. The word 'pro-create', after all, means 'to create for' — to create for God. Just as grace perfects nature by helping us humans to deal with sin and to transcend our fallen and imperfect lives in a moral sense, the elimination of inherited diseases, for example, by gene therapy, may also be done in cooperation with God and to the ultimate glory of God. In this case we can place assisted reproduction technology, along with both genetic research and gene therapy, and even stem cell research, in the context of this broadly religious perspective.

Christians should not, therefore, adopt a fundamental attitude of suspicion and fear, let alone condemnation, with respect to the application of human reason and research to the area of human reproduction and the elimination of human imperfection by tackling inherited defects and diseases, either by embryo research or by gene therapy. So the simple answer at this stage to the moral and ethical question of whether we intruding improperly into the province of God is: 'No. We are exercising our God-given abilities to act as stewards, to complete and help perfect the work of creation.'

† † †

However, that said, it is necessary to introduce a qualification. Rational control, it is true, is a distinctive achievement of humans. Whereas other animals are creatures of instinct, humans are able to reflect on their experience, and with language they can process and communicate knowledge and order their affairs both for their individual benefit and for the improvement of the lot of human society as a whole. Nevertheless, unfortunately not all human rational activity produces results that we would call beneficial. Humans can use their capacity to reason in inhuman ways: one can with deliberation and control do the most inhuman of things. Deliberation and rationality tell us only that a human being is acting, not that he or she is acting in the best interests of him or herself or of society.

From a Christian perspective the category of sin also reminds us of this, for, by definition, sin is a deliberate, rational, human choice of acts, either of commission or omission, that may be inhuman or anti-human and contrary to the will of God. Rational control clearly is not the guarantor of humane choices, but only the condition of their possibility: we can rationally and intentionally do what is right; but unfortunately we can also as easily do what is wrong.

This means that we need to bring to the developing world of human reproductive technology, embryo research and genetic research a set of criteria for determining what may be thought admissible, and for judging what would best be avoided. We must therefore address the question of whether reproductive and research procedures that involve the discarding or sacrifice of fertilised ova, whether in the process of achieving a successful pregnancy, or achieving some advance in genetic therapy, or perhaps for the purpose of harvesting stem cells, are acceptable at all.

It is at this point that the question of when a human life actually begins becomes crucial. It impacts on the question of whether IVF procedures are to be contenanced at all, given that some fertilised ova may be discarded once the choice is made about which to implant. Likewise, when fertilised ova are frozen for future use, legislation usually imposes a time limit on keeping them, after which they must be destroyed. In the area of stem cell research on embryos, the harvesting of stem cells results in the destruction of the blastocyst. In all these areas the question of when precisely a human life may be said to have begun, or when an embryo is to be accorded the status of an individual human being with legal rights to protection and care, becomes absolutely and literally vital.

Christians should not be confused about the fundamental moral principle of bioethics — the respect for human life and the derivative duty of the protection and preservation of human life. But the pressing question is: when exactly is the embryo to be accorded the status of an individual human person for whom these basic rights may be claimed?

† † †

When IVF procedures first came under scrutiny in the 1980s and we began to grapple with the difficulty of this question, there was an understandable human tendency to retreat into humour. Humans regularly seek to deflect the discomfort of an apparently difficult situation with humour. A story began to circulate about the different responses of a Roman Catholic priest, a Uniting Church minister and an Anglican priest to the question of when life begins. 'Life begins,' said the Roman Catholic priest, 'at the moment of conception. When the egg is fertilised by the sperm; that is when life begins.' The Uniting Church minister said: 'No. Life begins at quickening, around the eighteenth to twentieth week of a first pregnancy or around the sixteenth week of a second or later pregnancy. When the child in the womb begins to move and is felt to move, that's when life may be said to begin.' And then the Anglican priest had his say: 'No. You are both wrong. Life begins when the last of the children leaves home and the dog dies!'

This whimsy is an indication that the answer to this kind of question may be difficult to discern. To try and answer the question of when life begins is a little like trying to answer the question of when middle age begins. In one sense life does not begin at fertilisation since spermatozoa and oocytes are already alive in advance of fertilisation; they are living cells and spermatozoa, in particular, display great activity. A genetically novel kind of human cell comes into existence at fertilisation. We rightly speak therefore in an adjectival sense of *human* sperm and *human* ova or of a *human* blastocyst, just as we speak of *human* hair. But the crucial question is: at what point should a new creation of this kind be accorded the substantive status of a human *individual* or a human *subject*?

Certainly the most vocal opposition, first to the procedure of in-vitro fertilisation and more recently to research on embryos, including stem cell research, has come from those who recognise that the highest value must be accorded to the 'individual human person' and that the human embryo must be accorded this status from what is usually referred to as the 'moment of conception'. For example, the Roman Catholic position is stated clearly in the Catholic Catechism: 'Human life must be respected and protected absolutely from the moment of conception.'[3] Once the embryo is accorded the status of an 'individual human person', the loss and destruction of unwanted fertilised ova, the freezing and eventual destruction of embryos, the possibility of scientific experimentation involving their ultimate destruction, then assume an enormous moral problem because every human life is sacred.

At the outset a fundamental objection may therefore be expressed about IVF on the grounds of the possible harm, loss or destruction of 'newly conceived human beings'. Such objections are based on the assumption that the status of a conceived human individual with rights to care, protection and life dates from the moment of fertilisation of an ovum by a sperm.

Dr Daniel Overduin and Father John Fleming thus, somewhat unthinkingly, identify fertilisation with human conception: 'We are human from the moment of conception (fertilisation) ...'[4] But this raises the important question of whether what is grown in the glass dish to eight or sixteen cell stage is rightly described as a 'newly conceived human being'? Are fertilisation and conception in fact the same thing?

This is also the starting assumption of the Roman Catholic Archbishop of Sydney, Dr George Pell. In an article published in *The Australian* on 22 August 2001 provocatively entitled 'Another Lamb to Slaughter', Dr Pell spoke of human embryos, despite their minuscule size, not just as human in an adjectival sense but as 'human subjects' which are destroyed in the processes of embryo research. This expresses the received teaching of the Roman Catholic magisterium. During the Sunday Angelus on 3 February 2002, Pope John Paul II likewise said that science had demonstrated that we have a human individual with its own identity from the moment of fertilisation. This alleged scientific fact was said to have been supported by twelve professors from teaching faculties of medicine and surgery at five different universities in Rome. This raises essentially the same question: is a fertilised ovum rightly regarded as 'a human subject'?

It is probably not a coincidence that this language of 'human subjects' was again used when Dr George Pell and his Anglican counterpart in Sydney, Dr Peter Jensen, plus a number of other church leaders responded to the announcement of proposed New South Wales legislation to permit stem cell research. This followed the publication of the Report of the Commonwealth House of Representatives Legal and Constitutional Affairs Committee known as the Andrews Report. The New South Wales bishops' response, which was critical of the fact that their State's proposed legislation seemed designed to cut across the Andrews Report, assumed that the production of embryos for stem cell research would involve 'the manufacture of a new race of laboratory humans'. Indeed, the blastocyst was said to need parents or guardians concerned 'to protect his or her own interests'!

Those who argue that from the moment of fertilisation it is possible to affirm that a unique human individual has been conceived follow a teaching that originates with Pope Pius IX in 1869. Pius IX declared excommunicate all who procured abortion 'without distinction as to the method, direct or indirect, intentional or involuntary, or as to the gestational age of the fetus whether it were formed or unformed, animate or inanimate'. The Roman Catholic position since 1869 has therefore been that the destruction of life at all stages of pregnancy from the moment of conception is sinful and wrong.

But this has not always been the case. In the Christian tradition prior to 1869 it was commonplace to distinguish at least two distinct stages in the process of human conception. These separate stages are already reflected in the statement of Pius IX that the destruction of life is wrong regardless of whether is it 'formed or unformed, animate or inanimate'. The distinction between an animate and an inanimate fetus originated with Aristotle, who thought that the developing human fetus went through a number of stages, from vegetative, to animal, to rational. Christian theologians of the past have also tended to speak in terms of a process of delayed ensoulment, and of the inanimate embryo's being endowed with a human soul by God as an event subsequent to fertilisation. For example, early in the fifth century St Augustine thought of 'ensoulment' as a distinct additional animating act of God at around the forty-sixth day after fertilisation. In the thirteenth century, Thomas Aquinas, following Aristotle, thought that ensoulment happened forty days after fertilisation in the case of males and ninety days after fertilisation in the case of females. The medieval mystic Hildegard of Bingen thought of ensoulment as happening only at the moment of birth, which happens also to be the Jewish position.

Today soul-talk is more likely to be used not to suggest the introduction of a new animating creation as an additional act of God, but as a shorthand way of stating that, from the perspective of faith, at the moment of conception the genetically unique embryo is to be accorded the status of a human individual or a human subject in the eyes of God. As Christians we thus speak of each Christian or human 'soul', or of the loss of so many 'souls' by drowning at sea. However, the point is that different thinkers from Aristotle onwards, including Christian theologians, have tended to distinguish different stages in the development of the embryo.

Theologians of the past have also worked with the distinction between the 'unformed' and the 'formed' fetus. This element in the tradition can be traced back to Exodus 21:22, in the Greek translation of the Hebrew Old Testament known as the Septuagint. This was the version of the Old Testament most commonly used by the New Testament writers and the early Christian Fathers. This particular verse comes from a passage about taking 'an eye for an eye and a tooth for a tooth', and it addresses the question of the penalty to be imposed when somebody strikes and injures a woman who miscarries as a result of her injury. The Septuagint version of Exodus 21:22 provides that if the fetus is formed the penalty is death; if the fetus is not yet so formed as to be a copy or image of the human form, then the penalty is a fine. This text has been very influential in the moral tradition of Western Christianity. For example, St Augustine, writing in Latin, says: 'If what is brought forth is unformed but at this stage some sort of living, shapeless thing, then the law of homicide would not apply, for it could not be said that there was a living soul in that body, for it lacks all sense, if it be such as not yet formed and therefore not yet endowed with its senses.'[5]

In this way Christians have sought, using the best scientific information available to them at the time, to distinguish stages in fetal development, and to accord the status of an individual human being only from animation or ensoulment onwards, with the time variously defined, or by visual observation, from formation in recognisable human form as distinct from the unformed fetus.

In 1869 Puis IX foreclosed on this long history of Christian tradition influenced by Aristotle and Exodus 21:22, by declaring that all abortion was wrong from the beginning of conception, whether animate or inanimate, formed or unformed.

Curiously, at the time of this pronouncement a long-running debate about just how mammals are conceived had yet to be resolved. This was a debate between those known as Animalculists, who, once again following Aristotle, argued that the female provided only the environment for the implantation of all that was necessary for the development of a human individual by the male, and the Ovists, who insisted that the female contributed an ovum that was fertilised by the male. It was only in 1875, six years after Pius IX's declaration, that a Belgian, Edouard van Beneden, first reported the result of his research, that a meeting of gametes, the fertilisation of the egg by the sperm, was definitely how mammalian embryos come into being.

The question we must face today is whether subsequent scientific knowledge about fertilisation and the beginning of life that was certainly not available to Pius IX in 1869 must now also be taken into account. For a start, one signal that what we mean by 'fertilisation' and 'conception' may have to be reviewed is given by the new procedure of cloning by cell nuclear transfer (CNR), where the nucleus of an ovum is removed and replaced by DNA from an adult cell. This is the way the cloned sheep Dolly was conceived. If we define conception simply as the meeting of gametes — in other words, if we think of conception merely as the fertilisation of an ovum by a sperm — we are in the unfortunate position of saying that Dolly was not conceived. This alone should alert us to the fact that our understanding of exactly what we mean by both fertilisation and conception is bound to be conditioned by new discoveries.

Let me put my cards on the table: I think the scientific evidence now indicates quite clearly that 'fertilisation' and 'conception' are not the same thing. In other words, I do not think we can any longer assume that these are synonymous terms. This means that the initial problem with which our community is grappling today is a problem of semantic promiscuity, involving an illicit logical move from talk of 'fertilisation' to talk of 'conception' as though both terms referred to the same thing when they do not.

Given recent advances in the understanding of the development of the embryo, I think it is now clear that we must begin to think of conception less as a *moment* and more in gradual and continuous terms, as a *process*. Fertilisation may be a moment; conception is a process. This process is marked by a great deal of cellular fluidity. The embryonic stem cells are at this stage totipotent: they are uncommitted to any particular path of cell differentiation. Some of these cells may eventually form a fetus, and any of them can become any of around two hundred different kinds of body cells; but others will form a placenta and umbilical cord. This means it is not possible to photograph the early embryo when it is at four- or eight-cell stage and say that is the person at age so-many-days-after-fertilisation; some of those cells will not end up as part of a human person at all.

During the course of the process of conception, which takes some days, the embryo may divide and give rise to identical twins. If we insist that the embryo is endowed with a soul from the moment of fertilisation, are we then, in the case of twinning, to say that one unique individual soul has become two souls? Moreover, I understand from the literature that sometimes the two divided parts of an embryo may reunite in a process termed 'mosaicism'. In this case, instead of identical twins only a single child results. The late Professor A. E. Hellegers wrote: 'Twinning in the human being may occur up to the fourteenth day, when conjoined twins can still be produced. Less well known is the fact that in these first few days the twins or triplets may be recombined into one individual being.'[6] It would thus be logically necessary, according to the view being discussed, to suppose that two souls have united to become a single soul! This should cause us to exercise caution in relation to soul talk — and certainly in relation to the question of whether fertilisation of an ovum can be identified as being synonymous with the conception of a human individual.

What comes into existence at fertilisation has the potential to become a human individual only if a third condition is present. This is its successful implantation in the lining of the womb. It quite simply does not have this potential if it is not implanted. Norman M.

Ford, a Roman Catholic priest and Director of the Caroline Chisholm Centre for Health Ethics in Melbourne, has observed that developmental potential has to be matched by a favourable environment: 'It is to be noted', he says, 'not even adults can realise their potential without nutrition and fluids and the right temperature and environment.'[7] Although a fertilised ovum may possess a unique genetic identity, its genetic make-up will not by itself be sufficient for it to develop into a human individual. No less essential to the process of cell differentiation and growth are signals received from the mother's womb. It is only at implantation at the earliest that we can begin to say that conception has occurred. This begins to happen about seven days after fertilisation, but even here it is necessary to note that implantation is itself a process. During the days when implantation is occurring significant changes occur in the embryo, all of which must be completed before it is possible to say categorically that 'A unique individual has been conceived.'

Andre Hellegers, who was one of seven advisers to Pope Paul VI at the time of the preparation of *Humanae Vitae*, goes on to draw out the logical implications of this scientific information for the present debate:

> All these matters are brought forth to point out that although at fertilization a new genetic package is brought into being, within the confines of one cell, this anatomical fact does not necessarily mean that all this genetic material becomes crucially activated at that point or that irreversible individuality has been achieved.[8]

In an assessment of this, the Roman Catholic moral theologian Bernard Haring concluded: 'The consequence seems obvious: without individualization there is no personalization, that is, there has not yet emerged a human person.'[9] This is now accepted by Norman Ford. 'The fact that the genetic identity of the human individual is formed in the zygote does not mean the human individual is already formed … The first two cells, even if they interact, seem to be distinct cells, entities or ontological individuals and not a single organized two-cell ontological individual.'[10] Clearly, following the fertilisation of an ovum by a sperm a number of things have to occur before it is possible to say that a human individual has been conceived.

† † †

All this is not so new as it may seem. Hellegers was making this information available in theological circles already in 1970. I myself first learned the importance of distinguishing between fertilisation and conception in the mid-1970s from Professor Gordon Dunstan, who at that time taught moral theology and ethics at the University of London.[11] In *The Artifice of Ethics*, Dunstan said with admirable clarity that it 'is hardly apt to speak of a "moment" of conception, Conception is rather a process, beginning with the quick passage of the sperm into the cytoplasm of the ovum and extending surely over the first week of cell division'.[12] Before IVF procedures became a topic of contention, Dunstan, the leading Anglican moral theologian working in the field of medical ethics at the time, used this distinction in discussing the question of abortion after rape. He pointed out that in fact immediately after rape, even if an ovum had been fertilised, no human individual would have yet been conceived. There was therefore no question of talking of abortion. Rather, it was a matter of curettage.

In England, Dunstan contributed to the deliberations of the Committee of Inquiry into Human Fertilisation and Embryology chaired by Dame Mary Warnock. The report of this Committee, known as the Warnock Report, was published in 1984. It made the point that at the time the blastocyst begins to implant, a plate of cells, described as the embryonic disc, is formed between the two cystic spaces within the blastocyst, and within it the first recognisable features of the embryo proper begin to appear. The first of these features is the primitive streak, which appears as:

> ... *a heaping-up of cells at one end of the embryonic disc on the fourteenth or fifteenth day after fertilisation. Two primitive streaks may form in a single embryonic disc at this stage of development. This is the latest stage at which identical twins can occur. The primitive streak is the first of several identifiable features which develop in and from the embryonic disc during the succeeding days, a period of very rapid change in the embryonic*

configuration. By the seventeenth day, the neural groove appears and by the twenty-second to twenty-third day this has developed to become the neural folds, which in turn start to fuse and form the recognisable antecedent of the spinal cord.[13]

In other words, until the blastocyst stage has been reached, the embryo *in vivo* is unattached, floating first in the fallopian tube and then in the uterine cavity. From the sixth to twelfth or thirteenth day, internal development proceeds within the blastocyst while, during the same period, implantation is taking place. Both internal and external processes of development are crucial to the future of the embryo. If implantation does not occur, the blastocyst is lost at or before the next menstrual period; if the inner cell mass does not form within the blastocyst, it does not have the potentiality to develop into a human individual. Given that twinning can occur up to the fourteenth day of this process, it is not logically possible to talk of the conception of a unique human individual (as distinct from the fertilisation of an ovum) prior to the completion of this process. That is to say, the process of conception is a fourteen-day process. Each of us can say that we came to be in the sense that we were each conceived, as a human individual with potential, fourteen days after the fertilisation of an ovum and not before.[14]

† † †

There are, of course, many who unwittingly still follow the 1869 teaching of Pius IX that the human individual is formed from the moment gametes meet, the moment of fertilisation. At the time of the Australian Federal Parliamentary debate on stem cell research, Deputy Prime Minister John Anderson, in a passionate plea for all embryos to be protected,[15] correctly posed the most crucial unresolved question: 'Is there any sound reason for our not regarding each human embryo as a unique human life deserving our care and protection?' Curiously, John Anderson raised this question with apparent candour despite a rather more cavalier assertion earlier in the very same article which purported already to provide a clear answer to it. An individual's life, he said, must be held to start from the moment of fertilisation; 'Any other starting point is arbitrary.' Indeed, he alleged, from this moment onwards 'with time and nourishment' a human subject will grow to maturity.

However, there are some very sound scientific reasons for not according the status of a conceived human individual to a fertilised ovum until the other developments have occurred, which have been outlined above. John Anderson's contention is that a unique configuration of DNA is sufficient to establish that we are dealing with a newly conceived human individual that with 'time and nourishment' will grow to maturity. But this is, to say the least, very problematic. It is true that at the time of the fertilisation of an ovum by a sperm a new and living cell comes into being, with its own unique composition of DNA. A DNA profile is an index to a cell's uniqueness; but the question of human individuation (the achieving of the status of a conceived human individual) rests on additional criteria. After all, a unique DNA profile will be found in cells produced by a swab of the inner mouth. This is obviously not to be confused with the cloning of a human individual! In other words, the presence of a unique DNA profile in a fertilised ovum is a *necessary* but not a *sufficient* criterion for determining whether we are dealing with a conceived human individual.

This is a key point that John Anderson appears to have overlooked. In his speech to Parliament at the opening of the stem cell debate on 20 August 2002, the presence of a unique DNA coding was cited as a sufficient reason for classifying the newly fertilised ovum as 'a distinct human being'. This was said to signify the beginning of 'a new human existence' that is 'complete and equal to any adult'. Any other beginning point was said to be 'of necessity arbitrary'.

But a little more analytic rigour will show that it is these assertions that are scientifically speaking questionable. For the assertion that an individual human being has been conceived does not follow with logical necessity from the assertion of a cell's unique DNA coding. This is why it is important to note that in the early stages of the process of conception embryonic stem cells, though genetically identical, are not committed to any one developmental pathway. Because of the fluidity of the process there is no fixed or predetermined plan for each cell and its multiplying progeny. As we have already noted, some cells will eventually become part of the newly formed human individual, but others continue as extraembryonic membranes and the placenta. It is only at the primitive streak stage at around fourteen days after fertilisation that specific cells become committed to the formation of a multicellular human individual. Norman Ford's judgment is therefore right when he says: 'It seems a human individual and person could not begin before cells of the rudimentary embryonic organism form a distinct ongoing living body at the primitive streak stage ... ' It is only at this point that the embryo is 'animated by a divinely created immaterial life principle'.[16] If we wish to use soul talk, this is the point at which such talk becomes possible, because from this point onwards, but not before, we are able to speak of the conception of a human individual.

† † †

Now, this very fundamental information for the resolving of the moral conflicts involved in in-vitro fertilisation has not been recognised in this country and has been overlooked even in some professional literature. A Report of the Special Committee Appointed by the Queensland Government to Enquire into Laws Relating to Artificial Insemination, In-Vitro Fertilization and other Related Matters, known as the Demack Report, was confused, for example, at this point. After asserting that 'Conception results from the meeting of sufficient numbers of spermatozoa with the ovum ... '[17], the report then noted that at fertilisation:

> ... *usually only one sperm penetrates the corona and the zona pellucida. Once that happens, a reaction begins within the ovum which involves the release of granules within the zona pellucida, thus blocking the entry of other sperm. Enzyme actions produce a series of changes to both gametes and, within eight hours, two pro-nuclei have formed, one from the spermatozoon, the other from the ovum. The joining of these into a single nucleus* completes the conception [my emphasis].[18]

This last sentence discloses that fertilisation is being understood not as a 'moment' but at least as an eight-hour process, which is completed with the joining 'into a single nucleus', yet this process of fertilisation is then assumed to be 'conception'. No argument is offered in defence of this identification of fertilisation and conception. It is simply assumed.

Clearly, this teasing out of current confusion in our language is of the most momentous importance for the resolving of difficulties relating to the practice of IVF, not to mention the more recent development of stem cell research. It is important to note that, methodologically speaking, the question of when the embryo is to be accorded the status of a conceived human individual with rights to protection and care is, in the first instance, a physiological question, not just a theological question. It is certainly not a question which can be arbitrarily decided on the basis of scientific knowledge as it stood in the last quarter of the nineteenth century.

† † †

Once we come to terms with the physiological facts and are in a position to distinguish between the fertilisation of an ovum and the conception of a human individual, a number of troublesome difficulties fall away. First of all, the natural wastage rate of fertilised ova (which is said to be in the order of 60 per cent) because of failure to implant no longer throws up the problem posed by the apparent natural loss of very high numbers of 'conceived human individuals'. We quite simply are not talking of 'conceived human beings' who never see the light of day.

Also, strictly speaking all popular talk of the conception of human individuals in a test tube is incorrect. What occurs in the test tube prior to implantation, while being rightly called fertilisation, is not correctly called conception. What takes place in the test tube is at best the beginning of the process of embryo-genesis; we rightly talk of in-vitro *fertilisation*; it would be incorrect to speak of in-vitro *conception*, and I am gratified that we do not use this construction. We do not refer to IVC!

Just to clinch this argument, it is useful to note that the word *conception* is a translation of the Latin *conceptio*, from the root verb *concipere* which means 'to hold on to' or 'to retain'. It refers to the retaining of the menstrual blood by a pregnant woman. This occurs around day fourteen after fertilisation. This is why it is possible to say both 'a child has been conceived' and 'she conceived and bore a son'. Conception, which is complete at the end of the process of implantation, happens in relation to the woman 'who conceives' at the same time as a child 'is conceived'.

Furthermore, the status of the embryo in the first fourteen days is clearly different from its status with rights of protection and care as a 'conceived human individual' after the fourteen-day process of conception is complete. Though up to fourteen days we are dealing with human genetic material, a pre-embryo or pro-embryo, which as such, should be treated with respect, and certainly not frivolously, the inevitable loss of fertilised ova is not to be regarded as the killing of 'conceived human individuals' or the slaughter of 'human subjects'. Freezing of fertilised ova also seems more congenial once we are clear that we are not dealing with 'newly conceived human individuals'. We just do not have 75,000 frozen people at various places around Australia.

It also follows that growth of cells in the test tube is unlikely to be allowed after fourteen days under Australian law. However, if there is a utilitarian argument for the possible benefit to mankind of experimentation on embryos, this could be tolerated in a controlled way under licence up to that time. Stem cell research seems also permissible, for embryonic stem cells are harvested within the fourteen-day period prior to the completion of the process of conception. We may think of this in terms of a radical form of contraception, but not in terms of killing an already conceived human individual.

It is sometimes said that stem cells obtained from adults or from the umbilical cords of recently born babies could do just as well for medical purposes, and would not involve the destruction of the blastocyst. There are two problems with this. The first is that cells 'remember their age' or bear the stamp of their age. The cloned sheep Dolly was cloned from the cells of an adult sheep. Unfortunately, this means that Dolly was already old and arthritic before her time. It may therefore be very important to harvest stem cells at the earliest possible time.

The second problem is that stem cells obtained from sources other than the embryo may not be totally reliable for research purposes. For example, in order to deal with Parkinson's disease, appropriate adult cells would be hard to find and could require the removal of a section of brain! Cells derived from umbilical cords may not have the potential of embryonic stem cells. It might be possible to reproduce red blood cells from them but not nervous tissue, for example. Whether, after differentiation, blood cells can be 'de-differentiated' and taken back to a plenipotential state so as then to be turned into neural cells is yet to be confirmed, though this claim has been made. As the process of cell differentiation is yet to be fully understood it seems necessary for research to proceed on both embryonic and adult stem cells. The medical need for stem cells will not be answered by harvesting only adult or umbilical cord cells.

† † †

Once we are clearer about what actually happens at conception in physiological terms we can begin to see what ethical norms should be applied. However, we still have considerable work to do on wider questions relating to genetics. What are we to say, for example, about gene therapy and the whole prospect of producing so called 'designer babies'?

Christian moral thinkers tend to think of negative eugenics, on one hand, and of positive eugenics on the other — the first, generally speaking, being acceptable and the second morally dubious. For example, when a desirable therapeutic or corrective outcome is aimed at, such as the elimination or treatment of some inherited disease, this may be referred to as negative eugenics. This is quite a different thing from the use of genetic engineering for the positive outcome of enhancing personality or producing what the media might call 'designer babies' by choosing their sex, the colour of their hair and eyes, and the degree of their intelligence. Generally speaking, if it becomes possible through gene therapy to eliminate the inherited susceptibility to cancer from a particular patient, for example, I think we would all judge that to be good and acceptable. Likewise, in the case of haemophilia, instead of administering a clotting agent to stop bleeding, if it is possible by gene therapy to stimulate the natural production of what is lacking all the better. For in principle, there is very little difference between treating a child for haemophilia with the missing clotting agent known as Factor VIII and supplying the correct gene for the natural production of Factor VIII.

There are many hundreds of genetic diseases that cause very severe disability and/or distressing symptoms, and/or death. Furthermore, no effective conventional therapy exists for many of these conditions, and where some means of treatment is possible it may be burdensome and constant. Given all this a 'single shot' cure with an effective gene therapy would surely be highly desirable. The treatment of genetic disease by correcting defective cells in a culture using DNA transformation techniques and then returning the corrected cells to the diseased individual seems morally unexceptionable. So, from an ethical point of view, such phenotypic therapy, as it is called, raises few problems.

However, there are some moral and ethical concerns relating to germ line therapy. For another possibility seems to be that, instead of seeking to modify defective genes by inserting a gene into body cells (somatic cells), a decision might be taken to seek to alter germ or reproductive cells. In other words, the passing on of inherited diseases might be addressed in such a way as to eliminate the problem once and for all in much the same way that smallpox, to all intents and purposes, has been eliminated from the face of the earth. Instead of treating a patient with an inherited disease, we would be endeavouring to ensure that no further potential patients were actually born, either with an inherited disease or with an ability to pass one on. Strictly speaking this is not so much therapy as a preventative measure.

To some extent this outcome is already attempted through genetic counselling. Couples who risk having a baby with an inherited defect might be warned about it and urged not to try. However, these risks are often statistical. If there is a one-in-four chance of producing a child with such a defect, some couples will hope that their baby will be one of the three in four chances of escaping the defect. It is surprising how often I have heard of tragic cases where the risk is taken with a negative outcome, and then sometimes taken the second time, once again with a negative outcome. Germ line therapy may be a way of avoiding genetically inherited diseases altogether. In such cases, reproductive cells or gametes would be treated right from the very start so as to avoid genetically inherited disease altogether, rather than treat it in a patient long after it has been acquired. One theoretical difficulty at this point is that any damage to a gene as a result of the procedure would also affect the germ cells and would be transmitted to offspring, so the risks attaching to making DNA alterations to reproductive cells or germ cells could be enormous.

Let us suppose, however, that after fertilisation (in vitro) but prior to conception and implantation it were to become possible to inject what may be lacking into a fertilised ovum so that a possible inherited defect is screened out from the start, before the process of cell differentiation and the development of body organs. Then it would follow that the genetic change would be part of the resulting cells and the possible defect would not be passed on to the future generations of the resulting fetus.

The difficulty here is that if fertilised ova could be tested to determine whether there was a need for gene therapy of this kind (if we can call it therapy), then those requiring treatment would be better rejected than treated. In other words, if there is usually, let us say, a one in two or a one in four risk of genetic disease, a 25 per cent risk but not a 100 per cent risk, there will be some fertilised ova that would produce normal babies while others would produce affected babies. In distinguishing which was which before gene therapy could be used, we would in fact eliminate the need for gene therapy. Clearly, it would be a better procedure to select a normal fertilised ovum than by gene therapy to try to correct a defective one. For this reason germ line gene therapy of this kind, while thinkable, does not seem a practical possibility.

The conundrum for us is that in some places experimentation on embryos is not permitted by law. In Western Australia, for example, the *Human Reproductive Technology Act* originally did not permit experimentation even on pre-embryos (zygotes), but only procedures that could be considered therapy. There could be no intention to discard some embryos after testing. Procedures could only be performed with the intention of implantation for the purpose of assisting conception. The possibility of genetic testing of embryos and the choosing of the healthy and discarding the defective was not legally possible. For the reasons that I have already tried to make clear, I think this aspect of the legislation was based on an erroneous set of presuppositions in relation to the status of the embryo at this early stage of its development. Indeed, this legislation seemed to be motivated by the view that it is better not to know and to leave things to nature, by which is meant to leave things to chance. But then, in the course of a pregnancy, if genetic testing is done and it is found that, for example, cystic fibrosis has been acquired, it leaves the couple in the predicament of having to grapple with the possible termination of a pregnancy, which clearly involves a much more difficult ethical decision.

Geneticists often point to the possibility of avoiding the need for gene therapy simply by testing embryos in vitro and only implanting those known not to be affected as one of the great potential benefits that the new genetics will be able to offer couples who live with such risks. Indeed, elsewhere in the world, in Britain for example, this kind of genetic testing is now common.

At the moment the ethical debate about genetic therapy is in its infancy, and we must proceed with as much caution and care as is humanly possible to avoid mistakes. Generally speaking, however, genetic therapy for the replacement of a defective gene in a patient seems acceptable, while germ cell or reproductive cell therapy seems more questionable.

† † †

It might already have been noticed that at the beginning of this discussion on moral issues raised by genetics, I spoke not just of negative eugenics (the elemination of a disease) and positive eugenics (the use of genetic methods to enhance physical features or personality of already healthy individuals) but also of gene *therapy* (where the emphasis is on the elimination of disease) and genetic *engineering* (the enhancement of intellectual or physical characteristics). Somehow the word 'therapy' carries positive and welcome overtones, whereas the term 'engineering' carries a negative and more sinister colouring.

Most geneticists are very quick to point out that what I have called positive eugenics is somewhat fanciful, and certainly not what those involved in the new genetics are currently doing. The possibilities of positive eugenics are said to be 'far off', 'nothing to worry about right now', 'not even so much as in sight, certainly not over the next 30 years', and so on. A positive eugenics is not a part of the current scene and we need to keep our feet realistically on the ground. For example, as I understand it, a genetically inherited disease usually involves a defective member in a single pair of genes. It can be pinned down; the therapy is focused on a single gene. But in the case, let us say, of intelligence, what appears to be involved is not a single gene, but a combination of genetic elements that are far more difficult even to pin down and understand, let alone manipulate, than the single defective gene producing a disease. Many hundreds of genes are likely to be involved in influencing intelligence and personality. Moreover, variations between individuals in each of the many hundreds of genes influencing intelligence and personality are likely to be very subtle, by contrast with the more straightforward all-or-none type of differences that are encountered in genetic diseases. It may be, therefore, that humans will never fully understand the complexities that would be involved in this kind of genetic control.

It is, therefore, much less likely that gene therapy could move in the direction of enhancing normal characteristics such as intelligence, personality, physical features or abilities. Such interventions are not imminent, we are told, because we are nowhere near having the knowledge necessary to know which genes to manipulate.

Nevertheless, even if positive eugenics is not what scientists are currently doing, I suspect the general public will continue to be suspicious and understandably apprehensive about what may be just around the corner. What today is said to be impossible tends to become the possible of tomorrow in the modern world. And given the as yet theoretical and speculative nature of these possibilities, the moral and ethical question may certainly be asked: are there good reasons for not so much as taking a step in the direction of positive eugenics?

Or, to ask the same question in another way: why exactly is it that we can be happy with negative eugenics, involving the elimination of disease by gene therapy, but uncomfortable with anything that might be construed as personality enhancement? After all, either way we could be said to be involved cooperatively with God in the elimination of defects and the perfecting of humanity. If we are cooperatively involved in the perfection of humanity, why not address what might be termed personality defects as much as disease? Why exactly should we not want to improve personalities? Indeed, is not the improvement of personality one of the chief interests of religion? Are we not supposed to become less selfish and more loving, more placid and less aggressive? Why exactly should we be disinclined or discouraged to move towards designer children to eliminate personality defects if that were one day to become possible?

Well, I think that some inherited historical memories may be colouring our perception of what it acceptable and what is not acceptable at this point. Indeed, I suspect that talk of the *new* genetics is meant to distance what is currently being done from any negative connotations that may be associated with the *old genetics* which last century acquired a bad name. The overriding plan of Hitler, for example, was to produce a master race. That horror continues to stalk us. As a consequence, any move in the direction of personality enhancement is seen in an unwelcome light.

Perhaps we need to remember, however, that there are two basic reasons why we are repelled by what Hitler tried to do. First his hope of producing a master race was, in fact, racist. The idea was to produce a master race that would so excel as to dominate the world and keep other races in subjection as second-class citizens. That is perhaps the primary reason why we judge it to be objectionable.

Secondly, the German experimental programs were entirely without the consent of patients, or without their informed consent. In the light of the horror of experimentation on human subjects we are today rightly very conscious of the need for informed consent.

But what would the moral situation be if genetic therapy could be used for personality enhancement in a way that was not racist, was available to everyone, and was only done with the informed consent of subjects? If the overall aim to improve and perfect humanity and make it whole warrants gene therapy to eliminate disease, why should that same aim not warrant the attempt to improve intelligence, or musicality, or incline us to be more peaceable and easy to live with? What really would be wrong with that?

On the other hand, it may not always be easy to distinguish between negative and positive eugenics. For example, what are we to say about the alleged discovery of a so-called 'gay gene' which is sometimes said to trigger homosexuality, making it less a matter of choice than of inheritance? I do not believe that particular reported discovery is a scientifically substantiated outcome of the current human genome project which has mapped some tens of thousands of genetic markers; it may just be media talk. However, if there is something in it, the morally interesting question would be whether at some future point of time parents could choose to eliminate the 'gay gene' if it was found in their recently conceived child. What are we to think about that? Is this negative eugenics or positive eugenics? In other words, is it the elimination of a defect or would we be entering the arena of personality enhancement and control?

There is also a grey area relating to the question of the sex of a child. There is possibly less of an ethical problem regarding sex choice where this comes from the desire to have a child of a particular sex, for example, to lessen sex-linked genetic diseases. When the male is a carrier of an inherited disease, would it be better to decide to have a girl, so as to avoid the problems of the disease? Is it better to change the sex than to terminate the pregnancy and try again? Once again, this is a grey area that we may one day have to address and the question is whether this would be negative or positive eugenics.

To some degree the logic of the word 'perfection' may help us maintain the distinction between negative and positive eugenics. The concept of 'perfection' implies imperfection. One can only perfect what is judged to be less than perfect. So negative eugenics, which aims to eliminate a disease, may be judged to involve the elimination of a defect or imperfection in the interests of achieving perfection or wholeness. But whether a person has blue eyes rather than brown is, morally speaking, neutral. A brown-eyed person is not normally judged to be suffering from a defect or imperfection. Certainly a brown-eyed person is not normally judged to be more or less perfect than one with blue eyes.

So here is a clear criterion for distinguishing negative eugenics from positive. One is concerned with the elimination of what is clearly judged to be a physical defect or imperfection, whereas the other may be seen as idle tampering, a kind of trivial pursuit, genetic alteration rather than genetic therapy. That kind of criterion would not help us, however, where a judgment of degree, such as a level of intelligence, is at issue.

Once again, the fact that genetic alteration for the purpose of enhancement is not currently being done or that it is still 'a long way off' does not mean that we should not anticipate the possibility and think through the moral question of its desirability.

So, why should we not want to move in the direction of positive eugenics, by producing or attempting to produce designer children if that were to become an actual possibility?

The first reason is economic. I suppose Karl Marx will be heard at this point to be saying, 'I told you so'. In any event, surely resources should go to prioritised areas and the elimination of disease and suffering must come at the top of the list. Greater priority is to be given to putting resources into research that will eliminate disease and suffering than to the comparative triviality of personality enhancement.

But, apart from the obvious economic factor, what further reasons might there be for not moving in the direction of a positive eugenics of enhancement? The second reason is that, in general terms, the mentality of positive eugenics could lead to the view that unless a child is absolutely perfect, that is without any defect or disability, then he or she is to be regarded as somehow subhuman. In fact, humans are currently subject to all kinds of defects and imperfections that, generally speaking, do not trouble us. In all of us there are between five and eight mutant genes. This is quite normal. None of us is really perfect in this sense. The question is, should we allow ourselves to be coaxed into the view that this is somehow abnormal by pursuing a search for some kind of absolute designer perfection?

Thirdly, it is simplistic to claim that all questions of behaviour derive from our genetic make-up. Many factors are involved in what makes us what and who we are as persons, and while inherited genetic factors form a part of our make-up, they do not wholly define us. Our moral perfection or the building of a more peaceful world is unlikely to be achieved by genetics alone. There will be environmental, social and cultural factors to be addressed. Religion and morality will at this point surely continue to be crucial.

Fourthly, there are clearly some social problems that appear on the horizon in regard to designer children. The prospect of positive eugenics raises such questions as precisely who would decide what characteristics were to be favoured over others? Who would decide whether physical power was to be elevated over a love of music, for example? Who is to take the blame when a child's behaviour falls below acceptable standards? One can imagine the response: 'Well, it's all your fault, after all, you designed me!' And who would be responsible for mishaps and crimes — the child or the designer parent?

Fifthly, there are the difficulties involved in assessing risks and benefits. There is the danger of introducing further defects through introducing new genetic material and so on. In other words, the design may turn out otherwise than expected. And given the propensity in modern society for patients to sue doctors, would we not be entering a nightmare of litigation, given that children could well turn out a little differently from what parents thought was being designed. Would children themselves sue parents for faulty design?

These are some of the problems that we might anticipate as we consider the very speculative possibility of conceiving a child as the planned creature of another. That is a turning we may prefer not to take at all. Certainly these are all reasons that reinforce the view that the negative eugenics for the elimination of disease and human suffering is clearly one thing. The idea of positive eugenics is quite another. And it is not just that one is currently progressing while the other is not; it is that even what is not yet actually possible but still only thinkable may not be humanly desirable.

† † †

In the space of a single chapter, my purpose has not been to solve all the myriad questions that have arisen in recent years as a result of the advances of high-technology medicine. Rather, I am concerned to illustrate just something of what happens when the world of religious ideas and insights is brought to bear on the world of science and medicine. This is an example of the adequacy of the first-order insights of the biblical revelation for a regulative but not speculative purpose, not that we should know more but that we might do better. The fundamental moral insight that all life is sacred is sufficient for the pragmatic purpose of working out what kind of human behaviour is appropriate in specific circumstances and situations. We end up with a regulative truth. We are able to do the truth (see 3 John 3).

At the same time, what I have tried to do in this chapter is to illustrate the nature of ethical debate based upon what the Bible teaches. In relation to such complex matters as the treatment of human infertility and the question of embryo research and genetic research, we cannot simply go to the Bible for the answers to such questions. There are clearly no answers to these in the Bible. The Bible provides us with some basic first-order principles, such as the principle that all life is sacred, that murder is wrong, that we should love our neighbour, that our neighbour is anybody in need of care and protection, and that all human life must therefore be respected and protected. We then have to bring those principles to bear on specific situations of a highly technical kind. Christian ethics is the art of bringing the moral insights of the biblical revelation to bear on the world as it is, and we have to take time to try and find out by rational inquiry what actually is going on or could possibly in the future go on in the world before any progress in our ethical thinking can be made.

If the Church is to open people up to new possibilities and not automatically close their minds by a painful repetition of traditional positions and formulas, much more dialogue between disciplines appears to be needed. In the area of stem cell research, it is distressing to hear and read of Christian leaders of all denominational persuasions taking set positions on particular issues which often presuppose the uncritical repetition of late nineteenth-century views grounded in the scientific knowledge of that era. With a little more thought and dialogue with contemporary medical science, it could be possible to unravel and clarify issues for the ultimate betterment of humankind.

My suspicion is that the medical world might also be more open to neighbouring disciplines. The most basic methods of ethical argument often seem foreign to many medicos with whom I have discussed such issues as IVF and surrogate motherhood. Indeed, most seem to be at a loss to know where to start to untangle the moral problems that immediately face us. In the course of recent discussion I have found that the most expert medical minds have a very minimal acquaintance with the basic principles and procedures of ethical argument. For example, twenty years ago I was asked for an authoritative ethical or Christian moral opinion on the question of the rightness or wrongness of IVF, as though this might be handed down by fiat from on high or simply plucked from the miasma of abstract thought. And I observed some slightly startled looks when I said 'I can not do that until you tell me exactly what you do and unfold to me your understanding of exactly what happens'. Information gathering is quite essential before the implications of a moral judgment or insight can be discerned. The first-order moral insights of the Christian religion, such as 'all life is sacred' or the 'life of each human individual should be protected', have to be brought into conjunction with the hard facts of a particular circumstance or procedure in order to allow us to articulate the behaviour which will best embody them. Before the ethics can be formulated, there must be dialogue in order to understand as fully as possible what happens. This means that much more interdisciplinary work at the tertiary level should be done in the preparation of people for professional work, and that this should be matched by much more continuing dialogue in clergy–doctor groups. Certainly, the work of establishing moral and ethical norms is an exercise for the whole community, not something that can be left to individual moral choice.

But reproductive technology gives us only a sample of the way in which the world of value impinges upon medical matters. The fact is that modern medicine constantly leads directly into the world of value. Human affairs are never conducted in a value-free vacuum and every medical practice, no matter how trivial, is value laden — for each procedure will implicitly or explicitly express some vision of what is thought to be good or right, and it goes on within the context of a way of viewing the world. It will express virtuous ideals of justice, love and care. It will involve such additional issues as paternalism in dealing with certain communities, attitudes towards the future, cost-benefit analysis and so on.

Unfortunately, we all have finite minds which cannot hope to contain all there is to know. We usually cope with the sheer weight of possible knowledge and learning by familiarising ourselves with a section of it only; we thus tend to inhabit a reasonably self-contained world of ideas. The modern age is therefore the age of specialists; even the GP, as a doctor of primary contact, also specialises in medical matters to the exclusion of other fields of inquiry.

But, given the complexities we face, many of our modern problems can be solved by bringing different worlds of thought together: In the meeting of medicine and moral theology, for example, we stand on the threshold of an exciting new land which few have yet entered. The question facing conservative evangelical or Bible-believing Christians is that, given that there are no ready-made answers in the Bible itself to the moral questions that currently face us in the modern world, will they have anything to say at all in relation to these matters?

CHAPTER 9

LIBERALISM, ECUMENISM AND OTHER RELIGIONS

I said at the beginning that I do not see myself as a liberal Christian. I prefer the description of progressive or dynamic orthodox. Nevertheless, I am well aware that there is a tendency amongst conservative evangelical or Bible-believing Anglicans and Christian fundamentalists to think of most of the rest of the Church as 'liberal'. Thus, the true evangelical Christian is sometimes said to be one who adheres strictly to the Bible and its teachings, while all others are imagined to depart from scriptural norms by adopting more liberal and tolerant attitudes. Within the Anglican Church, Sydney Anglicans sometimes appear to imagine that only they stand for adherence to 'the teachings of the Bible'.

We noted at the outset that Anglicanism is often understood to be a religion of tolerance. It is a church of an extraordinarily inclusive kind which has a unique ability to hold people of a wide diversity of theological and moral viewpoint within its broad and generous embrace. It is a church suited to the times. In today's liberal Western democracies tolerance is a virtue, and intolerance is in very large part viewed as the source of the most of the world's woes. If the world were only a little more tolerant we would avoid the Northern Irelands, and

Bosnias, and the Palestinian West Banks of this world. Could not a peace in Northern Ireland have been won with far less tragedy through just a little religious tolerance; could not peace in the Middle East?

The curious thing is that while we pride ourselves as being a very tolerant, free and liberal society, this is exactly what Islamic people tend to recoil from. In Muslim eyes Western liberal democratic society is so tolerant as to become entirely beyond the pale and, in fact, intolerable to them. Indeed, the question we currently have to face is whether the ideal of tolerance is really robust enough to sustain a harmonious world community and to contribute positively to the elimination of terrorism, tension and fear, or is it in part the cause of tension and fear. For example, it appears that excessive tolerance in Western culture is what triggers forms of hatred of the West. Does the Western value of tolerance to the point of permissiveness therefore go some way towards explaining the origin of some forms of terrorism in the contemporary world?

Tolerance is, of course, the primary virtue of the European Enlightenment of the eighteenth century. After the sorry story of religious wars in the post-Reformation period, the appeal to reason and commonsense threw up a desire to promote tolerance of difference, particularly in religious matters, which seemed to be grounded in personal faith commitments that were not thought to be publicly resolvable by rational argument anyway.

In modern Australian society we are children of the Enlightenment insofar as we tend to assign religion to the private arena of personal belief and the inner spirituality of individuals. Our society is one in which we must all be tolerant of another's religious viewpoint. This means that religion is tolerated so long as it is contained within the realm of the private. It has no real place in the public arena. In 2002 the *Sydney Morning Herald* responded critically to Archbishop Peter Jensen's urging of evangelism in the workplace by declaring that because religion is essentially a private matter, religious people should keep their religious views to themselves — even in the workplace. I think we are all suspicious of aggressive proselytising by intrusive badgering of people, or the attempt to win people to a cause by exercising subtle duress or outright hostility to alternative viewpoints.

True public witness to truth, however, and the open discussion of religious issues in pursuit of truth, should surely not be objectionable in a free and open society.

On the basis of the prevailing privatised view of religion it is sometimes also argued that the Church should keep out of the public arena of politics. Indeed, Church and State should be kept entirely separate. In democracies such as modern America and Australia, individuals are thus left with the freedom to make their religious commitments for themselves. No religion is given preferential treatment for there is no religion established by law, and no individual is pressed into belonging to any specific religious group. The separation of Church and State means that people are free to identify with the faith community of their individual choice.

However, the separation of Church from State tends subtly to the elimination of Church from State, even inhibiting religion from making a positive contribution to public debate by relegating it to the realm of the private. Indeed, the ensuing privatisation of religion leads to its being marginalised and trivialised. There is often even a suggestion in the air that religious people should be entirely mute in relation to public or political matters. Hence, the *Sydney Morning Herald*'s view that religious views should not be expressed in public, not even to the next person in the queue at the office water fountain.

As a consequence of this thinking, we tend to live with the idea that the State cannot be seen publicly to support the work of the Church if it is an identifiably 'religious' project rather than more clearly 'educational' or 'charitable' or of 'social welfare'. Thus, for example, if we happen to be involved in building schools, it may be possible to obtain government funding, or at least tax deductibility for a fund-raising appeal, for an assembly hall or school auditorium, but certainly not for a chapel. The assembly hall might be used as a temporary chapel on occasion, but the separation of Church from State means that the State cannot be seen to be supporting anything overtly religious. Ironically, this means that all kinds of quasi religious and moral positions of a very general kind can be promoted in school assemblies, since nothing is value-free, but it is not possible to obtain government support to erect a building that might be explicitly or unequivocally identified as 'Anglican' or 'Roman Catholic' or whatever! Somehow, the separation of Church and State means not only that individuals are free to follow whatever faith they choose; it means that, having made their choice, they are supposed to keep their faith to themselves as a private matter.

In the public arena this means that religious ideas tend to be disallowed, not because they are necessarily bad ideas, or logically defective and incoherent ideas, but simply because they are *religious*. We thus tolerate religion in our kind of society provided it is individualised and not taken too seriously in public. The toleration of religious ideas that reduces them to the trivial in a context of excessive individualism may suggest to us Christians that 'tolerance' may not always be a good thing.

Some might argue that it is not just that Church and State should be kept apart and that religion should not be brought into politics, but that it is not even wise to mention religion as a subject of discussion at dinner parties for fear of breaking up the occasion. It is better for me as a private individual to tolerate your point of view and for you to tolerate mine, and for us both to keep our views to ourselves. Likewise, moral commitments, provided they do not transgress the law, tend to be regarded in our kind of society as purely private matters. For is not the area of lifestyle as well as of belief also a matter of personal commitment and private moral judgment? This means that morality tends to become a purely personal decision of the will, like faith itself, rather than a subject that can in principle be publicly settled by rational argument. The truths of morality and religion are both, in this way of looking at things, at best private truths, not public ones.

In liberal democratic societies like modern Australia we leave such matters as personal morality and religious preference to the freedom of individual choice. Each person is free to pursue his or her own religious practices, believe as a matter of private opinion his or her own set of religious doctrines, and adopt his or her own particular lifestyle, provided he or she respects the equal right of every other individual to do likewise. And then we handle the multiplicity of viewpoints in the resulting multicultural society by recourse to the virtue of tolerance. You tolerate my viewpoint and I will tolerate yours. So long as your beliefs do not intrude on mine, and we respect the equal validity of each other's positions, then all will be right with the world. Or so we think.

† † †

It seems to me that we Australians, at least outside academic circles, do not engage in a great deal of reflection about the philosophical underpinning of our society. We are rather more pragmatic than ideologically self-conscious. We are currently concerned to debate the question of the unlikely continuing role of the monarchy and the idea of an Australian republic, but our chief preoccupation seems to be a pragmatic concern to come up with an alternative constitutional arrangement that will work; certainly we do not seem to reflect together about the nature of our democratic freedom and individual rights, where those rights come from, whether they are really somehow inherent and inalienable in the individual (which tends to be the basic assumption) or somehow conferred by the community as a consequence of a kind of consensus decision, and so on.

In other words, I think it is fair to say that Australians do not pay much attention to the philosophical underpinning of liberalism, and its origins. Australians are not in the habit of quoting from John Stuart Mill, or from Edmund Burke, for example, in the way Americans do in their reflection on the nature of their individual liberty and democratic rights. In Australia we know we must live together within a broadly based tolerant, multicultural, polyethnic society, but our self-reflection about the reasons for this is not well developed.

Nevertheless, even if we do not spend much time reflecting on our political philosophy, we unwittingly absorb views that are important to us in a less direct kind of way through literature, film and art. In this way we sustain images of mythic individualism that somehow express a broad grasp of human destiny.

This mythic individualism is illustrated by Robert Bellah, the grand old man of American sociology, in two books, *The Good Society* and *Habits of the Heart*.[1] In *Habits of the Heart* Bellah points out that the individualism of the political philosophy undergirding all modern Western liberal democratic societies is drilled into our corporate unconscious where it operates as a residual quasi-religious commitment by its constant replaying in the mythic images that our society regularly holds before itself.

Let me illustrate with one or two of Bellah's examples. The paradigm of the individual hero in our culture in the 1950s and 1960s was almost certainly the cowboy. When I was a child, a cowboy suit was a regular must as a Christmas present; when we grew out of one cowboy suit it was time for Santa Claus to bring another: I can still smell the fresh leather. And our most regular pastime was to play cowboys and Indians in a cotton tent on the back lawn. Cowboy movies were a regular feature of the Saturday afternoon matinee. The image of the cowboy hero came from America but we acted as though it were thoroughly Australian. In any event, in a cowboy movie the stereotypical cowboy rides into a community and often does good work on behalf of the community, for he is not selfish, but he never finds his own destiny within the community. Rather, he finds his destiny essentially as an individual — as in the case of the Lone Ranger, who rides off into the sunset, or goes off with his Indian companion … leaving the community the better off for his ridding it of crooks, or cattle rustlers, or hostile Indians … but also leaving the local schoolteacher behind her picket fence looking wistfully after him. There is never — or only rarely — any suggestion that he settles down and gets married and has children and becomes part of the community — all that is a little too bourgeois, middle class and domesticated. Rather, he finds his fulfilment essentially alone and goes off to do his own thing somewhere else. He never quite belongs to the community he serves. His human destiny is worked out as an individual rather than as a belonging member of a community with others.

What impact this mythic image of the ideal hero might have on family life and the increasingly prevalent tendency of individuals to walk away from family responsibilities in our kind of society is anybody's guess.

Or take the more modern equivalent of the cowboy of the last generation. This is the detective waiting patiently by a telephone that rarely rings in a little office full of grey filing cabinets and with piles of papers on his desk in downtown Manhattan ... but it could be Sydney or Perth. He is often alienated from colleagues in the organisation he works for. We never see him in settled domestic arrangements, or participating in normal community life either. Sometimes, it is true, he has a female colleague but it is never quite clear if they are partners in a sexual sense; and whether they might ever marry is an entirely unanswered question. Their relationship is ambiguous; they are essentially separate individuals.

Then the phone rings or in comes a client with a problem. As the detective begins to investigate it he finds that it is a problem with more ramifications than at first appeared and, indeed, that society itself has the problem. Those who run the city are mixed up in a network of underworld activity of an unsavoury kind — and that is why the detective can never really belong to the community. It is corrupt to the core. So what started as an individual client's problem becomes a community problem. As the detective bores further and further into the community it becomes increasingly murky. And the hero finds his destiny independent of it. He has to stand apart from it to preserve his integrity. And when he is offered a bribe or enticed into it by offers of drugs or grog or sex, he transcends it by ultimately resisting such temptations.

James Bond movies provide a good example of this kind of stereotype. But we see the same action played out over and over again, week after week, in detective series on TV. The hero is an individual who finds his or her fulfilment in resisting being tainted by the community, preserving his or her individual moral integrity in the face of the erosive forces of society with its insistent power to corrupt. Always society is portrayed negatively.

These images of mythic individualism played against a negatively portrayed community are reinforced daily on TV news and in the press. Read the papers and we get the impression of Australian society as corrupt to the core — full of crooks, teenage violence, theft, joy riding in other people's cars, drugs, horse-race fixing, backpacker murders and even the dreaded beginning of political assassination by organised gangs. Society itself is fundamentally flawed. One heroically survives in such a society essentially as an individual. Human destiny is rarely, if ever, presented as finding fulfilment within it. Rather, we tend to get by with the belief that the individual should be free to do his or her own thing, within a kind of fragile truce based on the ideal virtue of tolerance: you do your thing and I'll do mine.

In the political philosophy of which these mythic images are simply an expression, society is also regularly portrayed negatively. It is a threat to the individual and his or her rights. It is the role of government in such societies to act as a kind of umpire so as to ensure that individual rights and freedoms are not eroded by the aggressive, the selfish and self-interested — all those who will not respect the rights and freedoms of others in their own individual quest to rise by elbowing people aside and getting on in the world at others' expense.

† † †

Now, the kind of individualism of modern Western liberal democratic societies that I am talking about inevitably finds expression in the moral pluralism of our age. Most of our moral debates are not about our responsibilities to others in the community or about finding our destiny together with others in the community, but about the preservation of individual rights, and they arise out of a fundamental concern that society might be involved in the subtle erosion of those rights. Once again, in relation to the individual, society tends to be portrayed negatively. There is very little about responsibilities to our neighbours in the press. The occasional press article on the person who does some unselfish thing is remarkable because it is so contrary to our normal expectation of what people do.

In an earlier age, the approach to ethics was to teach the virtues that enabled a person to move from where he or she happened to be to what they might become (more trustworthy, honest, caring). But in modern liberal democratic society concentration on the virtues has given way to a static ethic of the protection and tolerance of individual rights and freedoms. Provided I do not encroach on your patch of space, I am free to do as I will, in modern liberal democratic society. Being free of the moral restraints of the conventionally agreed-upon values of the community means standing loosely to the idea of community standards or a set of 'core values', and following one's own privatised set of values. Thus, we must be tolerant of diversity, and when somebody encroaches on our space or does not respect our rights, we rely on the law to impose limits to protect our individual rights.

Now I think there are some very concerning difficulties in handling the ensuing diversity of moral, religious and political viewpoint by appeal to the virtue of tolerance. And it is here that we can begin to discern more clearly that modern liberal democratic societies may be seriously flawed. For a start, the privatisation of morality means that there is less and less incentive even to try to work out by rational conversation and debate, what the best or most desirable set of agreed or shared values might be for the living of life well in community. Rather, a welter of conflicting viewpoints and sectional commitments are simply asserted, as though one is as good as another, and then it follows that just about everything must be tolerated — for who are you to say that your values are better than mine? The idea of moral truth tends to go out the window in liberal democratic society. We are schooled instead simply in liberal-minded tolerance, the tolerance of a plethora of alternative viewpoints, as though one is a good as another.

One outcome of this moral pluralism and the abandonment of the quest for something that might in the past have been termed public moral truth is that we have become more and more reticent about the teaching of morality to the young. For who are you to try to tell me how to live my life? Religious instruction becomes increasingly difficult to pursue publicly. This is surely why the will to sustain the teaching of morality and religion in schools has disappeared so remarkably from our secondary schools systems over the last generation. In some places it is apparently not possible to have Nativity plays at Christmas time in schools, when there are some Muslim children present, even despite the fact that the Koran itself has a place for Jesus. Should we not be tolerant of individual religious commitment as a private matter, and is not the best way to do this simply to do and say nothing publicly about any of them? It is easy to see how tolerance of religious belief so long as it is privatised gives rise to a culture of disbelief.

At best in schools we try to do something of a lowest common denominator kind, perhaps called the 'clarification of values', but leaving the individual once again with an alleged freedom of choice. Of course we have to be tolerant to, and sensitive of, the beliefs of others, but the resulting reticence concerning the teaching of morality to the young even in our own families and broadly religious denominational groupings might be something which we will live to regret should society become increasingly violent, less secure and trusting, and more threatening.

Can this be at least one basic reason why Western liberal democratic societies seem to be in such a parlous condition? We did not really need Osama bin Laden to tell us that things are not well in Western liberal democracies; still less did we need him to take misguided corrective action into his own hands to bring the West to its knees. We only have to look at some of the problems with which we are grappling at present: the difficulty individuals seem to have in sustaining relationships, divorce, even a reluctance to commit to marriage in the first place, youth suicide, the widespread prevalence of depression, the ubiquitous use of antidepressants, endemic child abuse, inequitable distribution of wellbeing between rich and poor, drug and alcohol abuse, and its associated crime and violence, and the ensuing need for security systems just about everywhere these days to protect us, not from international terrorism, but from ourselves.

† † †

Another outcome, in a world of moral pluralism, where the quest for moral truth is abandoned and practically everything is tolerated, is that protest tends to become the standard way of expressing a political or moral point of view. Strident assertion and marches with placards tend to replace reasoned community conversation and debate, because nobody really believes that conventionally agreed upon community standards are possible of achievement any more. Instead of open discussion and reasoned argument, we end up with a form of intolerance as everybody shouts louder in defence of their respective rights. Street rhetoric replaces public conversation and debate.

Because, in this increasingly individualistic society the individual must be free to do his or her own thing in the face of the possible erosion of those rights by society, the individual thus tends to survive in a state of siege. Moreover, with little public agreement on standards of morality or sense of duty to others individuals tend increasingly to exploit situations — that is, until somebody else screams or a Royal Commission is held to find out exactly what unfair benefit someone else has won.

In an atmosphere of mutual mistrust, then, society also becomes more and more litigious. Doctors of medicine, for example, currently have to pay huge premiums for professional indemnity insurance, even if that means that the community can hardly afford the very high medical fees that must necessarily be charged just to pay the insurance premiums. Certainly, there are signs that Australian society is already on the way to assuming the litigious character of its US counterpart.

Clearly, there never has been a time in Australian society, and probably this is the case in all modern Western liberal democratic societies, when individualism has been so aggressively at work amongst us and human self-interest so unrestrained. If we simply argue for individual freedom from society's constraints and for tolerance, where do we stop? Only at the point where individual freedom might encroach upon the rights of the neighbour. But conversely the pressure of the neighbour must be resisted in the protection and preservation of individual rights. We have to exercise as much tolerance as possible in such a society; but how then can we avoid having to tolerate the tawdry, the grotesque and the anti-human?

We surely cannot be expected to be tolerant of literally everything. Also, how do we prevent tolerance from slipping into indifference? We must be accepting of variety and diversity as social enrichment, but what are the limits of tolerance and how might we determine them?

In order to judge what is to be tolerated and what not, we clearly need community conversation and debate. And we might hope to see not just the development of a kind of multiculturalism where difference is merely tolerated, but a positive community engagement in which cross-cultural conversation flourishes. In a society in which there is a genuine meeting of cultures, some may experience a call to modify aspects of their assumptions and commitments, and to strengthen other aspects. We have to be open to the need to move beyond a stand-offish tolerance of difference and to the possibility of the transformation of difference. For we may be able to reach a common mind in the interests of the ultimate health of the community as a whole. Just to uphold the tolerance of individual diversity may be socially stultifying; individual interests and the tolerance of difference may need to be balanced by the discernment of community need and an appreciation of the public value of consensus.

Professor Max Charlesworth, in his spirited defence of liberalism and its ideal of individual autonomy, says that this ideal does not rule out an individual and free decision to choose to live lovingly, responsibly and in accordance with altruistic ideals such as those of the Christian religion. Charlesworth says:

> As for the criticism that the notion of autonomy is linked to an individualistic and a-social stance, there is absolutely no reason why an autonomous act must necessarily be self-regarding in intent and cannot be other-regarding. People may very well make conscientious and autonomous moral decisions about their responsibilities and obligations towards others and acknowledge their dependency on others.[2]

But it seems to me that this rider is in tension with his original exposition of individual autonomy, in which he speaks negatively and pejoratively of traditional societies with their shared religious commitments and their 'core values', and what he calls their paternalism. All this is presented as a bad thing from the point of view of liberalism and individual autonomy. A little later in the chapter the commitment to individualism is said to be able to accommodate the free choice of these same communitarian values, or at least the best of them, from which individual autonomy seeks to shake itself free. I think the difficulty here is that even if a more socially responsible and communitarian approach to life is theoretically possible as an individual choice in modern liberal democratic societies, in practice the weight of the culture is nevertheless against it.

† † †

If this understanding of modern Australian society is anywhere near the mark, the Church has a specific and unavoidably political role to play. For the Church works with a fundamental understanding of human destiny that is quite out of kilter with that of the surrounding culture. Indeed, one aspect of our mission may be to call into question the ideological underpinning of Western liberal democratic society as a fundamentally incoherent and inadequate set of ideas, which may even hold within it the seeds of its own self-destruction.

Let me say what I mean. I suspect that inherited Christian values of neighbourly care and fellowship, and indeed old Australian values of mateship, will not be sustained, with an adverse effect on the quality of life in society, when society itself tends increasingly towards an aggregate of autonomous individuals, all trying to get on at the expense of the other. It is difficult to love your neighbour when the pressure of the whole culture is to see your neighbour as your economic rival. Instead of thinking of human destiny in individualistic terms, as Christians most of us would be more inclined to affirm that humans can really only find their true fulfilment in community with others, by working cooperatively for the common good and not simply lobbying for the preservation of their own self-interest and individual rights. The Christian commitment to love and care entails that mutual *inter*dependence, rather than just individual autonomy or complete *in*dependence, is the value that we feel motivated to cherish and strive to uphold.

The difficulty is, of course, that the fundamental commitment of liberalism to the freedom of the individual and to tolerance, cannot *of itself* generate a positive set of values with respect to others. These must be derived from some other source which has to be married to the liberal ideal. Indeed, in the past the liberal ideal has worked because it has piggy-backed on the values of more traditional, religiously influenced societies, and it is only in the more secularised context of today, with the weakening of Christian influence, for example, that the inadequacies of the liberal ideology are beginning to be exposed.

For a start the liberal ideal of individual freedom held together by an ethic of tolerance has in practice constantly to be modified. In its own interests, society regularly has to apply communitarian values which come into conflict with individual interests and rights. This can be illustrated anecdotally. In the early 1980s I became involved in the debate about the banning of cigarette advertising. The Cancer Council, which has since become the Cancer Foundation of Western Australia, asked me if I could publicly support the banning of cigarette and tobacco advertising. As this was a cause with which I sympathised I wrote an article which was published in the Anglican *Messenger*, the provincial Church newspaper in Western Australia. The article, which noted the decrease in smoking amongst adults, but the alarming rise in smoking amongst teenagers and even younger children, was entitled 'Out of the Mouths of Babes Comes Smoke'. At the end of the article I then signalled support for a Bill to ban tobacco advertising, which was coming before the West Australian Parliament, and said that we would all watch closely how our politicians would vote 'because this might condition the way we ourselves cast our vote at the next election'. Very predictably, all hell broke loose. I was very roundly attacked by a variety of politicians, but notably by one from Carnarvon who accused me of encouraging people to determine their next vote on a single issue. At the other extreme the then member for South Perth and Shadow Minister for Health resigned from the Liberal Party because of its criticism of me and its opposition to the Bill to ban cigarette advertising. Public debate in the media raged for a week or two.

In the course of this I had a full editorial written against me in the press, which charged me with leading a fundamental assault on the principle of the freedom of the press. I decided to respond to it by writing a reply in the form of a Letter to the Editor. As I recall, the editorial appeared on a Saturday. I hand-delivered the letter in response on the Sunday. It was not published on the Monday or on the Tuesday. By the Wednesday I was wondering how I could apply some pressure to make sure the response was at least published. But on the Thursday it was finally published, one suspects somewhat reluctantly. In it I pointed out that we rightly value our individual and democratic freedoms including the freedom of the press, but that freedom is never quite absolute. It may have to be balanced and restrained by the needs of the whole community. We may not as a society be prepared to tolerate everything, or more or less anything. Moreover, I tried to point out that not all freedoms were of equal value, and cigarette advertising may no longer be tolerable. The final sentence of the letter read: 'The freedom to lure people to a premature death is not a freedom we should value.'

In other words, to urge a broad-minded tolerance that leads to the inclination to be accepting of everything, without some eye to the impact that unrestrained freedom might have on society, may be quite disastrous. The remedy will involve striking a balance between the interests of the one and the interests of the many. The liberal agenda of an ideological commitment to individual freedom, tolerance, independence and autonomy alone, simply will not do.

A final example may illustrate this. While I was living in Manhattan in 1993, there were regular press reports about violence, even killings, in schools. Some schools were beginning to install metal detectors at the school gate to prevent students from bringing in weapons. The commonplace experience before boarding an aircraft children had begun to have at the school door. But the really remarkable thing was the debate that this development triggered in the press and on TV and radio talkback. Some students argued that they had an inalienable human right to protect themselves as human individuals, and that the Second Article of Amendment of the US Constitution provided that 'the right of people to keep and bear arms shall not be infringed'. Curiously, in Manhattan the sale of fireworks was banned, but it was possible to go around the corner and buy a firearm!

This raises an underlying concern about the health of liberal democratic societies based almost exclusively on individualism and the virtue of tolerance. According to the official figures I was then able to put my hands on, there were 38,317 deaths from firearms in the USA in 1991. Of these 18,526 were suicides, 17,746 were murders, 1,441 were accidents and 604 were unspecified. That so many died as a consequence of the use of firearms cannot be entirely unrelated to the Second Amendment, and probably also indicates the place of the firearm in the hands of the heroes of mythic individualism, the cowboy and the detective. But there is something akin to an undeclared underground civil war going on in the USA; 17,746 people in one year represents a lot of casualties.

When the Howard Government in Australia brought in arms control legislation, following the Port Arthur massacre, communitarian interests and values more easily triumphed over individual interests and freedoms promoted by the gun lobby. When communitarian interests and concerns are expressed, as they were on that occasion, those who urged us to tolerate the presence of firearms in society argued that the rights of the individual must be protected at all costs. But individual rights and freedoms are not absolute. They have to be balanced by community interests. After the Oklahoma bombing, a letter to the editor of *Time* magazine by somebody signing himself Philip G. Plotica of Gettysburgh, Pennsylvania, responded with these words: 'For those concerned over the erosion of personal freedoms, forget it. We've already lost the most basic one of all: freedom from fear.'[3]

These are extreme examples, but they speak of a fundamental flaw with repercussions of a much more subtle but insidious kind in all liberal democratic societies. Liberal societies built almost solely upon an ethic of tolerance, which allow the exclusive operation of the principle of individual freedom with minimal communitarian concern for the ultimate good of society as a whole, may be a hazard to themselves. It may be that, like the Roman Empire, such societies are in danger of breaking up from within. Is a multicultural society based only on tolerance anything more than an uneasy truce amongst potentially conflicting options? This kind of society may not be robust enough to survive, unless we begin thinking in more overtly communitarian terms.

✝ ✝ ✝

One starting point for the development of a Christian response to the kind of individualism on which liberal democratic societies are based is the doctrine of the Trinity, which provides us with a quite different approach to the resolution of the tension between the one and the many. If I detect a basic unresolved tension between the one and the many in Max Charlesworth's otherwise very helpful exposition of liberalism, I think it is precisely at this point that the Church has something of importance to say. For if nothing else, the doctrine of the Trinity of identifiable and distinct persons in one unity of being is an attempt to hold in *balance* the one and the many. This doctrinal symbol of the mutual interdependence of persons, and of how the one and the many go together in one communion, is clearly incongruent with the liberal ideal of individual autonomy and independence from the restraints of the many. It explains why we Christians are not and cannot ever really be simply 'liberals'.

Indeed, if the Greek orthodox theologian John Zizioulas[4] is right, the very idea of a person was originally worked out in the first five centuries of the Christian era in the context of theological debate about the nature of God the Holy Trinity. The doctrine of the Trinity gives us both our fundamental notion of what it is to be a person and indicates how we may conceive the ideal human society. This is in radical contrast with the idea of the autonomous individual of modern Western liberal democratic ideology. For the difference between being a person and being an individual is precisely that, by definition, an individual is one, isolated and discrete, independent of others. Individual autonomy means independence of the restraints of others. The implication of this is the tendency for society to be portrayed negatively as a potential threat to the freedom, autonomy and rights of the individual. But the essence of being a *person*, as distinct from being an individual, is that a person is related to another. Just as God the eternal Father achieves his specific identity as Father in relation to the eternal Son and vice versa, so amongst humans personal identity is derived in relation to others. To be a person one must be involved in interpersonal give and take.

That is why, when Basil the Great in 374 AD expounded the nature of the divine in his treatise *On the Holy Spirit*, he spoke not so much of three persons and one substance, as of three persons and one communion. The Father and the Son do not lose their unique identities; indeed, it is in their relationships that their respective identities are defined. The Father could not be called Father without the Son and vice versa. And it is in this same relationality that they constitute one unity of being, for the Father and the Son are relationally one by mutual self-gift. The Son does the Father's will, not out of duress or in compliance with some imposed and restrictive requirement, but because the Son's own will *coincides* with that of the Father.

In other words, relationality is essential to the concept of a person as distinct from the ideal of the autonomous individual of post-Enlightenment liberalism. And it is not *in*dependence but the mutual *inter*dependence of persons in communion that is the ideal of human destiny, for Christians as 'partakers of the divine nature' (2 Peter 1:4). With the doctrine of the Trinity in mind, and a grasp of the essence of divinity in terms of the relationality of persons, we can view society in relation to the individual not always negatively, not as a potential threat to individual freedom and individual rights, but much more positively. The doctrine of the Trinity provides us Christians with a fundamental social ideal and a political agenda which is radically at variance with the ideal of human destiny in the cultural and political environment of the modern West.

Moreover, the communion of the Church which gives us a glimpse of how society as a whole could be, does not just *reflect* the communion of God in some kind of Platonic sense; rather, what we know and experience in the Church *is* the communion of God. The communion of the Church is the communion of the Holy. That is why Christians are not just called to be of one heart and one mind, but are called to align themselves with the mind and heart *of God*, and to participate by grace in the communion of God, the Holy Communion. This means that in liturgy, Sunday by Sunday, we are involved in nothing less than the remaking of society by calling people into the communion of God, making one family out of many strangers.

We thus have in the Church an unavoidably political concern that flows from our fundamental insights with respect to the nature of God. Indeed, in the context of what has been called the political monoculture of Australia, in which the differences between political parties is more a matter of degree than kind (for both major parties are hooked in one way or another on the ideal of individual autonomy of modern liberalism), this gives Christians a distinctive political agenda. This gives us an approach to the resolution of the tension between the one and the many which is far removed from the post-Enlightenment ideal of individualism, individual autonomy, and absolute freedom of liberal democratic societies held together by tolerance. By contrast we value not just independence, nor acquiesce in a stultifying dependency, but aim at something between the two. We shall continue to value the human integrity, identity and freedom of persons, but seek to balance these things by paying attention to the needs of the community. We also acknowledge the individual person's positive need of others. Our ethic, therefore, will not stop at a discussion of individual rights, but will embrace talk of responsibilities towards others, and seek to promote virtues as well as rights in a genuine community of mutual interdependence by self-gift.

This explains why most Christians believe that religion is not just a matter of holding certain private beliefs or opting for a purely private moral lifestyle, or just being tolerant and accepting of every or any lifestyle. It is also a matter of trying to work out together, by public conversation and debate, a set of values for living of life well in community. For us, the essence of the Gospel is a call into the new city of the Kingdom of God which is dawning in this world, and of which the Church is the anticipation. The invitation of the Gospel is to a public cohering as a single people living faithfully within the secular community. This sometimes brings with it a sense of being somewhat alien in the prevailing culture; we are always in the world but not of it.

† † †

If the Church is to move beyond a detached tolerance of the views of others, then it must also fully embrace the movement of modern ecumenism. It is fairly well known that the Diocese of Sydney does not support with any real enthusiasm the ecumenical work to which the rest of the Anglican Church of Australia is committed. For some years now Sydney has actually declined to contribute financially to this work. This is possible because finance for the budget of the national

Church is raised in two ways. First a statutory assessment is levied on all dioceses to support the administrative machinery of the national Church, its General Synod and General Synod Office, and any work that the General Synod explicitly resolves to pursue. Then there is a voluntary assessment from which contributions are made to the Anglican Communion for the support of international activities such as the work of the Anglican Consultative Council, the Primates' Meeting and Lambeth Conference, plus the funding of international ecumenical dialogues. These include the Anglican–Roman Catholic International Commission (ARCIC) and the newly formed International Anglican–Roman Catholic Commission on Unity and Mission (IARCCUM) and the Anglican–Orthodox Theological Commission. Because the Standing Committee of the Diocese of Sydney has regularly declined to pay its voluntary assessment, it is not materially involved in the support of these initiatives. At the General Synod of the national Church in Brisbane in July 2002, some years of unpaid voluntary assessment were simply written off.

Sydney's firm refusal to contribute financially to this segment of the work of the national Church is within its constitutional rights. It is, after all, a voluntary assessment. Instead, the Diocese of Sydney prefers to contribute to causes it deems worthy of support. The projects which it favours are usually referred to as 'gospel ministries'. There is no doubt that these are all worthy recipients of support. However, this without doubt sends a message about the lack of perceived worth of the various ecumenical dialogues in which the Anglican Communion is a partner. The National Council of Churches in Australia, the World Council of Churches, and the Council of the (Anglican) Church in Asia are likewise hardly the flavour of the month in the Diocese of Sydney. This leaves the rest of the national Church to carry the financial burden of supporting these activities.

Given this apparent lack of interest in ecumenical affairs, it is understandable that even within the Anglican Church of Australia, some Sydney folk have articulated the doctrine of 'two tectonic plates' (see the Prologue) and foreshadowed a looser association between Sydney Anglicans and the rest. The development of a self-contained fellowship of faith and moral belief within the legal structures of the national Church would amount almost to a bifurcated Church. What may not be so clearly understood is that this is essentially a form of liberalism: you do your thing and I'll do mine. It is as though the Church can tolerate two integrities, in a way that is a little oblivious as to truth.

What motivates some of us Anglicans to pursue the quest for unity, both internally within our own Communion and with other Christians, with a good deal of commitment and energy is the same ultimate goal. Both the Church's internal unity and the Church's ecumenical work are pursued as essential ingredients of an authentic 'gospel ministry'. Talk of a stratified church, or of two churches within one, like two overlapping tectonic continental plates is anathema. Indeed, perhaps the diversity of viewpoint within Anglicanism demands a kind of internal ecumenism to maintain the internal unity of the household of faith. Despite the obvious diversity of viewpoint both within our own Church and amongst Christian denominations, most of us feel impelled to work towards an ever-deepening unity and fellowship, to which we are called by the gospel of reconciliation. It is simply not possible to cut our losses and go our separate ways and do our own thing in a liberal minded, somewhat stand-offish spirit of tolerance.

In the Church we know ourselves to be a community of unlikeminded people, since we do not come together around a common ideology or around a common interest or simply to pursue a commonly held practical goal. We come together in the Church because we are called together by God and for no other reason. The ecumenical imperative to unity with other Christians and the imperative to maintain and nurture unity within our own Church are the same: we are motivated by an appreciation of the will of God. Most of us find this gospel imperative in St John's Gospel, Chapter 17, in Jesus' farewell discourse with his disciples, when Jesus prays that his disciples may be one. But not just one in any sense or in some minimal sense. Jesus' own earnest prayer for his disciples is that they should be one 'as he and the Father are one'.

Furthermore, we must be one, not that the world will take more notice of us if we speak with one voice, though that may be so.

We must be one, not that the world may know *that* there is a God of some kind somewhere. Rather, we must be one that the world may have a chance of knowing *what* God is like — a diversity of different persons who are finding their destiny together in one unity of being. The pursuit of ecumenism is thus one of the most clearly defined imperatives of the Christian Gospel. It is a 'gospel ministry' informed by the love of God, indeed an evangelical ministry 'that the world may believe' (John 17:21). The Church at its best — when we glimpse authentic Christian fellowship and the human unity it seeks to achieve — is a promise of what God has in store for all humanity when God comes in his Kingdom and his Spirit is poured out on all flesh. The Church is the anticipation of the Kingdom, advance publicity of coming attractions, and itself a sign of the human unity of which we earnestly hope for men and women of every race and nation.

† † †

This means that the work of human unity among men and women who are committed to other creeds and belief systems different from ours is important. The achievement of human unity under God has become a particularly pressing challenge for the Church in the context of contemporary Australian multiculturalism, and globally in the context of a world divided and troubled by terrorism and fear. Apart from simply tolerating ethnic and cultural diversity, multiculturalism and moral pluralism, we have therefore to find a way of being together as more positive contributors to the one harmonious society. The unity of the Church thus ministers to the unity and peace of the nation and of the world.

There are certainly today a number of international reasons why we need to engage with one another with much more energy than we have expended to date across our religious and cultural divisions. We need to build a more profound national and international community of genuinely shared moral commitment and belief as possible. We cannot be content with a kind of liberal-minded tolerance of one another. Rather, we have a vocation to enter into a partnership together to build a more sustaining world peace.

In the Australia which lies before us inter-faith dialogue seems inevitable. The release by the Australian Bureau of Statistics in 2002 of the results of the 2001 national census makes it clear that Australia is becoming increasingly multicultural and religiously diverse. While 69 per cent of Australians still claim allegiance to a Christian denomination, at least as fellow travellers, 5 per cent of Australians now claim to belong to a religion other than Christianity. There are now more Buddhists in Australia than Baptists, more Muslims than Lutherans, and more Hindus than Salvos. We can anticipate that in an increasingly multicultural society there must inevitably be increasing dialogue, particularly in the first instance amongst the three great monotheistic religions.

If ecumenical activity does not enjoy a very high priority amongst Sydney Anglicans they have been even clearer about their attitude to other religions. In his installation sermon as Dean in St Andrew's Cathedral in Sydney on Friday, 7 March 2002, the Very Reverend Phillip Jensen made it more than clear that he was suspicious of the liberal attempt to relativise truth by the tolerance of all religions as equally true. In a spirited attempt to defend the unique claims of Christianity he went on to say that as he interprets the Gospel, it is both inclusive and exclusive. It is inclusive in the sense that it is open to anyone to believe. But Christianity is exclusive in its claims, given that salvation is said to be available only to those who have faith in Jesus Christ. This means that the claims of other religions must simply be pronounced to be false. This is certainly not the most helpful approach to other religions in the context of the tensions of today.

We must all take care not to speak of other religious traditions in a self-righteously condemning, hostile and even aggressive manner which is hardly designed to promote interfaith dialogue.

However, we do not want to give the impression that the world's great religions are all more or less the same; for then none can be taken really seriously. Apart from what is common, genuine dialogue with other faiths will also therefore focus frankly and candidly on differences. But we have first to get to know and trust one another.

Amongst the religious diversity of contemporary Australia, Islam, almost certainly, is for most of us the most unknown and strange and in a sense threatening. We inevitably feel somewhat alienated from the Muslim world, particularly in the wake of the tragedy of 11 September; no doubt the Muslim world feels just as alienated from us since the US-led invasion of Iraq. But who can doubt the importance of the engagement of world religions in mutual respect for the future peace of the whole world given these horrendous historical developments?

Some have imagined that the traumatic and tragic events of September 11 have inaugurated an entirely new world order. That might be an overstatement. But it has become clear to many since that fateful day that we in the West have a good deal to learn about Islam, and probably nearly as much to learn about the Judeo-Christian roots of our own culture and civilisation if we are going to enter into a positive engagement with Islam in decades to come.

We all know with the top of our heads that we must be tolerant of the presence amongst us of Muslims in Australia. We note the steady increase in the number of mosques around this country. There are now sixty-six mosques in New South Wales and thirty-five in Victoria, these being the most concentrated communities of Muslim people in Australia. But what happens beyond their high walls is largely unknown to most Australians. We carry a stereotype of Muslims at prayer picked up from a few fleeting TV clips, and that is about the extent of it; exactly what the people behind those walls believe and the precise nature of their moral commitments by and large remain a mystery to most Australians. So the question is: can we move beyond this very minimal relationship of tolerance to enter more fully into community life as partners in dialogue?

And where might the conversation begin? I think we must acknowledge that Christians, Muslims and Jews have much more in common than any of them have with the secular materialists who predominate amongst our neighbours, side by side in our streets. For one thing, those of us who see ourselves as standing in the Abrahamic tradition of ethical monotheism all worship the same God. However, as soon as we begin to explore our respective ways of thinking about the nature of God and of his will for us in the living of our lives we tend to part company. I am not entirely sure if I can put my finger on precise points of shared belief that might inform a Muslim–Jewish dialogue; I think that is something for Muslims and Jews to begin to identify. But if I can focus, by way of example, on the less threatening possibility of Christian–Muslim dialogue, it is certainly possible to discern some common elements that can provide a basis for genuine engagement. This is despite the sad history of tension between Christians and Muslims, particularly since the Crusades, which gives us the impression that they are as religious systems almost irreconcilable.

Though the Muslim use of the name Allah tends to give us the impression that the God of Islam is somehow different from ours, it is perhaps useful to know that the name Allah was used by Arabic-speaking Christians to refer to God long before it was taken over by Islam. Indonesian and Sudanese Christians use the name Allah for God to this day.

Islam and Christianity work with different views of the unity of God, since for Muslims God is one in a simple numerical sense, whereas for us Christians the unity of God is achieved within complexity — it is the unity of love between persons that both makes God one and allows us to become one in him and with one another. But this difference of view about the unity of God is simply a ground for further dialogue.

Also, Christians and Muslims can together celebrate the fact that the Koran itself holds a positive place for Jesus as a prophet. For us Christians he is more than a prophet, the incarnation of the love of God. But in the Koran, the life of Jesus holds a positive place, at least up to the story of the crucifixion and Resurrection. For the Muslim, Jesus is the Messiah, the Son of Mary. As a prophet of God it cannot be imagined that Jesus suffered a humiliating death without calling into question the sovereignty of God in the world, and so Jesus is understood somehow to bypass the trauma of death to go directly to heaven, without passing Calvary and without passing through the tomb, but collecting glory on the way, as it were. But there is certainly ground for a positive conversation to take place with Islam about Jesus, and about being patient of suffering as an index to the character of God.

A friend of mine who was until recently dean of an English Cathedral and who is an Arabic scholar with many contacts with the Muslim community in Britain, decided after September 11 to told a forum on Muslim beliefs. After an address by an imam, at question time, a very angry fundamentalist Christian woman stood up and berated the dean for holding such a function in the first place, accusing him of confusing Christian believers. 'What do you think you are doing?' she demanded. At this my friend turned to the imam and said, 'Perhaps you would like to answer this question. What do you think we are doing?' The imam startled the assembly by saying: 'I am here because I love Jesus.' And turning to the woman he said: 'Do you?' Christian fundamentalists are not accustomed to having that kind of question put to them so directly by imams.

I think it may also be useful for all of us to know that when Mohammed gave Medina its constitution, and this is the earliest and most original way there is of being a Muslim State, Mohammed provided that there should be equality for Muslims, and Jews and Christians. It was only later, and particularly under the Ottoman Empire, that a more intolerant and aggressive regime emerged.

In the context of the present world we will not be able to avoid dialogue on the subject of violence. Islam sees itself as a religion of peace, Christians therefore will be interested to learn more about the religious restraints on violence in Islam.

So the point I want to make is that if Christians have a vocation to help the world to move beyond an uneasy truce and beyond the mere tolerance of one another, genuine and honest inter-faith dialogue is, if anything, more important today than ever. In dialogue with Islam we will hold up its own better insights; we demonstrate by good example our Australian willingness to grant freedom of religious observance to Muslims, and call for reciprocity for Christians and Jews in places where they are cruelly persecuted by a Muslim majority. Certainly, the future of Western society is in dialogue between the religious traditions. Indeed, the future peace of the entire world demands it.

I am personally pleased that the Churches of the Anglican Communion have over the last year set up an official dialogue with Al

Azhar Al Sharif, the esteemed centre of Islamic learning in Cairo, and possibly the oldest university in the world. But dialogue across the faiths must be pursued with much more energy at all levels of the community.

Let me ground this sentiment by providing just one small but concrete example of what stands to be achieved. Shortly after September 11 the then ambassador of the Taliban to Pakistan declared a jihad on Australia. As it happened this was announced in banner headlines in the Australian press on the very day that the national Heads of Christian Churches were meeting in Sydney. It was suggested that we should seize the initiative and visit a significant mosque as a way of assuring the Muslim community that we were well aware of the deep divide between ethical and religious Islam and political and aggressive Islam. It was clearly important at that moment to assure our Muslim brothers and sisters in Australia that they were not immediately thought of as terrorists, and to invite them to join us in building a relationship that would make for peace. Some heads of Churches were at first reluctant starters; a visit the very next day was said to be too soon; they needed time to think about it; they needed to go home and consult their constituencies; the time was not opportune. Had that view prevailed the opportunity would certainly have been lost.

To cut the story short, we visited the Lakemba mosque in Sydney at the end of Friday prayers and were very warmly received. The visit was widely reported both in the Australian press and around the world in the Arabic press, including Indonesia where there had been some quite horrendous attacks on Christians. Indeed, it was later reported to us that at one Indonesian meeting that was set up to try to broker a peace settlement after violent island massacres and church burnings on Sulawesi, a local imam held up a newspaper showing coverage of the Lakemba mosque visit, and used it as a positive example that in Australia Christian and Muslim leaders enjoy congenial relations. That report made a significant contribution to at least one Indonesian peace agreement. Clearly, the promotion of dialogue between the great religious traditions is of enormous importance to the future of the whole world.

† † †

But what are we to say about the prospects for a deeper dialogue today between Christians and Jews? Christians have, of course, long enjoyed reasonably cordial relations with Judaism in Australian society as in most Western societies. Since the Second World War, there have been regular signs of progress in Jewish–Christian relations, even in what might appear to be small and trivial ways. Indeed, even within my own lifetime, I can discern some quite positive changes for good. We Christians used to speak, for example, of the Old Testament scriptures and of specifically Christian writings as the New Testament. These days we are a little more sensitive to the possibly offensive sound in Jewish ears of talk of 'Old' and 'New' Testaments, as though we all think that the 'Old' is succeeded and replaced by the 'New'. Thus in university departments of theology and studies in religion, it is much more common these days to hear references to the study of the 'Hebrew Scriptures' rather than the 'Old Testament'. But I wonder if, with a little more open dialogue, Christians and Jews might yet move beyond even this to speak of 'The Shared Testament'.

Within my own lifetime we have been enormously helped in the understanding of Christian origins by the contribution of Jewish scholars. Jesus was, after all a Jew; his teaching in relation to the Torah and Jewish prophetic traditions cannot be understood other than in the original context out of which it comes. I think of the seminal work of Geza Vermes on the religion of Jesus, for example, or Pinchas Lapide on the idea of resurrection in the light of the traditions of pharisaic Judaism, or of the work of the American Jewish scholar Alan Segal on the historical Jesus and on St Paul[5], not to mention the huge contribution of those who since the late 1940s have studied the Dead Sea Scrolls and the religion of the Essenes to throw light on Christian origins. Certainly, Christian origins cannot be understood apart from Judaism, and Christian studies are no longer the preserve of Christians alone.

But let us not sidestep the need to confront some inherited difficulties posed by Christian texts that appear to be unhelpfully hostile to Judaism. I am thinking particularly of those Christian texts that from a Jewish point of view can justifiably be called 'texts of terror', for they have been used through the centuries for the evil purpose of fostering anti-Semitism, most notably and frighteningly in Nazi Germany.

The author of St John's Gospel regularly blames 'the Jews' for all the misfortunes that befell Jesus. There is a variety of texts that could be cited but Chapter 8 verses 31–59 of John is the most difficult section: we all become uncomfortable by the reading of John 8:44, a verse in which Jesus addresses the Jews: 'You are from your father the devil, and you choose to do your father's desires. He was a murderer from the beginning and does not stand in the truth, because there is no truth in him. When he lies, he speaks according to his own nature, for he is a liar and the father of lies.' John here says the Jews have the devil as their father, in other words they are the children of the devil. This is said to the Jews and it is attributed to Jesus. Jesus' claim is that his Father is God and that their father is the devil, and they are identified with murder and lying, and a complete disregard for truth. This must be as complete a condemnation as any of us could imagine.

This passage has historically been used by Christians against Jews and it has been used by others in an appalling succession of anti-Jewish polemics. In 1945 the propagandist Julius Streicher, the editor of the Nazi newspaper *Die Stuermer*, used it to defend himself at his trial at Nuremberg: 'Only the Jews had remained victorious after the dreadful days of World War One', he said. 'These were the people of whom Christ said: "Its father is the devil".'[6]

What is even more frightening, a visit to the neo-Nazi website www.stormfront.org, under the heading of 'What world famous men said about the Jews', shows that the words attributed to Jesus in John 8:44 are quoted there even today. How do we respond to the historical use of this text to justify the most terrible crimes imaginable against Jews, and its continued use to this day by Christians and others to vilify the Jews and to foment racial hatred and tension?

Some Christian responses have argued that this text is so objectionable that it should simply be left untranslated or certainly not read in churches: it has been omitted from the post-Vatican II Roman Catholic lectionary and from recent Anglican and ecumenical lectionaries.

Others seek to resist a fundamentalist interpretation, which suggests that the text somehow came down a golden chute from heaven with a semi-magical divine authority and refers to Jews of all times and places to this day, by placing the text in its historical context and asking: is this reference to be restricted to Jesus' time, or perhaps to John's time of writing? Is it geographically restricted to Judeans rather than to Jews of the international dispersion?

Others question whether these are authentic words of Jesus at all. In Matthew's Gospel the phrase 'the Jews' as distinct from specific subgroups with whom Jesus came into conflict, such as the scribes and the pharisees, is used only five times, in Mark six times and in Luke six times. John by contrast uses the expression 'the Jews' some seventy times. In John the polemical tone towards the Jews is intense. Indeed, we can demonstrate not just a proclivity of the author of John to use the blanket term 'the Jews' more than others do, but that he does so when in the parallel texts in Matthew, Mark and Luke, a more restricted term is used. In Matthew, Mark and Luke Jesus is locked in sharp controversy with some Jewish leaders and has harsh critical things to say about 'this generation', but in John that criticism is presented in terms of 'the Jews'. So there are good grounds for thinking that the use of this phrase is not so much characteristic of Jesus himself, but rather is John's way of telling the story of Jesus and of how his followers came into conflict with the Jews.

But who can these Jews be that John is so hostile to them? Is it that this reference is to the Jews particularly with whom the Johannine community itself came into conflict and who ejected it from the synagogue in that period when Jewish followers of Jesus were struggling for life and eventually for a separate identity? Is the context one of fearfulness of the larger parent community? We also note the power differential in John's account of the fledgling Christian community as 'the little flock', put down, rejected and shunned, by the larger surrounding Jewish community. In this historical context one can begin to see the offending text as a very human outburst in the heat of struggle. Are we witnessing a furious bit of polemical rejection of an adversary in the context of a community row in which hope of reconciliation has vanished? Does the condemnation of the

Jews arise in a desperate situation of total human deadlock? Well, I think almost certainly something like that.

A little of the harsh edge is also taken off this text when it is observed that the devil is not necessarily to be imagined in dualistic terms as a red-clad figure with horns and tail and a pitchfork. The devil (*diabolos*) is the accuser in the heavenly court (Job 1 and 2); he is something like a crown prosecutor seeking a conviction. The Johannine community is clearly still processing the trauma of what it saw as the condemnation of Jesus by false accusation. John 8:44 has to be read in this light.

What is clear is that there is no plain reading of this text. It is open to a wide variety of interpretation. And it is also clear that when texts are read in different historical contexts they are heard differently. We cannot hear the text of John 8:44 in the aftermath of the Holocaust, or the foundation of the State of Israel, and of events since then, even the suicide bombings of the Middle East today, without coming to an awareness of new and painful meaning.

† † †

Finally, let me focus attention on another Christian text which we are tending today to read with new insight. In the sixteenth century, at the time of the Reformation, Martin Luther drew enormous value from Paul's writing on the theme of justification by faith in order to find an answer for his own spiritual crisis and for resolving his deep concerns about the state of the Church of his day. Given his anxieties about the buying and selling of indulgences, apparently as a way of securing a heavenly reward, the basic question he brought to the scriptural text was: how can I, a sinful individual, attain salvation? Is it really by pious good works, such as the buying of papal pardons? The answer Luther drew from the text of Romans in particular was: no, justification before God is by grace alone though faith in Jesus Christ. One does not get to heaven by one's own good works, or by pulling oneself up by one's own bootstraps; one simply relies on grace appropriated by faith alone in the achievement of Christ who died for our sins as a perfect sacrifice once and for all upon the Cross.

In other words, Luther's was an individual spiritual or psychological reading of the justification passages of Romans, conditioned by a presupposed question about personal salvation. Some contemporary scholars, following this broad approach to the understanding of the epistle's central message, therefore regard Romans as Paul's final and mature treatment of this theme, a general summation of his thought, rather than a letter directed to specific problems within the Roman community. Günther Bornkamm, for example, regards Romans as Paul's 'last will and testament' in relation to this matter.[7]

However, in more recent times, an entirely different reading of the text of Romans has become fashionable. This is less personal and psychological and a more socio-historical reading of the text which takes particular cognisance of the original context in which it was written and the specific problem in Rome to which it was originally addressed. It has been noted, for example, that Romans was written by Paul around 54 or 55 AD, and that at this time large numbers of Jewish people had recently returned to Rome, having been expelled by the Emperor Claudius in 49 AD. We know that some 4000 young Jewish men were conscripted into the Roman legion to serve in Sardinia in 19 BC. It is therefore conjectured that there could well have been a Jewish community of possibly 50,000 people living in Rome in the area between the Tiber and the sea by the time they were all expelled in 49 AD.

The historian Suetonius mentions that the original cause of the expulsion of the Jews from Rome had to do with rioting, precipitated by quarrels about someone called 'Chrestus'.[8] Scholars have for many years conjectured that this is a misspelling of 'Christus'. Indeed, it is more than a conjecture. F. Blass demonstrated in 1893 that 'Chrestos' was commonly used for 'Christus' and that Tacitus not only knew of the 'Chrestianoi' (Annals, 15.44.2) but that their name came from 'Christus' (Annals 15.44.4). Indeed, we now know that 'Chrestiani' as a name for Christians appears throughout the first and second centuries. Almost certainly, the riots of 49 AD were triggered by Jewish and Gentile Christians rubbing up against the Jewish community over the claim that the hoped-for Messiah was Jesus the Christ. It can thus be conjectured with a fair degree of confidence that the original disturbances which caused Claudius to expel the Jews from Rome were focused in synagogue disputes amongst Jews and Christians of mixed Jewish and Gentile origins.

In any event, the exit of the Jewish community from Rome in 49 AD resulted in economic recession and chaos in the city. Perhaps that is what we would today expect from the sudden withdrawal of the Jewish community from the commercial activities of a city. Imagine Melbourne tomorrow without the contribution of its Jewish citizens! As a result, for economic reasons, in 52 AD the Jews were allowed to return to Rome, but without right of assembly. When Claudius died and was succeeded by Nero in 54 AD an even more liberal policy meant that many more Jews would have been encouraged to return to Rome.

Now, it is into this highly volatile historical context that Paul wrote his letter to the 'beloved of God' as he calls them in Rome. He wrote around 54 AD or a little later. It may well have been that Gentile, and more politically correct, Christians who were not condemned to the fate of expulsion would have remained when the Jews left the region, possibly even occupying the synagogues vacated by them. We can imagine the difficulties and tensions that would have been thrown up upon the return of the Jews in relation to the reclaiming of synagogue property.

It is significant that while in Galatians Paul wrestles with the question of Judaising Christians, Christians who were tending to revert to Jewish practices, in Romans the problem is not Judaising Christians but the relationship between Christians and Jews. Amongst the questions Paul addresses in this letter to this very mixed environment is: How is it that the promises that were originally made to Abraham and his descendants, the Jews, are being fulfilled with respect to Gentiles? Paul's answer is 'justification is by faith' and not works. Abraham was a person of faith, and those who inherit the promises made to him are those who likewise have faith. In this reading of Romans it is understood as a missiological tract, a *Missionsdokument*, as the Germans speak of it. Rather than being Paul's mature thought on the theme of justification by faith, it is a letter specifically intended to address a basic issue that is of vital importance for the future development of a harmonious and unified Church community or *ecclesia* in Rome. It is interesting that, as he writes into this volatile mix, Paul nowhere refers in the body of the letter to the worshippers of God in Rome as an '*ecclesia*'; it is addressed to the 'beloved of God' in Rome. At best there are some peripheral and fragmented house groups to whom he sends greetings at the end of the epistle (Chapter 16). But it is significant that while Paul's other letters were addressed to the Church — the Christian community or *ecclesia*, in Corinth or Thessalonica for example — the term *ecclesia* never appears in the greeting or the body of the letter to the Romans, and perhaps this is because the communion of the Church is yet to be actualised in the context of a situation of controversy and division. Can it be, given the prevailing tensions, that there was not yet a community with sufficient coherence to be called the *ecclesia* of God in Rome? It may well have been that a harmonious and unified Christian community has yet to emerge in this city and that Paul is having to address the obvious difficulties resulting from a returning Jewish community of significant proportions including some Jewish Christians, but without right of assembly, and Gentile Christians occupying the very synagogues they had vacated.

Furthermore, in Chapter 11 of Romans it is significant that Paul warns his Gentile Christian readers not to be too self-confident. He speaks of Israel as a cultivated olive tree: some parts have been lopped off, and the wild olive of the Gentiles has been grafted in. In this circumstance Paul warns the Gentile Christians not to be proud (verse 20). If it was possible, he argues, for a wild olive to be grafted into the cultivated olive tree, how much more possible is it for God to regraft in the Jewish branches that were lopped off (verse 24)? There is still time for faithless Jews to come to faith and fulfil their vocation. It may yet be that those who have been lopped off the original stock may be regrafted in. Can it be that while Galatians is addressed to Judaising Christians who were reverting to Jewish customs, Romans is addressed more particularly to Gentile Christians in Rome who were thinking too highly of themselves in the context of the challenge posed by the returning Jews?

All this is, of course, open to discussion and debate. But the point is that this is a letter about relationships between Jews and Gentile Christians, and perhaps between Jewish and Gentile Christians, and how in the mission of God to the world all can be included as beneficiaries together as the covenant children of Abraham. For Abraham is accounted righteous in the eyes of God, not by virtue of his Jewish blood or genetic identity, but because of his faith — hence justification by faith. This is Paul's attempt to resolve a pastoral and human problem of Christian–Jewish relations. But if this text comes out of such a context in the middle of the first century, is it not a text with which Christians and Jews might well grapple today? Can we together wring a blessing and not a curse from this ancient text?

The point is that Christians must wrestle with these texts and a few others like them, and do so in the context of a newfound willingness to engage with Jewish brothers and sisters. We must enter a public discussion in which we are prepared to interrogate one another and gain a shared truth from them. Just to be content to retreat into our own bunkers, or even to retreat into a cool and liberal-minded tolerance bordering on indifference — you believe what you want and I'll believe what I want — is not enough.

This kind of mutual wrestling with inherited texts to find a blessing in them and not a curse, must be on the agenda of all three of the Abrahamic religions. We all worship the same God, and if God is in some way interested in what goes on in this world, then the question that currently confronts us all in the context of our heightened awareness of religious pluralism today is: what is God doing in such a world? What is God up to in the context of the religious plurality of our time? How are we intended to live together under the sovereignty of God? And what is our role together in building a more peaceful and just world?

What I am seeking to express here is summed up in some words I recently came across in a newly published book by one of the priests in my Diocese of Perth. He raises the question of whether God might be offering humanity 'a new opportunity by nudging each of the world religions out of their tendency to introspective self-definition and self-reference, forcing all of us out of the comfort zone of our self-enclosure to become public', so that we genuinely engage together, and insistently interrogate one another and learn from one another. We thus 'enter into a more lively, healthy, and life-giving cross fertilisation, a healthy "theology of cross reference".'[9]

I certainly hope that we may all be helped by that kind of cross-referencing exercise to move beyond the mere liberal-minded tolerance of others to a more life-giving and positive human engagement, for the ultimate good of all God's people and the peace of the whole world.

ENDNOTES

PROLOGUE

1 See this pattern of preaching in the early sermons recorded in Acts, Chapters 2 and 3. All biblical quotations throughout this book are from the New Revised Standard Version (*The New Oxford Annotated Bible with the Apocrypha*, ed. Bruce M. Metzger and Roland E. Murphy, Oxford University Press, New York, 1991).

2 The Christian conviction is that it is in and through the unique claims of Jesus, which bring us to an understanding of his own identity and significance specifically as 'Son', that God is in turn known as 'Father'. Because the Father is eternally the Father, and the Son is eternally the Son, it follows that one comes to a knowledge of God as Father through the Son. Thus Jesus may be said to be the 'only way to the Father'.

3 *Sydney Morning Herald*, 21 January 2003.

4 Rowan Williams, *Open to Judgment: Sermons and Addresses*, Darton, Longman & Todd, London, 1994, p. 35.

5 Garry J. Williams, 'The Theology of Rowan Williams', *Latimer Studies* 55, p. 21.

CHAPTER I — GOD: MANIFESTATION OR MYSTERY?

1 Erasmus, Letter to Cardinal Campegio, 5 February 1520, *Opus Epistolarum Des. Erasmi Roterodami*, ed. P. S. Allen, Oxford University Press, Oxford, 1906–, Vol. 4, no. 1062 (substantially repeated in a second letter dated 6 December 1520, ibid., no. 1167).

2 Lambeth Resolution 6(5)/1988.

3 Iris Murdoch, *Metaphysics as a Guide to Morals*, Penguin Press, Harmondsworth, 1992, p. 453.

4 Though not a Demea theologian himself, Berkeley may have provided Hume with the name Demea. Berkeley was unsympathetic towards the fideistic negative theology of his day, and in a passing reference to 'honest Demea', he somewhat unfairly makes Demea represent those who are rigidly orthodox and afraid to think. See George Berkeley, *Alciphron*, ed. David Berman, Routledge, London and New York, 1993, VII:27.

5 David Hume, *Dialogues Concerning Natural Religion*, ed. Stanley Tweyman, Routledge, London and New York, 1991, p. 109.

6 Ibid., p. 129.

7 Ibid., p. 98.

8   Ibid., p. 99.

9   Ibid., p. 120.

10 Ibid., p. 152.

11 'It is only as a science, replied Demea, subjected to human reasoning and disputation, that I postpone the study of natural theology.' Ibid., p. 97.

12 Ibid., p. 122.

13 Ibid., p. 123. Not least amongst these is St Paul himself in Romans 11:33.

14 Preached at Christ Church, Dublin, before the Irish House of Lords, on 15 May 1709.

15 Edward Copleston (1776–1849), after having been Fellow (1795), became Provost of Oriel in 1814 and held in plurality appointments as Bishop of Llandaff and Dean of St Paul's from the following year. Richard Whately (1787–1863) was Fellow of Oriel (1811), then vicar of Halesworth (1822) and principal of Alban Hall (1825), until he became Archbishop of Dublin in 1831. Given the inclusive sympathies that he shared with other Oriel fellows who desired to increase the comprehensiveness of the Church of England, he was to align himself as an opponent of Newman and the Oxford movement.

16 Richard Whately, *The Right Method of Interpreting Scripture, in what relates to the Nature of the Deity, and His Dealings with Mankind, Illustrated in a Discourse on Predestination by Dr King*, John Murray, London, 1821.

17 Richard Whately, *Elements of Logic* (1826), William Jackson, New York, 1834, pp. 254–256. Note also the discussion of the category of 'person' included in the Appendix on ambiguous terms (see pp. 289–301).

18 See *The Letters and Diaries of John Henry Newman*, ed. C. S. Dessain et al., Clarendon Press, Oxford, 1978, Vol. I.

19 The British Prime Minister William Ewart Gladstone was also touched by this theological movement (see Chapter 2).

20 *The Right Method of Interpreting Scripture*, op. cit., p. 121.

21 Ibid., p. 125.

22 A classic example of the Demea position, including its emphasis both on the mysterious incomprehensibility of God and at the same time on the practical usefulness of doctrine for making us 'better men', is found in Newman's Trinity Sunday sermon, preached on 14 June 1829, on 'The Christian Mysteries' (No. 199 in Newman's numbering), *Parochial and Plain Sermons*, Ignatius Press, San Francisco, 1987, pp. 129–136.

23 In a Sunday morning sermon on 31 October 1824 (No. 29 in Newman's own sequential numbering of his sermons). See *John Henry Newman, Sermons 1824–1834*, ed. Placid Murray OSB, Clarendon Press, Oxford, 1991, Vol. I, p. 272.

24 Ibid., p. 272.

25 John Henry Newman, *University Sermons, Chiefly on the Theory of Religious Belief*, Longmans Green, London, 1843, p. 59.

26 Ibid., p. 59.

27 Ibid., p. 18.

28 Ibid., p. 63.

29 See the sermon entitled 'Faith and Reason, Contrasted as Habits of Mind' (1839), in which Newman questions the appeal to reason as an indispensable preliminary to faith, for faith is 'independent of what is commonly understood by Reason'. *University Sermons*, op. cit., p. 211.

30 Ibid., p. 195.

31 *Sermons 1824–1834*, op. cit., p. 211.

32 See Newman's Tract 73, 'On the Introduction of Rationalistic Principles into Revealed Religion' (2 February 1836), in *Essays Critical and Historical*, Pickering, London, 1871, Vol. I, pp. 30–90 (esp. pp. 31–71). The distinction between a theology of manifestation and a theology of mystery may be found on pp. 40–41.

33 Ibid., p. 41.

34 Ibid., p. 40.

35 Ibid., p. 41.

36 Ibid. pp. 41–42.

37 H. L. Mansel, *The Limits of Religious Thought*, John Murray, London, fourth edn, 1859, p. 94.

38 H. L. Mansel, *A Second Letter to Professor Goldwin Smith*, Oxford, 1862, p. 40. A contemporary of King, Peter Browne vigorously expounded the Demea position in his *Things Divine and Supernatural Conceived by Analogy with Things Natural and Human*, W. Innys & R. Manby, London, 1733. Indeed, Browne thought that King had taken his argument from Browne's own *A Letter in Answer to 'Christianity not Mysterious'* (by John Toland), J. Ray for J. North, Dublin, 1697.

39 Something of the nuances between the thinking of King and Browne may be discerned in Mansel's footnote xvii to p. 98, *The Limits of Religious Thought*, op. cit., pp. 261–262.

40 Ibid., Preface, p. xii.

41 For a discussion of Mansel's view of 'regulative truth' see Don Cupitt, 'Mansel's Theory of Regulative Truth', *Journal of Theological Studies*, N.S., Vol. xviii, 1967, pp. 104–126, and D. W. Dockrill, 'The Limits of Thought and Regulative Truths', *Journal of Theological Studies*, N.S., Vol. xxi, 1970, pp. 370–387.

42 John Henry Newman, *An Essay in Aid of a Grammar of Assent* (1870), Doubleday, New York, 1955, p. 309.

43 In reply to Mary Holmes, who wrote to Newman after reading the first part of the *Grammar of Assent*, Newman said he was anxious to hear her views on the last hundred pages, which contain his essential concern about an approach to God through conscience and which he hoped lay people might understand. See M. Trevor, *Newman, Light in Winter*, Macmillan, London, 1962, p. 486.

44 G. Kittel and G. Friedrich, *Theologisches Wörterbuch zum Neuen Testament*, W. Kohlhammer Verlag, Stuttgart, 1933–, ed. and trans. as *Theological Dictionary of the New Testament* by G. W. Bromiley, Eerdmans, Grand Rapids, Michigan, 1964–, Vol. 4, pp. 802–828.

45 John Henry Newman, Tract 73, op. cit., p. 54.

46 Ibid., p. 45. Newman's explicit reference here is to the mystery of the Atonement.

47 Gregory of Nyssa, *Adversus Eunomius*, 12.

48 Richard Hooker, *Laws of Ecclesiastical Polity* (1594), collected by John Keble and revised by R. W. Church and F. Paget, Via Media, Ellicott City, Maryland, 1994, Vol. IV, p. 201.

CHAPTER 2 — THE NATURE OF DOCTRINE

1 British Library Additional MS 44719, ff. 237–240.

2 See Peter J. Jagger, *Gladstone, The Making of a Christian Politician*, Pickwick, Allison Park, Pennsylvania, 1991, p. 128. Peter Jagger points out that these notes appear to be those referred to by Gladstone in his diary as having been begun on 20 June 1830.

3 British Library Additional MS 44801, ff. 33–34. See also *The Gladstone Diaries 1825–1854*, ed. M. R. D. Foot and H. C. G. Matthew, Oxford University Press, Oxford, 1968–1974, entry for 20 June 1830.

4 Ibid. Gladstone notes on a visit to Cuddesdon on 23 August 1828 that 'Mr Newman of Oriel, dined here.' It may also be of interest that another entry during this Cuddesdon sojourn reads: 'An excellent sermon from Mr Pusey.'

5 Sermon 177 in Newman's numbering (21 September 1828), *Sermons 1824–1834*, op. cit., p. 206.

6 Sermon 411 on 'The Mysteriousness of our Present Being', preached on 29 May 1836, John Henry Newman, *Parochial and Plain Sermons*, Ignatius Press, San Francisco, 1987 edn, p. 912. See also Sermon 390, preached on 8 November 1835, on 'The Gift of the Spirit': '... we shall unite conceptions the most lofty concerning His majesty and bounty towards us, with the most lowly, minute, and unostentatious service to Him' (ibid., p. 647).

7 Edward Copleston, *Enquiry into the Doctrines of Necessity and Predestination in Four Discourses*, John Murray, London, 1821.

8 George Lindbeck, *The Nature of Doctrine*, Westminster Press, Philadelphia, 1984.

9 Unitarians deny the divinity of equal status of the Son with the Father — and thus deny the Trinity.

10 Dr Knox cited a canonical prohibition of the Sydney Church Ordinance, 1912. His letter to Howard Mowll is dated 21 September 1956.

11 The word is repeated three times in the course of the letter.

12 Augustine, *Confessions*, 4:17.

13 *Australian Church Record*, 16 June 1966, pp. 2 and 5.

14 Cyprian, *De Oratione Dominica*, 12–27.

15 Aidan Kavanagh, *On Liturgical Theology*, Pueblo Publishing, New York, 1984, pp. 91–92.

16 Ibid., p. 150.

17 John Henry Newman, *Essay on Development*, in *Conscience, Consensus, and The Development of Doctrine*, Image Books, Doubleday, New York, 1992, p. 88.

18 For the most developed expression of this view see H. R. McAdoo, *The Spirit of Anglicanism*, A. & C. Black, London, 1965.

19 John Henry Newman, *On Consulting the Faithful in Matters of Doctrine*, ed. John Coulson, Sheed & Word, Kansas, 1961. While the view he promoted was congenial to those Anglicans who were supporting a positive role for the laity in the definition and expression of the Church's doctrine, Newman's views were not so well received within the Roman Catholic Church. Indeed, the views he expressed on the role of the laity were what drew the charge from Monsignor George Talbot that Newman was 'the most dangerous man in England'.

CHAPTER 3 — SCRIPTURE

1 James Packer, *Fundamentalism and the Word of God*, Eerdmans, Grand Rapids, Michigan, 1958.

2 Peter Jensen, 'Evangelicalism and Anglicanism Today', one of three addresses delivered at Anglican Evangelical Conferences, UK, published by Anglican Media Sydney on 30 January 2003, p. 1 (see also Chapter 4, endnote 17).

3 *Fundamentalism and the Word of God*, op. cit., Chapter 2.

4 Letter from the Reverend Richard J. Condie, Chair of The Evangelical Fellowship in the Anglican Communion (Victorian Branch), dated 25 May 2000.

5 Gabriel Hebert, *Fundamentalism and the Church of God*, SCM Press, London, 1957.

6 *Fundamentalism and the Word of God*, op. cit., p. 19.

7 Ibid., p. 21.

8 Ibid., p. 73.

9 Ibid., p. 73.

10 Ibid., p. 79.

11 Ibid., p. 73.

12 Ibid., p. 80

13 Ibid., p. 102.

14 Ibid., p. 102.

15 Ibid., p. 108.

16 Ibid., p. 90.

17 Ibid., p. 110.

18 Ibid., p. 112.

19 Ibid., p. 164.

20 Ernst Käsemann, 'The Canon of the New Testament and the Unity of the Church', first published in English in *Essays on New Testament Themes*, SCM Press, London, 1964, p. 95.

21 Ibid., p. 103.
22 Doctrine Panel of the Anglican Church of Australia, *Faithfulness in Fellowship: Reflections on Homosexuality and the Church*, John Garratt Publishing, Mulgrave, Victoria, 2001.

CHAPTER 4 — CROSS AND RESURRECTION

1 For example, St Paul speaks of 'the Twelve', whereas elsewhere he usually does not use this term. He also speaks of 'the forgiveness of *our sins*', using the genitive plural, whereas elsewhere Paul usually speaks only of sin in the singular as an all-pervading 'gone-wrongness' of the whole created order.

2 There are in fact three accounts of Paul's Damascus Road experience in Acts (Chapters 9, 22 and 26). The details of the experience vary, given that in one, for example, those travelling with Paul are said to have heard, but to have seen nothing (Acts 9:7), and in another they are said to have seen, but heard nothing (Acts 22:9). These traditions consistently attest to the heavenly or visionary nature of the experience, described as a light from heaven and a voice.

3 See Robert Jenson, *Systematic Theology*, Oxford University Press, Oxford, 1997, Vol. I, pp. 204–205, for this idea.

4 Ibid., p. 205.

5 Peter Carnley, *The Structure of Resurrection Belief*, Clarendon Press, Oxford, 1987.

6 See E. G. Selwyn, 'The Resurrection', in *Essays Catholic and Critical*, ed. E. G. Selwyn, Society for Promoting Christian Knowledge, London, 1926, p. 319.

7 H. E. G. Paulus, *Das Leben Jesu, als Grundlage einer reinen Geschichte des Urchristenthums*, 2 vols, Heidelberg, 1828.

8 N. T. Wright, *The Resurrection of the Son of God*, Society for Promoting Christian Knowledge, London, 2002.

9 Nanog: from Tir Nan Og, the Land of Everlasting Youthfulness in Celtic mythology.

10 His death was 'a ransom for many' (Matthew 20:28). See also Galatians 3:13, I Corinthians 6:20 and I Peter 1:18–19.

11 Acts 20:28.

12 Ephesians 2:6 and 12–13.

13 See Mark 10:45, Ephesians 5:2, I Timothy 2:6 and I Corinthians 5:7, where the sacrifice is of Passover. For sacrifice of Atonement see Romans 3:25, Galatians 1:4, Hebrews 2:17 and I John 2:2.

14 John Knox, *The Cross of Christ*, Collins, Fontana Books, London and Glasgow, 1967, p. 11.

15 See Gustaf Aulen, *Christus Victor*, trans. A. G. Hebert, Collier Books, New York, 1986 (first published by Macmillan Paperbacks, 1969).

16 Stephen Sykes, *The Story of Atonement*, Darton, Longman & Todd, London, 1997, p. 52. In reference to defenders of the theory who now use the language of metaphor, he cites James Packer, 'What Did the Cross Achieve?', *Tyndale Bulletin* 25, 1974, pp. 3–45.

17 Peter Jensen, 'The Gospel and Mission of Anglican Evangelicalism', one of three addresses delivered at Anglican Evangelical Conferences, UK, published by Anglican Media Sydney on 30 January 2003 (see also Chapter 3, endnote 2).

18 John Calvin, *Institutes of the Christian Religion*, Book II, xvi:2.

19 Richard Southern, *Saint Anselm: A Portrait in a Landscape*, Cambridge University Press, Cambridge, 1990, p. 214.

20 St Anselm, *Cur Deus Homo*, Part I, Chapter 11.

21 Stephen O'Shea, *The Perfect Heresy*, Profice Books, London, 2001, pp. 187–189.

22 *Cur Deus Homo*, op. cit., Part II, Chapter 16.

23 R. C. Moberly, *Atonement and Personality*, John Murray, London, 1902.

24 Ambrose also said that penitential works could never merit forgiveness (*De Poenitentia* II.9 [80]). Though called 'satisfaction', the idea of 'full compensation' was absent.

25 *Laws of Ecclesiastical Polity*, op. cit., Book VI, v:I.

26 Ibid., Book VI, v:I.

27 Ibid., Book VI, v:6.

28 Hooker discusses this at length, ibid., Book VI, vi: 5–10.

29 Hooker was well aware of the analogical nature of religious language about God. He noted, for example: 'Anger and mercy are in us passions; but in him not so. "God," saith St. Basil, "is no ways passionate, but because the punishments which his judgments do inflict are, like effects of indignation, severe and grievous to such as suffer them, therefore we term the revenge which he taketh upon sinners, anger; and the withdrawing of his plagues, mercy." "His wrath," saith St. Augustine, "is not as ours …" ' Ibid., Book VI, v:4.

30 Ibid., Book VI, v:2.

31 See Ephesians 2:18: 'for through him both [Jews and Gentiles] have access in one Spirit to the Father'.

32 *Atonement and Personality*, op. cit., p. 382.

33 This is expressed by Anselm in *Cur Deus Homo*, Part I, Chapter 2, and Part II, Chapters 16 and 19.

34 *Institutes of the Christian Religion*, op. cit., Book II, xvi:2.

35 Tract 73, op. cit., p. 66.

36 Jaroslav Pelikan, 'Fundamentalism and/or Orthodoxy?', in *The Fundamentalist Phenomenon*, ed. Norman J. Cohen, Eerdmans, Grand Rapids, Michigan, 1990, p. 13.

37 Kenneth E. Kirk, 'The Atonement', in *Essays Catholic and Critical*, Society for Promoting Christian Knowledge, London, 1926, p. 270.

38 William F. Arndt and F. Wilbur Gingrich, *A Greek-English Lexicon of the New Testament*, Cambridge University Press, Cambridge, 1957, entries under '*dia*' and '*anti*'.

39 'Fundamentalism and/or Orthodoxy?', op. cit., p. 13.

CHAPTER 5 — LAY AND ORDAINED MINISTRY

1 General Synod Resolution 42/98: 'That this General Synod requests the Standing Committee to undertake production of a report on the meaning and place of the three-fold ordained ministry in the life and mission of the church, the report to be prepared in time to be debated fully at the next meeting of the General Synod. As part of its brief, the report should specifically canvass the implications for ordained ministry of the Appellate Tribunal majority opinion on the constitutional status of lay and diaconal presidency at the Eucharist.'

2 The membership of the group was as follows: the Most Reverend Dr Peter Carnley, Archbishop of Perth (chairman), the Venerable Trevor Edwards (Sydney), the Reverend James Minchin (Melbourne), the Reverend Dr John Woodhouse (Sydney). Subsequently, the Right Reverend David McCall, then the Bishop of Willochra, South Australia, became a member of the group.

3 The report of the House of Bishops of the Church of England, *Eucharistic Presidency*, Church House Publications, London, 1997, is a good example of recent Anglican work on the issue.

4 Paul actually contrasts *pneumatika* and *charisma*, to distinguish spiritual gifts independent of ministry within the Church from those brought to the service of others.

5 The General Synod of the Anglican Church of Australia, meeting in Brisbane in July 2001, received this report and commended it in the following resolution, 41/01:

> *That General Synod:*
>
> *1. receives the report entitled: "For the Sake of the Gospel" dated 18th February 2001;*
>
> *2. welcomes the presentation on essentials on faith and ministry as contained in the report in Sections 4 to 6;*

  3. *refers it to the Doctrine Panel and the Inter-Anglican Standing Committee on Ecumenical Relations;*
  4. *requests the Standing Committee to bring a report to the next General Synod on the above matters and after further study at all levels of our Church.'*

6 'For the Sake of the Gospel', 5.7.1.

7 Robin Greenwood, *Transforming Priesthood*, Society for Promoting Christian Knowledge, London, 1994.

8 Ibid., p. 185.

9 See also Anglican Articles of Religion, Article 36.

10 *Ministry and Ordination*, ARCIC Canterbury Statement, 1973, para. 13.

11 Australian General Synod, Resolution 19/1985.

12 Lambeth Resolution 1988/8.

13 Ibid.

14 Paul Gibson, *Anglican Ordination Rites — The Berkeley Statement: 'To Equip the Saints*, Grove Books, Cambridge, 2002.

15 Ibid., p. 4.

16 *Transforming Priesthood*, op. cit., p. 130.

17 *The Berkeley Statement*, op. cit., p. 4.

18 *Transforming Priesthood*, op. cit.

19 Robin Greenwood, *Transforming Church, Liberating Structures for Ministry*, Society for Promoting Christian Knowledge, London, 2002.

20 *Transforming Priesthood*, op. cit., p. 142.

21 Ibid., p. 163.

22 *Transforming Church*, op. cit., p. 115.

23 Ibid., p. 114.

24 Ibid., p. 173.

25 Ibid., p. 114.

26 Ibid., p. 115.

27 R. C. Moberly, *Ministerial Priesthood*, John Murray, London, 1897, p. 114.

28 *Transforming Church*, op. cit., p. 114.

29 At this point I have benefited enormously from reading the doctoral thesis of Peter M. Waddell of Fitzwilliam College, Cambridge, entitled 'The Eucharistic Priesthood of the Ordained Ministry: A Contemporary Anglican Proposal', 2001. This thesis is yet to be published.

CHAPTER 6 — LEADERSHIP AND PRIESTHOOD

1 This line of argument was articulated by the then Bishop of Bathurst in his reasons, Appellate Tribunal Opinion, General Synod of the Anglican Church of Australia, PO Box Q190, QVB Post Office, NSW, 1230, 1997, p. 85, and followed by other members of the Tribunal.

2 Ibid., pp. 87 and 88–89.

3 *The Constitution of the Anglican Church of Australia*, Part II: The Government of the Church, Chapter 3, section 7.

4 Tertullian, *De Praescriptione Haereticorum*, ed. R. F. Refoule, Series Latina I, Corpus Christianorum, Brepols Publishers, Turnhout, Belgium, 1954, 41:2–8, pp. 221–222.

5 I am indebted to the Reverend Professor J. Robert Wright of the General Theological Seminary in New York for drawing my attention to the significance of this directive to the presiding priest in both the first and the last of the classical English Prayer Books.

6 Bishop Wilson makes the same argument in the Appellate Tribunal Opinion, 1997, p. 85.

7 *Ministerial Priesthood*, op. cit., p. 238.

8 *Laws of Ecclesiastical Polity*, op. cit., Book V, lxxviii:2.

9 This liturgy was framed by the Scottish bishops and submitted, by the King's command, to the review of Archbishop Laud of Canterbury, Juxon, the Bishop of London, and Wren, the Bishop of Norwich. Though Archbishop Laud was himself reluctant to approve the requests of the Scottish bishops, which included replacing the term 'priest' with the term 'presbyter', the Scottish bishops eventually prevailed upon the King. They were insistent that their proposed changes to the 1604 Prayer Book would 'relish better with their countrymen'.

10 *The Constitution of the Anglican Church of Australia*, Chapter 2 — Ruling Principles.

11 See Roland de Vaux, *Ancient Israel*, Darton, Longman & Todd, London, 1961, pp. 348–349.

12 See J. Pedersen, *Israel*, Geoffrey Cumberlege, London, 1959, Vols III–IV, p. 158.

13 Archbishop Cranmer, *The Sacrament of the Lord's Supper*, ed. John Edmund Cox, (Parker Society) Cambridge University Press, Cambridge, 1844, pp. 345ff.

14 *Institutes of the Christian Religion*, op. cit., Book IV, xvii:13–16.

15 *Laws of Ecclesiastical Polity*, op. cit., Book V, lxxviii:3.

16 *Ministerial Priesthood*, op. cit., pp. 238–242.

17 Appellate Tribunal Opinion, op. cit., p. 85.

18 A catalogue of the functions synthetically associated with priesthood from time to time is found in the Appellate Tribunal Opinion of The Honourable Mr Justice Young, ibid., p. 27.

19 Ibid., p. 27.

20 Fifth International Liturgical Consultation, Dublin, 1995, Principle 4, adopted by the whole Consultation.

CHAPTER 7 — WOMEN IN THE EPISCOPATE?

1 Australian General Synod, Resolution 23/77.

2 Ibid., Canon 18 of 1985.

3 Ibid., Resolution 24/89.

4 Ibid., Resolution 25/89.

5 Martyrs at Carthage in 203 AD.

6 Elisabeth Behr-Sigel and Kallistos Ware, *The Ordination of Women in the Orthodox Church*, WCC Publications, Geneva, Switzerland, 2000, p. 89.

7 Ibid., p. 89.

8 J. Erickson, 'The Priesthood in Patristic Teaching', in *The Place of Women in the Orthodox Church and the Question of the Ordination of Women*, ed. Gennadios Limouris, Inter-Orthodox Symposium, Rhodos, Greece, 30 October to 7 November 1988, Katerini, Tertios, 1992, p. 115.

9 Michael Slusser, 'Fathers and Priestesses: Footnotes to the Roman Declaration', *Worship*, Vol. 51, No. 5, September 1977, pp. 434–445.

10 Irenaeus, *Adversus Haereses*, I, 13:2.

11 *De Praescriptione Haereticorum*, op. cit., 41:2–8, pp. 221–222.

12 Cyprian, *Epistle*, ed. G. Hartel, Corpus Scriptorum Ecclesasticorum Latinorum, III, 2, Vienna, 1868, 75:10, pp. 817–818.

13 Origen, *Fragment 74 on I Corinthians 14:34–35*, ed. Claude Jenkins, *Journal of Theological Studies* 10, 1909, pp. 41–42.

14 *Parnarion*, ed. G. Dindorf, Leipzig, 1859–1863, 49:3 (II:445–446); 78:23 (III:524); and 79:1 (III:528).

15 An Addendum by the Reverend Canon D. B. Knox in *The Ministry of Women, A Report of the General Synod Commission on Doctrine*, 1977, p. 31.

16 Ibid., p. 30.

17 Anthony C. Thiselton, *The First Epistle to the Corinthians*, Eerdmans, Grand Rapids, Michigan, and Cambridge, UK, 2000, pp. 800–823.

18 Oliver O'Donovan, *Resurrection and Moral Order: An Outline for Evangelical Ethics*, InterVarsity Press, Leicester, 1986, pp. 42–45.

19 In the technical language of classical theology, this is referred to as the divine arbitrium, the exercise of the divine freedom in individual vocation.

20 J. J. Gundry-Volf, 'Gender and Creation in I Cor 11:2–16: A Study in Paul's Theological Method', *Evangelium Schriftauslegung, Kirche, Festschrift fur Peter Stuhlmacher*, ed. J. Adna, S. J. Hafemann and O. Hofius, Vandenhoeck & Ruprecht, Göttingen, 1977, p. 152.

21 Sydney Diocesan Doctrine Commission, 'The Doctrine of the Trinity and its Bearing on the Relationship of Men and Women', Sydney, 1999.

22 The heresy of Docetism held that Jesus was not truly one but only 'appeared' to be, and thus called into question the reality of the Incarnation.

23 'The Doctrine of the Trinity and its Bearing on the Relationship of Men and Women', op. cit., para. 15.

24 Kevin Giles, *The Trinity and Subordinationism*, InterVarsity Press, Downers Grove, Illinois, 2002, p. 30.

25 From the Greek verb 'to empty' oneself. The seminal work on twentieth-century revisions of kenotic Christology includes C. F. D. Moule, 'Further Reflections on Philippians 2:5–11', *Apostolic History and the Gospel*, ed. W. W. Gasque and R. P. Martin, Paternoster Press, Exeter, and Eerdmans, Grand Rapids, Michigan, 1970, pp. 254–70, and 'The Manhood of Jesus in the New Testament', *Christ, Faith and History*, ed. S. W. Sykes and J. P. Clayton, Oxford University Press, Oxford, 1972, pp. 95–110; E. Kasemann, 'A Critical Analysis of Philippians 2:5–11', *Journal for Theology and Church* 5, pp. 45–89; J. Macquarrie, 'Kenoticism Rediscovered', *Theology* 77, pp. 115–24, and 'The Pre-existent Christ', *Expository Times* 77, pp. 1299–1302; and P. Schoonenberg, 'He Emptied Himself', *Concilium* 2, 1965, pp. 47–66, 'The Kenosis or Self-Emptying of Christ', *Concilium* 3, 1966, pp. 27–36, and *The Christ*, Sheed & Ward, London, 1969.

26 This nineteenth-century form of kenoticism was strongly advocated in slightly different forms by Bishop Charles Gore, the Congregationalist theologian P. T. Forsyth and others. It appears also to be accepted by Kevin Giles, *The Trinity and Subordinationism*, op. cit., p. 30.

27 A. N. Whitehead, *Process and Reality* (1929), Harper Torchbook, New York, 1960, p. 520.

28 *The First Epistle to the Corinthians*, op. cit., p. 822.

CHAPTER 8 — DOING THE TRUTH

1 Dr Megan Best, 'Untested treatments bring huge cost', *Southern Cross*, August 2002, p. 1.

2 Ibid., p. 12.

3 *Catechism of the Catholic Church*, Geoffrey Chapman, London, 1994, cl. 2270.

4 Dr Daniel Overduin and Fr. John Fleming, *Life in a Test-Tube*, Lutheran Publishing House, Adelaide, 1982, p. 35.

5 St Augustine, *Quaestiones in Heptateuchum*, I:2, no. 80.

6 A. E. Hellegers, 'Fetal Development', *Theological Studies* 31, 1970, p. 4.

7 Norman M. Ford, *The Prenatal Person*, Blackwell, Oxford, 2002, p. 68.

8 'Fetal Development', op cit., p. 5.

9 Bernard Haring, *Medical Ethics*, St Paul Publications, Slough, 1972, p. 80.

10 *The Prenatal Person*, op. cit., p. 65.

11 See G. R. Dunstan, *The Artifice of Ethics*, SCM Press, London, 1974 (The Moorhouse Lectures, 1973), and Dunstan's review of the Warnock Report, 'Warnock Reviewed', *Crucible*, October–December 1984, pp. 148–153. The Reverend Dr J. L. Morgan was amongst the first to signal an awareness of Dunstan's conclusions with regard to the status of the early embryo. See 'Anglicanism, Ethics, Moral Theology and Contrived Conception' in *Making Babies*, Anglican Social Responsibilities Commission, Acorn Press, Canberra, 1984, pp. 37–46.

12 Ibid., p. 68.

13 *Report of the Committee of Inquiry into Human Fertilisation and Embryology* (Warnock Report), Her Majesty's Stationery Office, London, 1984, 11:5.

14 Ibid., 11:22.

15 *The Australian*, 7 August 2002.

16 *The Prenatal Person*, op. cit., p. 66.

17 *Report of the Special Committee Appointed by the Queensland Government into Laws Relating to Artificial Insemination, In-Vitro Fertilization and other Related Matters* (Demack Report), Brisbane, 1984, p. 20.

18 Ibid. p. 21.

CHAPTER 9 — LIBERALISM, ECUMENISM AND OTHER RELIGIONS

1 Robert N. Bellah et al., *The Good Society*, Knopf, New York, 1991; and *Habits of the Heart: Individualism and Commitment in American Life*, University of California Press, Berkeley, 1985.

2 Max Charlesworth, *Bioethics in a Liberal Society*, Cambridge University Press, Cambridge, 1993, pp. 22–23.

3 *Time* magazine, 22 May 1995.

4 *Being as Communion: Studies in Personhood and the Church*, Darton, Longman & Todd, London, 1985.

5 See, for example, Geza Verme, *Jesus the Jew*, Fortress Press, Minneapolis, 1993; Pinchas Lapide, *The Resurrection of Jesus: A Jewish Perspective*, Wipf & Stock, New York, 2002; and Alan Segal, *Paul the Convert*, Yale University Press, New Haven, Connecticut, 1992.

6 Francis J. Moloney, *The Gospel of John*, Sacra Pagina Series 4, Liturgical Press, Collegeville, Minnesota, 1998, p. 274.

7 See Günther Bornkamm, 'The Letter to the Romans as Paul's Last Will and Testament' in *The Romans Debate*, ed. Karl P. Donfried, Augsburg Press, Minneapolis, 1977, pp. 19–31.

8 Suetonius (c. 75–160 AD), *Vita Claudii*, 25:4 (cf. Acts 18:2).

9 David Wood, *John Vincent Taylor, Poet, Priest, and Prophet*, Churches Together, London, 2002, p. 2.